Y0-BXV-996

ETHNICITY AND CONFLICT IN A
POST-COMMUNIST WORLD

Also by Kumar Rupesinghe

CONFLICT RESOLUTION IN UGANDA (*editor*)

EARLY WARNING AND CONFLICT RESOLUTION (*co-editor with Michiko Kuroda*)

ETHNIC CONFLICT AND HUMAN RIGHTS (*editor*)

INTERNAL CONFLICT AND GOVERNANCE (*editor*)

Ethnicity and Conflict in a Post-Communist World

The Soviet Union, Eastern Europe and China

Edited by

Kumar Rupesinghe
Senior Research Fellow
International Peace Research Institute, Oslo

Peter King
Director, Centre for Peace and Conflict Studies,
University of Sydney

and

Olga Vorkunova
Research Fellow
Institute of World Economy and
International Relations, Moscow

St. Martin's Press

First published in Great Britain 1992 by
THE MACMILLAN PRESS LTD
Houndmills, Basingstoke, Hampshire RG21 2XS
and London
Companies and representatives
throughout the world

This book is published in association with the International Peace
Research Institute, Oslo

ISBN 0–333–56951–2

A catalogue record for this book is available from the British Library.

Printed in Great Britain by Antony Rowe Ltd, Chippenham, Wiltshire

Reprinted 1994

First published in the United States of America 1992 by
Scholarly and Reference Division,
ST. MARTIN'S PRESS, INC.,
175 Fifth Avenue,
New York, N.Y. 10010

ISBN 0–312–08565–6

Library of Congress Cataloging-in-Publication Data
Ethnicity and conflict in a post-communist world: the Soviet Union,
Eastern Europe, and China / edited by Kumar Rupesinghe, Peter
King, and Olga Vorkunova.
p.   cm.
Includes bibliographical references and index.
ISBN 0–312–08565–6
1. Soviet Union—Ethnic relations.   2. Europe, Eastern—Ethnic
relations.   3. Soviet Union—Politics and government—1985–1991.
4. Europe, Eastern—Politics and government—1989–   5. Post
–communism—Soviet Union.   6. Post-communism—Europe, Eastern.
I. Rupesinge, Kumar.   II. King, Peter, 1936–   .   III. Vorkunova,
Olga, 1951–   .
DK33 . E835   1992
305 . 8 ' 009171 '7—dc20   92–11320
                                                           CIP

Contents

Preface

Three years ago, a new commission devoted to internal conflicts and their resolution (ICON) was established within the International Peace Research Association (IPRA) in response to the growing recognition that internal conflicts within existing state boundaries would become the dominant form of conflict. ICON has become a loose network of scholars working in the area of internal conflict and governance pursuing an interdisciplinary, global approach to conflicts and their transformation. ICON aims to stimulate and support scholarly work on early warning and conflict prevention, and holistic studies on conflict transformation. The present three volumes, and others planned for the future, are intended to contribute to the field, not least by encouraging scholars from regions of conflict to contribute to the discussion.

Acknowledgements

We would like to thank the various donors who financed the preparation and publication of these three volumes, containing contributions by nearly 50 scholars from many regions of the world who met at IPRA's XIII General Conference in Groningen in the Netherlands, from 3-7 July 1990. Without our donors' support, these publications would never have materialized. Particular thanks to Jan Ryssennars of the Netherlands Organization for International Development Cooperation (NOVIB), to Halle Jørn Hanssen and Ann Bauer of the Norwegian Ministry of Foreign Affairs, and Werner Lottje of the Evangelical Church in Germany, to Jan Erichsen of Kirkens Nødhjelp, and to Hiroshi Fuse, President of the Institute of Peace and Justice of the Risho Kosei-Kai.

Our special gratitude to Belinda Holdsworth of Macmillan Press Ltd who encouraged us to proceed with publication, and to Macmillan's obliging cooperation throughout the editorial process.

viii   *Preface*

The editors would also like to thank Beth Steiner and Per Olav Maurstad for helping to organize the Groningen conference participation, and Arild Engelsen Ruud, Morten Løtveit, and Jan Helge Hordnes for careful pre-editing of the papers included in this volume, and for their painstaking work with references. Jan Helge Hordnes did particularly fine work in getting all the manuscripts into camera-ready form. Susan Høivik has given much of her spare time in language editing; Erik Ivås typed some of the manuscripts. I would like to thank Tord Høivik, my colleague and friend, for carefully reading the manuscripts and offering many suggestions for improvements. And my thanks also to more than 40 referees who provided valuable suggestions and criticisms at an early stage.

The International Peace Research Institute (PRIO) provided an excellent scholarly environment for the pursuit of this work. Finally a special debt of gratitude to our families and friends, who patiently bore with us throughout the many evenings and vacations which were devoted to this work.

Oslo, March 1992   Kumar Rupesinghe

Notes on the Contributors

Harald Bøckman (b. 1945) received his main degree in Chinese from the University of Oslo, 1980, following studies in history, geography and anthropology. 1970-90 various study and research trips to China, Japan and Burma. Considerable shcolarly and popular production (books, articles, conference papers and translations). Connected to the Department of East Asian Studies, University of Oslo, since 1979.

Györgi Csepeli (b. 1946) Ph.D. in Social Psychology at the Hungarian Academy of Sciences 1981; Professor of Social Psychology, Eötvös Loránd University; Visiting Professor (Department of Sociology, UCLA 1989-90, Department of Political Science, OSU 1991); Recent books: *Structures and Contents of Hungarian National Identity*, Frankfurt/Main, New York: Peter Lang; *Twilight of State Socialism*, (co-authored with Antal Örkény) London: Pinter Publishers.

Sergej Flere (b. 1944) LL.B. and M.A., the University of Belgrade; PhD in Sociology, University of Zagreb in 1973. Taught Sociology at the University of Novi Sad during the period 1971-91. Presently full Professor of Sociology at the University of Maribor. He has done extensive empirical research, particularly in the sociology of religion and ethnicity. Fulbright Professor in the USA during 1986.

Miroslav Hroch is the head of the Faculty of History of the Karolyi University, Prague. His publications include *Social Preconditions of National Revival in Europe: A Comparative Analysis of the Social Composition of Patriotic Groups among the Smaller European Nations* (Cambridge University Press, 1985) and Ecclesia Militants: The Inquisition, co-authored with Anna Skybová (Leipzig, 1988).

Abdulaziz Kamilov (b. 1948) is a Senior Research Fellow at the Institute of World Economy and International Relations (IMEMO). He received his Ph.D. from IMEMO for a study of the Middle East conflict. He is the author of several articles on conflict resolution in the Middle East and nationality problems in Soviet Central Asia.

Peter King (b. 1936) is Senior Lecturer in Government and Director of the Centre for Peace & Conflict Studies, University of Sydney. He is currently an executive member of the Council of the International Peace Research Association (representing the Asia-Pacific region), and has been Professor of Political Studies at the University of Papua New Guinea.. In 1976 he was a visiting fellow at the Faculty of Law, Moscow State University. He has published widely on ethical issues in nuclear strategy and conflict resolution in the South Pacific and South East Asia.

Aksel Kirch (b. 1949) is a Senior Research Fellow at the Institute of Philosophy, Sociology and Law in the Estonian Academy of Sciences since 1975. In 1979 he became a Candidate of Sociology at the Institute of Sociology of the USSR Academy of Sciences in Moscow. He has published approximately 50 works, including eight articles in the journal *Sociological Researches*.

Marika Kirch (b. 1951) has been a Senior Research Fellow at the Institute of Philosophy, Sociology and Law in the Estonian Academy of Sciences since 1989. In 1983 she received her Candidate degree in Sociology. She has published approximately 30 scientific articles, currently on the problems of national processes in Estonia.

Douhomir Minev, is a Senior Research Fellow at the Institute of Sociology, an advisor to the Bulgarian Council of Ministers.

Viktor Nadein-Raevski (b. 1949) is a Research Fellow at the Institute of World Economy and International Relations (IMEMO), USSR Academy of Sciences, where he received his Ph.D. for a critical analysis of modern Pan-Turkism. He is the author of several articles on problems of nationalism in the Soviet Union.

Kumar Rupesinghe (b. 1943) Ph.D. in Sociology, City University, London; BA, (honours), London School of Economics; Senior Researcher at the International Peace Research Institute, Oslo (PRIO); Secretary General of International Alert, 1992-; Chair of the International Peace Research Association's Commission on Internal Conflicts and their Resolution, (ICON). He has published and edited many articles and books, including: *Conflict Resolution in Uganda*, James Curry Ltd., London, 1989 and *Ethnic Conflicts and Human Rights, a comparative perspective*, United Nations University, 1989.

Talib Saidbaev (b. 1937) was Professor in the Higher Party School, Moscow, until August, 1991. His main research interests are Islam and nationality problems. Publications in Russian include: *Islam and Society* (1978 and 1984); *Islam: History and Present* (1985); *Dialogue on Islam* (1988). At present he is working to establish an Institute of Islam in Moscow.

Galina Soldatova (b. 1956) is a Research Fellow at the Institute of Ethnology and Anthropology, Russian Academy of Sciences. She received her B.A. from Moscow State University in psychology, and her Ph.D. from the Institute of Ethnography. She is the author of several articles on psychological aspects of nationality problems in the Soviet Union.

Borislav Tafradjiski (b. 1958) has, among other things, participated on a research team studying the new system of health-care organization in Bulgaria and the transition from state budget financing to health-security funding. Attended University of Oslo International Summer School 1991; considerable involvement in studies of ethnic conflict in Bulgaria.

Tair Tairov (b. 1937) is a Professor of Juridical Science at the Youth Institute, Moscow which he joined after a long period as a Research Fellow at the Institute of World Economy and International Relations (IMEMO), Russian Academy of Science. His main research interest is the political development and nationality problem of the former Soviet Union. He has published more than thirty articles, including *The Soviet Union after the Coup: The Rise of National States*, and *After the Wall, New Iron Curtains*, both published in Swedish.

Valery A. Tishkov (b. 1941) is currently Minister of Nationalities of the Russian Federation; M.A. from Moscow State University; Ph.D. from the Institute of General History, USSR Academy of Sciences. He was General Secretary of the Division of History of the Russian Academy of Sciences (1976-82), Head of American Ethnic Studies at the Institute of Ethnology and Anthropology (1982-), and became the Director of the same institute in 1989; he has published numerous articles books, including *National-Liberating Movement in Colonian Canada,* Moscow, 1978; *History and Historians in the USA*, Moscow, 1985; and co-authored *Native Peoples of the US and Canada in a Contemporary World*, Moscow, 1990.

Mara Ustinova (b. 1943) is a Senior Research Fellow at the Institute of Ethnology and Anthropology, Russian Academy of Sciences. She received her B.A. from the Latvian State University and her Ph.D from the Institute of Ethnography - a study of the transmission of ethnocultural traditions in the contemporary family. Publications in Russian include *Family Customs of Latvian Urban Dwellers* (1980), and of 65 articles on etnocultural process in the contemporary family in the Baltic region. She is co-author of The *Contemporary Lithuanian Family*, (1989).

Olga Vorkunova (b. 1951) is a Research Fellow at the Institute of World Economy and International Relations (IMEMO), Russian Academy of Sciences. She received her B.A. from Moscow State University in history and her Ph.D. from IMEMO. Her doctorate was a study of development strategies in the Scandinavian countries. She is the author of several articles on the problems of assistance and conflict resolution in the Third World and the Soviet Union, as well as 'Skandinavia i mezhdunarodnie konflikti' [Scandinavia and International Conflict] in *Konflikti v "Tretem Mire" i Zapad*, 1989.

Anatoli Yamskov (b. 1956) is a Research Fellow at the Institute of Ethnology and Anthropology, USSR Academy of Sciences. He received his B.A. in International Geography from Moscow State University and his Ph.D from the Institute of Ethnography in 1987. His doctorate was a study on ecological anthropology - the cultural adaptation of peasant communities in the Caucasian pasturelands. He is the author of more than 20 articles on Caucasian ethnology. He is now working on the problem of ethnic conflicts in the Transcaucasus.

Introduction

Kumar Rupesinghe, Peter King and Olga Vorkunova

This book anticipates and celebrates a momentous historical series of events which have transformed the world – the end of the Cold War, and the collapse of Communist totalitarian regimes in the former Soviet Union and in Eastern Europe. One event above all has encapsulated this transformation: the dismantling of the Berlin Wall, which symbolised how people can regain their own history, breach boundaries which had contained them, and take part in debates on a common future which had been long forbidden and driven underground. And Berlin Walls have continued to collapse, with the dismantling of the remnants of the Soviet Empire and now, perhaps, even the dismantling of the Russian empire. This book then is all about the deconstruction of Empire and the emergent reconstruction of new identities and sovereignties.

It seems to be incontestable that we are living through the end of several eras – in a time of fundamental transition:the end of the Cold War and the Post War; the end of the superpower era; the end, perhaps, of power politics in its old mould – even the end of War or, at least, of great power wars. We need to study intensely the precise consequences of the demise of European Communism, and the problematic nature of the transition now under way. What this volume reflects on, then, is precisely the problem of a transition where, in the absence of liberal ideology and a an established middle class, reassertive nationalism is shaping the politics of the post-Communist world.

Certainly the Cold War seems to have largely disappeared from Europe and the major regions of what used to be called the Third World; and therefore the Post War era has largely come to an end. In Eastern Europe Soviet military power is almost gone – and with it the satellite regimes whose successors now look to NATO for security; to Germany for investment, and to God for reassurance that they will not be permitted to slide from socialist into capitalist degradation. Outside Europe all that remains of the Cold War are some atavistic regimes (Cuba, Vietnam, China, North Korea) and movements (the Khmer Rouge), which have not yet yielded to the force of US-Soviet *rapprochement* and its peace *Realpolitik*.

As for the demise of the superpowers, in the post Cold War event only one of them collapsed, as was vividly illustrated by the Gulf War. But in the United States itself the theory of American decline has been enjoying a rising popularity. The theory holds that the USA will overstretch itself in pursuing a post Cold War global security role and must change its priorities to domestic social and political reform and economic restructuring. Old style imperial power politics can no longer be sustained in Washington, according to many philosophically minded experts; but the point is strongly contested by many conservatives who say that the USA is still 'bound to lead'. No, the USA is 'bound to bleed,' economically at least, if it makes the attempt, reply the declinists; and the apparent triumphs of the Gulf War have not been decisive proof either way. The riots and social unrest in Los Angeles, California, is a result of the neglect of domestic issues in favour of irrelevant arms races and foreign adventures, constantly undermining the economic, social and technological bases of American power, as well as American prosperity.

The end of power politics – at least in its aggravated form, involving a quest for big power imperium through nuclear supremacy and global interventionism – therefore remains a possibility. And the new global agenda which was meant to replace the agenda of *Machtpolitik* – ecological sanity, social justice, a world human rights regime and a strengthened global political order through rejuvenation and then reform of the UN – all of these are at least still under discussion, together with the rival – or perhaps complementary – agenda of a global productivity race.

In which(or either) case there would be no more War – only trade wars – and much socio-political and economic-ecological summitry. But we already know that things aren't going to be so simple. For every Third World armed conflict liquidated or waning under Big Power duress, there is one under way or threatening to erupt in the world of post Communism (Yugoslavia plus the former Soviet empire), and the combustion chamber for conflict in every case – the Balkans, Caucasia,

Russia, Central Asia – is the subject of this book: post-Communist ethno-nationalism. Far from the demise of European Communism ushering in the end of History, a new, utterly non-Marxist spectre is haunting Eurasia – from the Sea of Okhotsk to the borders of the new Germany, and from the Soviet Arctic to Afghanistan: an ethnic war of all against all. On the one hand, as noted above, the total collapse of European Communism has meant the collapse of Soviet/Russian imperialism – first in Eastern Europe; then in the Baltic republics, and now, increasingly,everywhere Stalin once ruled, including non-Russian, Muslim areas of the Russian Federation itself (Tatarstan; Bashkiria; Checheno-Ingushetia) and, most momentously, the Ukraine. On the other hand, amidst the Soviet imperial rubble, many a nation and people whose identity has been blurred or lost for a generation or more has rediscovered its language and voice, and begun to remake its social and political habitat.

Ethnic self-assertion has been so strong – and so subject to political manipulation – that it even seems capable of providing a reprieve for Communist leaders whose other sources of appeal, apart from still occupying positions of power, are almost non-existent. Red coats have been hastily exchanged for those displaying the colours of the national rainbow, and patriotism has been the first refuge of many Bolshevik scoundrels (neo-Stalinist mafiosi, often), first in Romania and Bulgaria; later in Uzbekistan, Azerbaijan, the Ukraine and elsewhere. Conversely, many formerly liberal anti-Bolshevik nationalists have readily adopted or adapted the traditions of Red authoritarianism for their own fledgling dictatorships, as in Georgia.

But the main achievements of Soviet imperial deconstruction have survived, even if full democracy might have to wait for another day. The chapters in this collection were all completed before the military/Party/police coup attempt in Moscow of 19-21 August, 1991. Happily, the provisional title of this book survived this event, together with Presidents Yeltsin and Gorbachev; and the world has now indubitably entered the era of post-Communism, which may soon yield relief also for China's Han majority and non-Han minorities.

In the wake of the coup that failed to wind back the imperial clock, the changed balance of forces in Moscow finally gave the nations of the USSR as well as the liberals and democrats their best chance so far to consolidate their gains under *perestroika* and *glasnost*. For all the larger nationalities, this meant a chance to push for full sovereignty and independence – political, economic and cultural – without fear of military/police intimidation and economic blockade from the now fatally weakened Soviet Centre. The leading Moscow reactionaries in the Communist Party, the government, the military and the police/KGB, who were previously rendered respectable by Gorbachev, had by now committed suicide, been arrested or were scrambling to prove how passive they were during the coup.

Within days of Yeltsin's victorious stand against Vice-President Yanaev and his co-conspirators, most of the 15 Soviet republics had declared independence, and the process of decentralization through a new union treaty, which the coup leaders had intended to destroy, was now renewed with a vengeance in the absence of any immediate imperative to actually conclude a treaty or preserve the USSR at all. A ghost of the Gorbachev vision of a renewed union was finally conjured up in November 1991 – albeit without the three Baltic states, whose independence had by now been recognized by the two Moscows (Gorbachev's and Yeltsin's), as well as the rest of the world. But Georgia said it would not sign a new treaty; Armenia and Moldova said they would sign an economic treaty only; the three Slav republics (Russia, the Ukraine and *Belarus* – new nationalist name for Belorussia) and the six Muslim republics (Azerbaijan, Kazakhstan, Uzbekistan, and Kyrgyzstan (formerly Kirghizia), Turkmenistan and Tajikistan) all signalled that they would join; but it was not clear who would really join or who would stay if they did join – and this was as true of Russia as of the other nine. In any case, the demise of Gorbachev at the end of 1991 signalled the demise of his Union of Sovereign States as well, and the Yeltsin-sponsored Commonwealth of Independent Stated has fared little better in attempting to coordinate foreign and defence policy and economic, monetary and fiscal policy for twelve separate actors.

It was always clear that politics in the post USSR would include international politics of some kind, and possibly power politics, as first the larger and then the smaller republics jockeyed to inherit the Soviet Army, Navy, Airforce and strategic missile units, bases and weapons (including nuclear weapons) on their soil – and to raise or consolidate their own armies, militias and national guards.

The post USSR also posed several other problems and threats for the non-Russian nationalities which had seized the post-coup moment to attempt their independence:

•   A second conservative coup, leading to a fresh attempt at Soviet (or Russian) imperial reassertion from the Centre through surviving neo-Soviet institutions and leaders.

•   Russian imperial reassertion, through Boris Yeltsin or another leader exploiting the powerful institutions of a revivified or reasserted Russian republic.

Yeltsin's first impulse after the coup was to simply either take over or scrap all surviving Soviet institutions. Later he threatened that Russia would want to re-draw republic boundaries in the interests of the Russian diaspora (in Kazakhstan, Ukraine, Moldova, etc.) if the non-Russian republics insisted on going their own way. This threat was soon retracted, but the republics remain fearful of Russia's long-term intentions.

•   Neo-Stalinism (or neo-fascism, authoritarian ultra-nationalism or Islamic extremism) in individual states or republics, especially in the Caucasus and Central Asia.

•   Civil war – whether within recognized sovereignties, between them or against a reconstituted imperial Centre. The East European model of a disintegrating Yugoslavia racked by civil war over borders is an all-too-vivid reminder of what might lie in store for the post USSR.

After the coup the civil/international wars between Armenia and Azerbaijan, and between Georgia and South Ossetia continued as before; and Russia, in November 1991, barely avoided starting one of its own, thanks to another impulse of President Yeltsin – this time to crack down on national reassertion by one of the 'punished' (i.e., deported by Stalin) peoples of the Northern Caucasus, the Muslim Chechens of Checheno-Ingushetia. Yeltsin was happily checked by the democratic forces in the Russian parliament. Russia herself, the Russian Federation, must find a balance between, on the one hand, the desire of a radically reforming Centre under Yeltsin to prevail by authoritarian means if necessary (including the despatch of proconsular plenipotentiaries to the ends of empire); and the desire of long-suppressed nationalities and localities, on the other hand, to restore or discover democratic and consultative processes which will permit them to settle their own affairs in their own way. In the end Yeltsin, like Gorbachev before him, may have to let go – at least of those large Muslim 'autonomies' within the Russian Federation which have made a strong case for treatment on a par with the former Soviet republics.

All of the dangers identified above are being exacerbated by the fact that in the post Soviet Union, as in the new Eastern Europe, the chronic structural problems of a failed socialist economic model seem almost impervious to reform, which promotes political uncertainty and the eventual likelihood of an authoritarian relapse. At least the recent victories of 'market democrats' in much of the USSR and most of Eastern Europe affords a hope of a better future, even if it will take years to overcome the Soviet legacy of 45 (or 75) years of forced-labour tyranny, over-centralization and economic monumentalism – and a profound lack of rudimentary capitalist infrastructure and managerial skills.

'Civil society' on the political side, which is a more or less cost-free good, has developed much faster and farther than in economic life, where the costs of market reform can be protracted and painful – as Poland and others have discovered since 1989 – and where reform is therefore very difficult to begin. It would be foolish to expect a painless transition to 'market relations'. Political tolerance and institutional stability are therefore essential to cope with the difficulties of transition. One key to this in the post USSR is creative, long-term resolution of inter-nation conflict at all levels, but how this can be achieved will be the substance of debate and discussion for year to come. There is likely to be a series of cross border conflicts which may lead to inter-state wars, such as the one between Armenia and Azerbaijan. It is also likely that other ethnic groups and nationalities living within republics are going to clamour for greater independence. And profound psychological adjustments will be necessary in coping with cross-border loyalties, especially on the part of the Russian diaspora which numbers 25 million. Perhaps the inclusion of all the new republics as full members of the Conference on Security and Cooperation in Europe (CSCE) will lead to good behaviour, and the adoption of human rights standards, including measures for the protection of minorities. But no framework really exists to prevent conflicts from escalating into violence, and no framework yet exists for effective mediation and negotiation.

Likewise in Eastern Europe, there must be a settlement of ethnic differences, especially those concerning national boundaries and national autonomy, before economic and social reconstruction can begin or really work. Genuine democratization is undoubtedly the key first step; and is still lacking in Romania, Bulgaria – and above all in Yugoslavia, where Serbs in the name of Greater Serbia or Lesser Yugoslavia have conducted a war of aggression to 'liberate' ethnically Serbian and geopolitically important areas of Croatia and Bosnia while suppressing the autonomy of over a million (Muslim) Albanians in Kosovo within the borders of Serbia itself.

***

This book is predominantly the work of scholars who have experienced the nightmare of 'proletarian internationalism' (in Eastern Europe) and the 'flourishing and merging of peoples' (in the Soviet Union) in their own minds and on their own bodies over the past generation and longer. 'Actually existing socialism' is no more; but contending with its various legacies is also potentially nightmarish, and there is a fund of wisdom in these chapters for averting or minimizing catastrophe. The authors from the former USSR are clear that the legacy of Stalinism and 'stagnation' from the Soviet period has been to exacerbate nationality conflicts, both through the effects of 'imperial' migration patterns (whether industry-driven or induced by deportations and forced migrations), and in other ways. Everywhere the trauma and waste of failed socialism has left the nation as the most accessible and fulfilling point of reference for disillusioned peoples, including the imperial people themselves, the Russians, whose enormous diaspora is at once a source of concern for Russians in the Russian heartland and a source of neo-imperial threat to the newly liberated non-Russian republics. The authors in this volume are clear that, while re-drawing ethno-political boundaries is a Pandora's box, there must be operative treaty guarantees of human and group rights for the Russian diaspora as well as for the newly liberated ethnoses and *their* diasporas.

All are convinced of the positive value of democracy in that it helps to build a civil society, the rule of law and market mechanisms for the allocation of goods and services. But none of them think that these achievements will be painless or automatic for they all draw attention to the danger of unbridled nationalism and violence. The process of the transition from totalitarian regimes to democracy requires imagination and courage in building mechanisms and insti-tutions for the peaceful resolution of violent conflicts in particular.

The authors – both Soviet and East European – have several grave reservations about contemporary post-socialist nationalism – above all that it can be a source of authori-tarianism as well as liberation; of pogroms as well as normal, fruitful intercourse with other peoples and cultures; of atavism as well as progress after the long sleep of Stalinist feudalism. Yet nearly all are agreed that national feeling and self- expression must now be given their due, even at the expense of rational-seeming federal or confederal structures, if necessary. At the same time new mechanisms, processes, norms and legal orders for the resolution of nationality conflict, and for the defence of national and human rights, must be developed – and the outside world must play its part in easing and encouraging peaceful change.

To that task this book is dedicated.

1

The Future of the Soviet Union: Deconstruction versus Disintegration

Peter King

1. INTRODUCTION

The Soviet Union was beset by a triple crisis as the reform process launched by Mikhail Gorbachev in 1986 ran out of steam and began to reverse course during 1990. *First*, a crisis of the economy and society, because economic *perestroika* had palpably failed to move beyond rhetoric towards market reform, or indeed towards any significant change whatever in those 'command economy' patterns of ownership and control in industry and agriculture which had previously immiserated the country and were now beggaring it. *Second*, a crisis of the regime, as *glasnost* and partial democratic reform failed to produce either a legitimately elected national leader or a parliament capable of genuine autonomy free of Communist party tutelage and arbitrary Presidential *dirigisme*. *Third*, a crisis of the union, as the dissenting minority nationalities, taking the promises of *perestroika* and the Soviet constitution literally, moved from the assertion of sovereignty towards a demand for independence.

This chapter explores the contemporary sources, scope and intensity of nationality conflict in the USSR; assesses the effectiveness of the various methods of political struggle being used on all sides (including at the Soviet Centre); canvasses the arguments for and against continuation of the USSR as an authoritarian federation; surveys the various mechanisms and principles of conflict resolution available to the embattled parties;

and focuses finally on workable alternatives to the present forced union of 15 republics, with a preference for *deconstruction* of the Union (consensual dismantling of Union structures, with Moscow allowing the graceful departure of all republics which wish for it) over *disintegration* (where Moscow resists the exit of the reluctant to the bitter end, with potentially disastrous consequences for future cooperation).

The chapter proposes that there is no way out of the triple impasse confronting President Gorbachev, except by allowing a break-up of the USSR to the extent that the major nationalities desire;[1] no route to regime legitimacy or economic recovery and social renovation except by allowing genuine self-determination in all of the 15 Soviet republics. Gorbachev himself may not survive such a process in view of his growing unpopularity, but it is certain that no part of his original programme – and probably not him either – would survive the kind of military, police and 'partocrat' reaction which has been building through, around and (perhaps) despite him since early in 1990.

2. THE NATIONALITY CRISIS

The crisis of the Soviet federation is predominantly a crisis of nationality – and not only for the minority nationalities, but for the majority Russians as well. (For Soviet population figures by republics and nationalities, see Tables 1-3. Table 1 also shows current political alignments of the republics on the issue of sovereignty and independence.) Boris Yeltsin, so-called President of the Russian Soviet Federative Socialist Republic (actually Chairman of its Supreme Soviet), the anti-Tsar of all the Russians (and many millions of other Soviet citizens as well), has tapped an urge towards specifically Russian, as opposed to Soviet, renewal since his break with Gorbachev in 1987 and his departure from the Communist Party in mid-1990. He proposes that Russia should shed her self-imposed authoritarian leading role in the union: she must not only recover her pre-Soviet past, but acquire an appropriate post-imperial identity. Hence the Russian President's strong commitment (which there may be grounds for doubting later) to build new relations horizontally among the constituent members of the Union of Soviet Socialist Republics with a view to replacing the 1922 Soviet union of coercion with a voluntary federation, confederation, economic community or whatever. There is in fact now a strong likelihood that more than one form of inter-republic or interstate relations will emerge in a deconstructed or reconstructed Soviet polity.

At present, Gorbachev stands for the continuity of the ruling *nomenklatura* (party, government, military and police);[2] the continuity of the imperial federation, and the containment (at least) of *glasnost* and *perestroika* in the interests of maintaining the fundamentals of the economic and political status quo.

Boris Yeltsin by contrast stands for a genuine disempowering of the *nomenklatura*;[3] a voluntary federation of the republics, and a bold attempt to turn the economy around with some version of his advisers' 500 Days programme, including rapid privatization in the agrarian and industrial economy. At present (early 1991) there is no other serious policy choice facing the country – the process of democratic party formation is still embryonic, and, given Gorbachev's unpopularity and lack of support even on the Right, all that stands between the people and reaction is Yeltsin with his five million supporters in Moscow, his millions of working class supporters in the rest of Russia, in the Ukraine and in Belorussia and his important following in the smaller republics.[4]

Democratic politicians everywhere are clear about this – the leaders of the Baltic secession, for instance, look to Yeltsin not only for political protection, but for fruitful economic ties to replace Moscow's policy of industrial *diktat*, which has given Estonia and Latvia (especially) military production combines which are not needed or wanted; have caused serious pollution problems; have drawn in Slav settlers by the hundreds of thousands, and have become the social and organizational basis of the imperial counter-revolution in the Baltics since 1989.

The Baltic case for national freedom is as painfully straightforward and morally compelling as the Russian case is tortuous and paradoxical. The Latvians, Estonians and Lithuanians have had their substance drained as victims of the Soviet experience since 1940, to the point of national exhaustion and even extinction. (Indeed Latvia is now only 52% ethnic Latvian.) The Russians, by contrast – exploiters and 'ethnocrats' in the eyes of all except themselves – have reached the brink of deracination (at least according to Alexander Solzhenitsyn) through bearing the burden of upholding an empire in which Russians, although they are still a majority of the Soviet population and the leading core in all institutions of central power, have had no separate capital,

Academy of Sciences, or (until 1990) Communist party of their own. In many ways, they have retained only a tenuous cultural identity in a multinational federation which was supposed by many critics to cater exclusively for Russian interests (Dunlop 1983). The Russian birthrate is also now dropping alarmingly, which suggests that high birthrates in the Central Asian republics could quite rapidly make the Russians themselves a Soviet minority people.[5]

If the Balts aspire to the condition of Finland (or Sweden or Norway), and the Russians (or at least tens of millions of them, especially in Moscow and Leningrad) aspire to rediscover themselves, the Moldavians will probably aspire mainly to become citizens of Romania, whence they were plucked in 1939-40, at the same time that Baltic independence was being annulled by Stalin in collusion with Hitler. For them – and for the Uniate Catholics of the Western Ukraine (Orthodox in ritual; papal in loyalty), who were forcefully detached from Poland in those years – there is no question of Russian or Soviet 'protection': incorporation in the Stalinist empire has been pure tragedy and loss. (The Uniates have had Marxism *and* the Orthodoxy of the Moscow Patriarch imposed on them.) For the rest of the Ukraine's 52

Table 1: *The USSR Population by Republics, 1989 (in millions)*

Pro-Sovereignty		Pro-Independence	
Slav		**Baltic**	
Russia	147.4	Lithuania	3.7
Ukraine	51.7	Latvia	2.7
Belorussia	10.2	Estonia	1.6
	209.3		**8.0**
Central Asian and Muslim		**Caucasian**	
Uzbekistan	19.9	Georgia	5.4
Kazakhstan	16.5	Armenia	3.3
Tajikistan	5.1		
Kirghizia	4.3		**8.7**
Turkmenistan	3.5		
	49.3		
Caucasian and Muslim			
Azerbaijan	7.0	Moldova	4.3

Total population in 1989 was 286.7 million and in 1990 it was 288.6 million

Source: *Ezhegodnik...*, 1990, pp. 8, 12.

Table 2: USSR Republics, Nationality Distribution, 1989

Armenia		Kazakhstan		Russia	
Armenians	90%	Russians	41%	Russians	83%
		Kazakhs	36%	Tatars	4%
		Ukrainians	6%		
Azerbaijan		**Kirghizia**		**Tajikistan**	
Azeris	78%	Kirghiz	48%	Tajiks	59%
		Russians	26%	Uzbeks	23%
		Uzbeks	12%		
Belorussia		**Latvia**		**Turkmenistan**	
Belorussians	79%	Latvians	54%	Turkmen	68%
Russians	12%	Russians	33%	Russians	13%
				Uzbeks	9%
Estonia		**Lithuania**		**Ukraine**	
Estonians	65%	Lithuanians	80%	Ukrainians	74%
Russians	28%	Russians	9%	Russians	21%
		Poles	8%		
Georgia		**Moldova**		**Uzbekistan**	
Georgians	69%	Moldavians	64%	Uzbeks	69%
Armenians	9%	Ukrainians	14%	Russians	11%
Russians	7%	Russians	13%	Tajiks	4%
Ossetians	3%	Gagauz	4%		

Source: *Time*, 12 March 1990

Table 3: The USSR Population by Nationalities, 1989 (in millions)

Russians	145.2	Georgians	4.0	Jews	1.4
Ukrainians	44.2	Moldavians	3.4	Adigei	1.3
Uzbeks	16.7	Lithuanians	3.1	Mordvinians	1.2
Belorussians	10.0	Turkmen	2.7	Poles	1.1
Kazakhs	8.1	Kirghiz	2.5	Chechens	1.0
Azerbaijanis	6.8	Germans	2.0	Estonians	1.0
Tatars	6.6	Chuvash	1.8	Abkhazians	1.0
Armenians	4.6	Latvians	1.5		
Tajiks	4.2	Bashkirs	1.5		

Source: *Ezhegodnik...*, 1990, p. 10.

millions (including eleven million Russians) the situation is more complex – the large Russian-speaking minority has brought about linguistic Russification of several million Ukrainians and the Orthodox Church has remained loyal to Moscow – at least until recently when the autocephalous heresy resurfaced. However Rukh, the Ukrainian independence movement, rules in Lvov, capital of Western Ukraine, and is making steady headway elsewhere. A hunger strike and mass demonstration outside parliament in Kiev not only forced the resignation of the Ukrainian Prime Minister in October 1990, but also a decision that Ukrainian youth should undergo military service outside the republic only on a voluntary basis, and a promise that the question of handing back Party and Komsomol (Party youth league) property to the government would be reviewed, together with the question of fresh parliamentary elections.[6] The future trajectory of Ukrainian nationalism is likely to be almost as important as the trajectory of Russian nationalism in settling the fate of the USSR.

Belorussia with its eleven millions has faced the same Russifying pressures as the Ukraine, and is certainly more vulnerable to them. It has been conventionally written off as a force for radical change in the era of *perestroika*; but, under the impact of the Chernobyl disaster, of intimate contact with the Baltic nationalist movements and new revelations about Stalinist atrocities in Belorussia – and in response to Gorbachev's harsh new economic policies – Minsk during early 1991 became a leading centre of strikes and agitation for a U-turn in Moscow and the resignation of Gorbachev.

Likewise, Georgia and Armenia, Christian civilizations older than Russia herself, which have looked to Russia historically for protection against both Shiite (Iranian) and Sunni (Turkish) Islam, have now turned decisively against Moscow. In neither republic was the desire for protection strong enough to prevent efforts to achieve independence after the October Revolution – efforts which were crushed by Stalin as General Secretary of the Communist Party and Commissar for Nationalities at the end of the Civil War. Now, any lingering desire for protection has evaporated in the fierce light of *glasnost* and under the impact of disillusioning trauma: in Georgia the bloody crackdown on nationalist protest of April 1989; in Armenia the failure of Soviet protection during the anti-Armenian pogroms which have erupted since 1988 in Baku (the capital of Azerbaijan) and in

Nagorno-Karabakh (the ancient Armenian territory deliberately awarded to Azerbaijan by Stalin after the Civil War for purposes of divide and rule – and to appease Turkey). Armenia's only close friend in the region is the Kurdish nation – victim of Soviet, Turkish, Iranian, Syrian and Iraqi oppression.

Moving east from the Christian Caucasus, there is less interest in independence among the Islamic republics than one might expect from the history of Russian and Soviet conquest, colonization, annexation, exploitation and despoliation in the region. Caucasian Azerbaijan has perhaps suffered least. The Central Asian republics (Turkmenistan, Uzbekistan, Kazakhstan, Kirghizia, Tajikistan) have variously had to contend with the influx of a Russian plurality (Kazakhstan), or large minority (Kirghizia); the imposition of a cotton monoculture and the drying up and pollution of the Aral Sea under the impact of Tsar Cotton, thanks to over- irrigation, over-fertilization and pesticide run-off (Uzbekistan is worst affected); pollution from nuclear testing (Kazakhstan); suppression of nomadic life-styles, and persecution of Islam (until recently) in all republics.

Despite these impediments to fraternity in Central Asia, President Gorbachev's March 1991 referendum on the future of the Soviet Union confirmed that, notwithstanding catastrophic youth unemployment, poverty and ecological decay, and the religious, cultural and ethnic attraction of neighbouring powers (Iran and Turkey especially), Central Asians – at least under existing neo-Brezhnevite leaders – are not yet prepared to part with the union that has devastated, but also, at least in some ways, modernized and subsidized them for the past 70 years, even though the recent departure of Russian specialists and technicians has crippled and even closed down industry in many places.

What, then, do the Central Asians want? Pan-Turkic and pan-Islamic sentiment runs freely alongside cross-cutting conflictual tribalisms: Kirghiz versus Uzbeks over land and housing in Kirghizia; forcibly transplanted Meskhetian Turks (from Georgia) versus Kirghiz; Persian-speaking Tajiks left high and dry by the retreat of Abbasid power in fear of all the Turkic peoples and resenting Uzbek control of their ancient city, Samarkand. Nevertheless, as in Ukraine, the national and religious resistance movements of Central Asia – whatever their present shape and status – probably still have far to evolve in the direction of demanding self-determination and independence.

One straw in the wind is the phenomenon of Central Asian pro-
fessionals and intellectuals at the Centre, Russified and
Sovietized by years of Party service, suddenly rediscovering their
Islamic and national roots.

Meanwhile the process launched by Boris Yeltsin, whereby
a core of four republics (Russia, Ukraine, Belorussia and
Kazakhstan) will try to negotiate separately the fundamentals of
a new federation open to all,[7] could quite sensibly incorporate
all of the Central Asian republics at an early stage, since they
remain collectively and individually pro-union. As for the
Azerbaijanis, they are strongly placed: their various blockades
of the Armenian adversary have never been effectively contested
by Moscow;[8] and their military attacks against the Armenian
enclave of Nagorno-Karabakh inside Azerbaijan have been
routinely condoned and even supported by the Centre. They
outnumber the Armenians two to one and can look for support
not only to a large Azeri minority in Iran, but to mono-cultural,
multi-racial Turkey on Armenia's western border. They (like
Armenians, Georgians, Lithuanians and Latvians) have been cut
down in the street by Soviet security forces on the rampage
against independence movements;[9] but they voted for prolonging
the union in the recent referendum.

3. THE RUSSIAN DIASPORA

A word, finally, about the Russian diaspora outside the Russian
republic – numbering no less than 25 million in the early 1990s,
after Tsar-driven and free Russian colonization in the old
Empire; after the upheavals of the Civil War; after Stalin's
kulak deportations during the collectivization of agriculture;
after the Terror of the 1930s and the Gulag (whose penumbra
of human suffering was the prolonged or permanent exile of
millions); after the pre-war, intra-war and post-war deportations
of supposedly disloyal Balts, Caucasians, Crimeans and others
(whose places were often filled by Russians), and after the
economic migrations of the 1960s and 1970s.

To these 25 million Russians can be added perhaps half a
million Russian troops and dependents still pullulating anomal-
ously on the territories of the former Warsaw Pact allies who
have been abandoned (and are very grateful for it!) by Soviet
power since 1990. The *aus*-Rus, survivors of a vast 'creole

pilgrimage' (Anderson 1985; see also Stavenhagen 1989) to all
points of the compass from Muscovy, have a multifold bearing on
the future of the Union. Certainly they are upholders of the
status quo (i.e., bearers of reaction) and colonizers who threaten
the demographic (national) integrity of certain republics
(Estonia, Latvia, Kazakhstan, Kirghizia – see Table 2). But
many of them are also peacemakers and good citizens of the
emerging would-be independent states, where some Russian
communities are long-established and living under authentic
local guarantees. (Estonia has even incorporated the UN Declaration of Human Rights into its draft constitution).

Nevertheless, even in Estonia and Latvia, where the proportion of independence sympathizers among the local Russians is
probably highest,[10] the Russian threat is not merely demographic, as I have mentioned. In Estonia, for instance, the combination of a Russian-dominated military establishment, a predominantly Russian-staffed military-industrial complex, together
with large-scale mining of oil shale driven by Soviet rather than
Estonian needs, has created disastrous environmental degradation from military fuel dumping and possibly nuclear and chemical weapon waste dumping as well, and from industrial and
mining pollution of Estonia's major river systems at source.[11]
Estonia and Latvia are forced to consider restrictions on Russian
in-migration. They must address an ethnic imbalance which
makes it impossible for these republics to mount the special
majorities required to qualify for secession under Gorbachev's
legislation of April 1990 which is supposed to implement Article
72 of the Soviet constitution.[12] (In any case, of course, the
Baltic republics do not legally or morally recognize their forced
incorporation in the Soviet Union – and so there can be no
question of jumping through hoops fabricated in Moscow to earn
the right of exit.) Latvia and Estonia also need leverage to check
the military and military-industrial push behind in-migration.
Lithuania has actually legislated against any right of settlement
for non-Lithuanian retired military officers.[13]

The final form of the Russian threat to the independence-
seeking republics is the Interfront movement, dominated in
Estonia by the local captain of military industry, and mobilizing
the militarized production workers, the 150,000 occupation
troops and the ranks of the KGB as well.[14] (The locally-based
Interior Ministry *miilits* were taken over by the Popular Front
government during the short tenure of Gorbachev's liberal ally

Vadim Bakatin as Minister of the Interior.)[15] The climactic point so far of the Russian/Soviet threat to Baltic self-determination has been the National Salvation Committees which appeared during the crisis of early 1991 – groups of Army/Party-sponsored reactionaries, who would have headed (at least temporarily) the quisling regimes which a full-scale Moscow-ordered crackdown would have produced. In the event, however, the Right, or Gorbachev, or both, held back; and, although 21 people died in Vilnius on the night of 12 January, the would-be independent republic held firm as the people mobilized behind President Landsbergis to physically defend the parliament building.[16]

A military crackdown by Moscow probably cannot be fully repulsed anywhere, at least in the short run; but it is now really only in the two Protestant Baltic republics, Latvia and Estonia, that there is still a firm demographic basis for a Russian-led counter-revolution. The large Russian minorities in Kirghizia and Kazakhstan are in retreat, as local industry collapses and Slav fear of resurgent Islam, Turkic nationalism and ethnic eruptions continues to grow.[17] The push of minority national-ism against the Russians in the Soviet periphery (and of Ger-man, Polish and other nationalisms against the lost Russian tribe in Eastern Europe) both encounter the friction and resis-tance arising from lack of jobs and housing in the Russian heartland. The Russians *would* be in-gathered by the millions, but they *cannot* be. There is potential for trouble in Eastern Europe as well as in the Soviet periphery flowing from this fundamental lack of demographic flexibility, which would be only partly alleviated by Moscow's consent to massive emigration from Russia westwards – which will be part of a promised new emigration law to operate from 1993.

4. TYPES OF NATIONALITY CONFLICT

Observers of the present ethnic turmoil in the USSR have distin-guished three kinds of conflict: between the Centre and the periphery (the republics); between the republics; and within individual republics.[18] The centre-periphery problem affects every republic, but especially those which have declared or would like to declare independence – and above all Lithuania, which led the way with its independence declaration of 1 March 1990. *All* republics, including Russia, have now passed declarations of sovereignty (at least), asserting the superiority of their laws over those of the Centre; but those republics whose Supreme Soviet (or Supreme Council) did *not* boycott the March 1991 referendum – the three Slavic and six Muslim republics – must be accounted least likely to try to secede at the moment.

Developments during 1990 confirmed that Georgia, Armenia and Moldova wish for secession (leading probably in Moldova's case to eventual reunion with Romania)[19] as ardently as the Baltic republics (Georgia finally declared independence in April 1991);[20] that the Muslim republics may evolve towards demanding separate or collective independence (possibly Uzbek-dominated)[21] as the economic situation worsens; that the two 'junior' Slav republics, Belorussia and (most critically) Ukraine, seem likely to demand independence soon, and that Russia's quest for sovereignty will not be appeased until Boris Yeltsin has prevailed in his epic struggle with Mikhail Gorbachev.

Inter-republic strife affects Armenia and Azerbaijan most severely – the ancient historical legacy of religious strife is compounded by the Karabakh conflict, which has seen the Armenian-majority enclave of Nagorno-Karabakh (an autonomous republic within Azerbaijan) seek reunion with Armenia. This precipitated an inter-republic military stand-off as, first Armenia, and then Azerbaijan, mobilized behind their territorial claims for Karabakh, which Moscow has declined to settle in Armenia's favour since the troubles of 1988 and which therefore seems bound to continue. Although the Armenia irregular militias which were raised to support Karabakh and defend the republic against Azerbaijani incursions have been partly disbanded, and Soviet army and police forces seem capable of containing the inter-republic confrontation, clashes and tension continue. Other inter-republic territorial disputes – between Moldova and Ukraine; Georgia and Armenia; Russia and Ukraine; and Russia and Kazakhstan, for instance – seem unlikely to involve violence. But in Central Asia, where there has already been considerable communal bloodshed, such conflicts could be deadly – for instance those between Uzbekistan on the one hand and Tajikistan and Kirghizia on the other.

As for the third kind of nationality conflict, within the republics,it seems bound to continue in Azerbaijan – but also in the Central Asian republics, where embattled refugees (e.g., Armenians) and emigré populations (e.g., Meskhetians) are involved as well as established populations. There are also serious conflicts within Georgia (pro-Soviet Muslim minorities in Abkhazia and Southern Ossetia in conflict with aroused and authoritarian Georgian nationalism under the Round Table government); in Moldova – where Russian and Turkic-speaking (but Christian) Gagauz minorities wish to uphold Gorbachev's status quo against the independence movement, and in the Russian Republic where Tatars (land-locked, but numbering 3.5 millions – larger than the indigenous titular population of any of the Baltic republics), Karelians, Bashkirs and others have asserted sovereignty against the RSFSR Centre.[22] In other words, centre-periphery politics are being played out in the Russian as well as Soviet outlands; and, although outright independence is probably not a serious option for any of the RSFSR autonomous republics, autonomous regions or national areas, their problems are in some cases worse than those of the Central Asian republics and their case for enhanced autonomy is strong.[23] The overall picture is one of extensive, intensive and expanding conflict – *Moscow News* in March 1991 identified 76 'cities, towns, districts and regions where Soviet people are in mortal conflict on ethnic grounds'.[24]

5. MEANS OF NATIONAL STRUGGLE AND THE CENTRE'S RESPONSE

Five years into *perestroika*, the various national movements aiming for full independence, which are at the heart of the nationality crisis in the USSR, are mostly about three years old. In this time their methods of struggle have become as diverse as the nationalities themselves, while the Centre also has developed a rich repertoire of suppressive strategies and tactics. The Centre of course has the entire panoply of means available to the authoritarian power state in the late twentieth century – military, ideological, political and economic; but the independence-seeking republics have waged a determined struggle. Let us consider the various arenas of struggle in turn, in order to assess the long-term prospects for republic independence.

5.1. Military

Since early in 1990 there have been military or military police crackdowns on the nationalists in the Baltic republics, in Georgia, in Armenia and in Azerbaijan. The military means available to the dissident republics for resistance against Moscow have been minimal; but several republics have at least partially liberated their local Interior Ministries during the reign of Gorbachev's liberal ally Vadim Bakatin as All-Union Minister, giving themselves some military or quasi-military capacity against the Centre,[25] and irregular militias for the direct defence of independent republican institutions (parliament, press, TV, etc.) have appeared in all of the Baltic republics. There are no illusions that these militias could prevail against a determined Soviet Army or Interior Ministry force;[26] but their symbolic value is high, and their traditions include the long guerrilla struggle of the 'forest brothers' against Soviet occupation in the Baltic states, which was not finally extinguished until the 1970s when the last individuals were captured or killed.[27]

Yeltsin in his less wary moments has called for Russia to exercise more control over her military destiny by establishing a Russian army 'to defend the sovereignty' of the republic.[28] In addition, there is a widespread feeling that conscripts from one republic should not be used for repression or the control of civil disorder in another, as is the current practice; and that persecution of representatives of dissident nationalities among the Army draftees (especially the Balts) has reached unacceptable levels.[29] The campaign against conscription by most of the republics (including the Ukraine) can be viewed as a form of indirect military struggle, one which could greatly sharpen national antagonisms in the future if it leads to an overwhelmingly Russified Soviet army. Meanwhile the republics are beginning to regularize their militias for defensive purposes, with or without the draft resisters who in many cases are officially protected and provided for in the republics.

5.2. Ideological

Gorbachev's government has released, published, permitted to be published or tolerated the publication of a vast documentation on nationality injustices in the Stalin period, especially concerning the unconscionable and unconscionably brutal occupation and annexation of the Baltic states in 1940-41; but also covering the conquest and annexation of the Ukraine, the Caucasus and Turkestan (Soviet Central Asia) after the Civil War, and the arbitrary deportation of small nationalities to the East during and after the Second World War. Gorbachev has thus abandoned the kind of mythical claims to legitimacy which previous Soviet regimes depended upon in the Soviet periphery – voluntary adherence to the USSR; the 'flourishing' of nationalities; the 'friendship of peoples' (in the short term) under socialism, followed by their 'merging' under communism (in the long run). But no sooner were the fundamentals of Stalinist mythology effectively disowned than the regime began to recoil in consternation from the consequences of ideological retreat, especially the accelerating independence movements in the Baltic region.

Yes, the Balts had been forcibly occupied and annexed in collusion with Hitler; yes, tens of thousands had been deported to Siberia in 1941, and more tens of thousands following re-occupation, re-annexation and collectivization after 1944: but, no, that was in another decade; new facts have been created (including a vast military infrastructure, more than a million 'economic' settlers, and tens of billions of rubles worth of industrial investment), and it is therefore imperative that the Baltic states stay in the federation. Or, if they do leave, why then they must pay full compensation to the Centre.

However, the Baltic leaders also have a bill to present to the Soviet authorities, and they seem to have won this particular ideological skirmish hands down on the merits.[30] Moscow has been left to argue that upholding 'law and order', and ensuring the effective functioning of the economy, requires discipline on the part of the republics – a far cry from the ideology of the progressive multinational Soviet federation under Stalin or even Brezhnev.

5.3. Political

In the absence of any firm ideological footing, *divide et impera* is the order of the day in the Soviet approach to the breakaway republics – Azeri versus Armenian; Russian against Balt, Moldavian or Central Asian Turk; Ossetian against Georgian. (Stalin, ironically, had an Ossetian father and a Georgian mother.) This is the unspoken dimension of political struggle between Gorbachev and the republics over national self-determination. The public struggle in recent times has mainly concerned the drafting and re-drafting of a new union treaty by

the Centre, and the promulgation of declarations of sovereignty
and independence by the republics.[31] Referendums on the question of the Soviet future have also proliferated – the Centre has
sought support for a *renewed* union, on the one hand, while the
republics have sought endorsement of independence or sovereignty. Fitfully but forcefully coordinating the pro-sovereignty,
pro-independence stand of the republics was Boris Yeltsin with
his grand scheme to reconstruct the union from the bottom up.

However, Yeltsin did not burn his bridges with Gorbachev to
the extent of boycotting the climactic (or perhaps anti-climactic)
referendum of March 1991, in which the voters were asked:

> *Do you consider it necessary to preserve the Union of Soviet*
> *Socialist Republics as a renewed federation of equal sovereign*
> *republics in which the human rights and freedoms of people of*
> *any nationality will be fully guaranteed?*[32]

Six republics (the Baltics plus Moldova, Georgia and Armenia)
did boycott the poll; but the 'yes' vote for Gorbachev's proposal
was 71% in the RSFSR and even higher elsewhere. Nevertheless
in Kazakhstan, where the republic government added a question
about a future 'union of equal sovereign *states*' (emphasis added),
and in the Ukraine, where the extra question concerned 'an independent state', there was an overwhelming 'yes' response (over
90%) – higher than said yes to Gorbachev's rather tendentious
and arguably self-contradictory question. In the RSFSR Yeltsin's
proposal for an elected Russian Presidency received as much
support (70%) as the Gorbachev proposal, despite heavy Communist Party opposition;[33] and, if Yeltsin wins a popular election
for this Presidency in June 1991 (as now seems inevitable,
barring 'accidents' which have dogged Yeltsin in the anti-
bureaucratic phase of his career), then Gorbachev, who has
never stood for popular election as Soviet chief executive, will
find himself more than ever embattled and lacking democratic
legitimacy in his defence of Soviet institutions.

While the republics mobilize around assertions of sovereignty and independence[34] – and in the Baltic case are forced
to physically defend the symbols and institutions of national
integrity – elsewhere the threat to self-determination is
less militarized and less urgent, and the work of national
consciousness-raising proceeds more normally. In the struggle for
nationhood the crucial audience may be purely local, or may
include the international media and the governments which will

eventually arbitrate on the USSR's murky economic and political future, the big powers of the OECD especially.

In addition to the individual efforts of the republics there is substantial inter-republican cooperation – not only among the geographically contiguous and historically self-conscious (as a collective) Baltic republics,[35] but among the Central Asians as well, who have also instituted summitry among the republican Presidents.[36] Moldova is essentially on its own (its most important backer is across the border in Bucharest); and, while Armenia and Georgia should be able to cooperate closely against their common Soviet and Turkish adversaries, Armenia's plight is deeper than Georgia's – the Azerbaijani blockades have prevented full recovery from the 1988 earthquake, and effective Russian or Soviet support of Armenia against Azerbaijan depends importantly on Georgia's cooperation for geographical reasons. There is also a territorial/ethnic dispute between the two Christian republics of the Caucasus.

As for the three Slav republics, Solzhenitsyn (in the United States) has appealed for them to recall their common destiny and remain together while shedding the imperial burdens assumed by Russia:

> We have to make a hard choice: between the empire, which has been ruining primarily us, and the spiritual and bodily salvation of our people.... Did Russia grow poorer from its separation from Poland and Finland?... we will straighten up even more without the crushing burden of our Central Asian underbelly, so thoughtlessly conquered by Alexander II.[37]

Yeltsin also sees a cooperating core of Slavic republics as essential for the future, but he has aligned himself closely with the secession-minded republics, and appears to hold out more hope for a (transformed) federation than Solzhenitsyn, who would (in the last analysis) force the non-Slav republics from the future Russian Union which he has in mind. Yeltsin supported Lithuania against Gorbachev during the economic blockade of 1990, and flew to Estonia during the crisis of January 1991, when it seemed that there might be a military crackdown throughout the Baltic region. In Tallinn he signed an agreement with the three Baltic republics to the effect that their respective soldiers would not attack each other.[38]

The main official Soviet site for protection of nationality rights is the new Federation Council which was set up in March 1990 and includes the Presidents of all the republican Supreme

Soviets (or Councils) – potentially a powerful diluter of Russian personnel dominance at the highest level of power.[39] Although it has been boycotted by the Baltic republics and others at times, it has offered some protection to the nationalities, for instance in the Baltic crisis of early 1991 (Kux, 1991, p.6). Although its role was only advisory at the beginning (Kux, 1990, p.88), it had apparently acquired decision-making powers by late 1990 when it virtually replaced the Presidential Council, which was also rather cavalierly established through the Congress of People's Deputies by Gorbachev.[40] The Federation Council has served to bring the President of Kazakhstan, Nursultan Nazarbaev, to all-union prominence in the role of loyal critic of Gorbachev's approach to the republics. Unfortunately Gorbachev's next exercise in constitutional tinkering, a Security Council consisting of his hard-core conservative and institutionally powerful allies – Valentin Pavlov (Prime Minster), Boris Pugo (Interior Minster), Dmitri Yazov (Defence Minister), Vladimir Kryuchkov (KGB) and Gennadi Yanaev (Vice-President) – plus two decorative liberal (or at least ex-liberal) allies, Vadim Bakatin and Yevgeni Primakov, suggests that the Federation Council may go the way of the Presidential Council if the trend to the Right resumes.

Likewise the protection of the republics and the minority nationalities generally – and also of the Russian interest personified by Yeltsin – is not very brilliantly served by the new parliamentary institutions which are supposed to represent nationality interests: a somewhat revivified Soviet of Nationalities ('upper house' of the Supreme Soviet) and a standing commission on nationality questions of the same Supreme Soviet. Gorbachev's ability to use his party, government and military connections to steamroller the indirectly elected and only partially democratized Supreme Soviet is notorious.[41] All Soviet institutions at the Centre can be construed, ultimately, as serving Gorbachev's cold war of attrition against the independence-seekers.

5.4. Economic

Since Lithuania's declaration of independence on 11 March 1990, Moscow has wielded economic carrots and sticks in a variety of ways to secure the return of Vilnius to the Soviet fold and to warn off other would-be independentists. Economic blockade was tried for some months, and finally deemed counter-productive – it was not decisive and was also offensive to Gorbachev's supporters in the West. (This did not prevent the subsequent

abortive coup attempt -if that's what it was – of January 1991.)
But the ordinary economic policy of Moscow towards the republics is experienced as a kind of permanent blockade or at least
economic cold war. That is, the republics feel dominated,
exploited and frustrated by the militarized monopolism of the
all-union economic ministries. The aspiration to get control of
local resources (for environmental as well as economic reasons),
enterprises and revenues; to expand republican budgets and
reduce Moscow's leverage over strategic economic decisions; to
initiate real privatization of industrial and agrarian property,
and to develop local banking and launch a local currency[42] – all
of this has entailed perpetual friction with the Centre, whose
own economic room for manoeuvring has steadily shrunk in
parallel with the collapsing economy and its own failure to settle
on a strategy of economic reform.

The bankruptcy (literal and metaphorical) of the Centre in
general and Gorbachev's team in particular, progressively shorn
of its liberal reformers during 1990 and early 1991, was clear in
the shock withdrawal of 50 and 100 ruble notes from circulation
in March 1991 and the draconian price rises of April – carried
through in the absence of any other steps likely to arrest economic implosion,[43] and rendered almost pointless by accompany-
ing wage, salary and pension rise. These measures were meant
to reduce the 500 billion ruble overhang which is plaguing the
Centre's attempt to control inflation.[44] But in early 1991 the
Centre was facing a kind of fiscal strike by the republics, who
are no longer meeting either their normal or their reduced-
by-agreement revenue contributions;[45] and the resulting ruble
underhang means that the Centre will be unable to meet its own
commitments for defence and welfare spending – or, dare one
suggest it, for *nomenklatura* pay and privileges – except by
printing money: a formula for political disaster, or, perhaps,
economic self-determination in the republics.[46]

Voices are being raised in Moscow for a dramatic response to
the economic troubles now pressing in on Gorbachev – a full-
blooded return to the past, with labour conscription (as under
War Communism during 1918-20 – and, in effect, for most of the
Stalin period) and the forcible imposition of budgetary discipline
on the republics through confiscation of assets. There would
be Presidential rule in the republics, as necessary; the
'administrative- command economy' would return with a vengeance, and the KGB would expand its newly-conferred role as

spearhead of the Gorbachev campaign against speculation and corruption – a role which gives personnel of the 'blue organ' the right to raid any premises (including joint Soviet and foreign investment companies) to search for evidence of economic crimes.[47]

Of course, with the military and the police in the ascendant, the Centre could – whether with, without or despite Gorbachev – try to crush republican economic autonomy and the hesitant steps being taken to establish a new economic order from the bottom up. These steps include inter-republican trade agreements (often involving barter, which Lithuania employed to resist the blockade of 1990) and even deals between individual republics and cities. (Estonia has agreed with the reforming city government of Leningrad to supply food in return for industrial goods.) This is the preferred path of the dissident republics for escaping from the supply and distribution crisis brought about by moves towards local autarchy during 1990. (The autarchic regime includes shopping only with a valid locally-issued ration card or internal passport; a ban on 'export' of scarce republican consumer goods, and so on.)

The Centre can try to crack down and impose iron economic discipline under General Staff auspices, as I have noted; but – as Academician Georgi Arbatov has remarked – the military which, according to Gorbachev himself, has been consuming 18 per cent of GNP (not 15-17% as in the higher range of American CIA estimates), cannot in the final analysis do anything constructive for the economy, and would eventually have to call the civilians back.[48]

6. Should (Must) the Soviet Union Survive?

The struggle for small (and large) nation independence in the USSR is all very well, some observers would say; but it is, firstly, doomed to fail, and is in any case, secondly, undesirable from a wider perspective. Is the struggle of the nationalities fated to bring a reprise of 1919-20 (and 1940)? Does the Soviet imperial regime represent a higher interest of stable geopolitics and an irreversible trend towards integration (the merging of sovereignties) in the contemporary world? Arguments for and against Moscow's involuntary union of less than sovereign republics typically combine *moralism* (ethical reasoning) and *realism* (prudent deference to the allegedly inevitable) – the 'socialist commonwealth' confronts national self-determination, and 'Moscow (or NATO) won't stand for it' rebuts 'Moscow (even with NATO) can't stop it'. The moral values invoked range from the lower interests of one's tribe to the higher interests of humanity; and historical analogy or precedent is deployed in partisan fashion, as one would expect, to demonstrate the inevitability of what is held to be desirable. Let us try to elaborate summarily the main parameters of the world's 640 billion ruble question.

6.1. Pro Union
'Secession is not a real option' – Paul Goble

Economy
Break-up of the union would be economically irrational since the constituent republics have no serious alternative for the foreseeable future but to trade with each other. Russia's special contribution to the union – the abundant supply of cheap energy and the generous subsidy and technical staffing of the 'backward' republics – would be lost.

Society
Only a revived union can guard against debilitating, destructive and potentially disastrous ethnic conflict – and the forced migrations and relocations within and between republics which could ensue. Of course, Russians are particularly at risk in outlying republics (and it would simply be impossible to resettle all of them in Russia proper); but so, also, are Central Asians and Caucasians and Moldavians at risk – from each other.

Strategy
Only a revived union can check the growing potential for outside strategic pressure and even military meddling in Soviet affairs. Moreover, without a Soviet counter-balance to the Western powers generally and the United States in particular, the outlook for progressive and independent forces in various parts of the Third World must be clouded. Russia herself, shorn of her internal as well as external European and Asian imperium, will be in a vulnerable and threatened position – but still armed to the teeth, including with nuclear weapons. In reality,

Washington, Bonn, Paris and London (and even Tokyo and Beijing) need a stable, intact Soviet Union as much as Moscow does. Secession from even a fitfully functioning polity is in general unacceptable to contemporary international society: that is why it is so rare, and usually requires war to bring about.

Polity
The federation has been renovated to some extent and can be further improved through a new treaty of union if the republics show due forbearance. Small-nation nationalism is anachronistic – and the attempt to force through independence of the republics against the wishes of the Soviet patriotic establishment will only precipitate a military/police crackdown against the nationalities *and* the democratic reformers.

6.2. Pro Independence

'We are a Third World country' – Yuri Levada
'All our life is nonsense' – Peter Vares

Economy
The All-Union economy is in free fall. The Centre is now bereft of ideas and authority, and the only workable approach to reform is decentralization – with privatization and free-market reform through local and republican initiatives. Organic links in the economy must be rebuilt voluntaristically, by market driven inter- enterprise and inter-republic domestic trade and republic-managed international trade.

Society
National independence has a 'profound emotional legitimacy' (Anderson 1985, p. 14) for those who have been forcefully deprived of it; for those who have suffered prolonged torments and deprivation in the name of internationalism, and for those who need resolute measures to preserve demographic self-sufficiency. Normal, non-antagonistic relations between divided communities can be achieved only when national borders have been restored or redrawn, purged of cynical *Realpolitik* consider-ations – and when the people themselves can play a direct role in re-structuring inter-ethnic relations and national constitu-tions.

Strategy
The multinational involuntary empire is dead: the new Europe cannot be soundly built while the USSR remains what it is. Russia must be content to play a modest strategic role *qua* the Russian lands alone, while continuing the path of strategic cooperation with the West started by Gorbachev – or there will be no Western aid and no end to economic disintegration in the USSR. Trying to hold down the empire by force will precipitate civil war and wars of intervention, and is in fact now beyond the resources of the regime.

Polity
The healthiest forces in Russian society already accept that the empire of 'barracks socialism' is finished. Russia's self-renewal will not in practice survive the attempt to sustain the union, whether renovated or not. Nor will democracy and civil liberties in any of the 15 republics.

The arguments above are one version of what divides the partisans of union, on the one hand, and deconstruction on the other. History will, as they say, decide. My own view is by now perhaps sufficiently clear: deconstruction (even disintegration) is an essential preliminary to any federation, confederation or whatever – and, I believe, most of the republics will eventually wish for independence alone.

7. COALITION-BUILDING AND THE STRUGGLE FOR INDEPENDENCE

A cold war of (mainly) political, ideological and economic struggle between the dissident republics and Moscow is deciding the fate of the USSR. Can the republics, in the last analysis, really prevail without precipitating disaster for themselves? Stephan Kux (1991) envisages four types of coalition politics emerging to decide this question as non-Communists take over power in the republics and the Soviet authorities lose their grip:

1) a 'centre-left' coalition at the Centre;

2) a 'co-imperial' coalition of Gorbachev and Yeltsin;

3) a 'vertical coalition' (power sharing) between Centre and republics, and

4) a 'horizontal coalition' between the republics against the Centre.

This list is both puzzling and incomplete – puzzling because a 'co-imperial' coalition could well entail Gorbachev accepting Yeltsin's commitment to decentring the empire, in which case it would be mis-named; incomplete because it misses two central features of the present situation where the Centre often plays a divide-and-rule game in relations with the republics, and Gorbachev has moved since 1990 to constitute a powerful coalition of convenience with the Right.

A more satisfactory typology of the most potent varieties of coalition politics likely in the 1990s would include the following:

A) a coalition of the centre-right (Gorbachev – or a centrist successor – plus the 'partocracy', the government apparatus, the police, the military and the captains of military industry);

B) a coalition of the centre-left (as advocated by Stanislav Shatalin of the Inter-Regional Group of Deputies in the Supreme Soviet);[49]

C) periphery coalitions (dissident republics – with or without Russia – versus the Centre);

D) Centre-periphery coalitions (involving Gorbachev – or Yeltsin, if he begins to assume all-union responsibilities[50] – in the leading role).[51]

Of course many permutations are conceivable within and among these broad possibilities. As for which type is likely to prevail in the long run, there seems little doubt that a democratized USSR would give the victory to some combination of coalition types B and C – which would probably offer the best hope of economic, social and political renovation. But even if the 'concrete heads' of the Right prevail in conditions of chaos,[52] it is hard to see the USSR re-emerging in either a Stalinist, Brezhnevian or Gorbachevian form.

The broad reform movement, although still an incoherent combination of national fronts and independence movements, unofficial unions, fledgling political parties, a turbulent half-free press and embattled parliamentary minorities – and Boris Yeltsin – is surely strong enough to veto a dictatorship of the Right in the long run. It may even be capable of forcing radical change, as happened in Eastern Europe, by some combination of those two potent instruments of non-violent resistance – a general strike, and a series of mass demonstrations in major cities which refuse to disperse.[53]

8.   NATIONALITY GOALS – AND A RESTRUCTURED FEDERATION

The ultimate goals of the dissident and not-so-dissident republics continue to cover quite a wide spectrum – from assertions of sovereignty,[54] through claims of a right to full independence, to outright declarations of independence. The spectrum of loyalist constitutional debate under *glasnost* has ranged from upholders of the *status quo ante* Gorbachev to proponents of a fundamental restructuring which would preserve the federation intact but give real power to a much larger number of constituent units. Thus under one proposal the Russian Federation, which presently includes 16 autonomous republics, five autonomous regions and ten autonomous areas, would be broken up into at least four components with republic status: European Russia, Western and Eastern Siberia and the Far East (Kux, 1990, p.104).

The Centre has so far shown little interest in this kind of restructuring. Gorbachev prefers to work within the given framework dominated by a giant RSFSR including more than half of the country's population and two-thirds of its land area.[55] Boris Yeltsin has been both sympathetic and ambivalent towards assertions of sovereignty by the smaller national 'autonomies' of the Russian Federation; but he would probably not tolerate any splitting up of the Russian land from Smolensk to Vladivostok, even though he is being forced to contend with a certain amount of collusion between the Union Centre and the minority RSFSR nationalities, which is intended to keep his own political ambitions in check.[56] The smaller republics (Georgia, Azerbaijan, Moldova) are even less interested in self-determination for their national minorities, and so it seems that the drama of USSR deconstruction, reconstruction or imperial reimposition will be played out primarily between the 15 republics of Stalin's later years. The most likely – or at least prominent – potential outcomes seem to be:

- the *status quo* (continuing strife, muddle and ambiguity);

- the *status quo ante* (a return – or at least, an attempted return to the Brezhnev order, presumably by means of a military/police crackdown);

- a (genuinely) renewed federation;

- a confederation of sovereign states;

- full independence for the republics;

- some combination of outcomes (3-5);

- civil war (perhaps in the aftermath of an attempted crackdown).

In other words, potential outcomes are extremely diverse – and even the civil war 'option' could arise from a struggle primarily at the Centre (between partisans of Russia and partisans of the USSR), or between the Soviet (or even Russian) Centre and various parts of the periphery (possibly in alliance with each other), or could involve uncontrolled escalation of conflicts in the periphery. Clearly a disastrous outcome to the definitive failure of the Gorbachev reform programme is possible – and nationality conflicts would be a prominent part of any worst-case scenario. Such scenarios are now being luridly depicted in Moscow, particularly by those with neo-imperial axes to grind, including Gorbachev and some right-wing nationalists. The Moscow and other liberals (like ex-foreign minister Eduard Shevardnadze, or Academician Arbatov)[57] are forecasting a possibility of military/police dictatorship with or without Gorbachev if things go on as they are.

The Moscow reactionaries (like the leader of the *Soyuz* group in the Supreme Soviet, Colonel Alksnis) prophesy a pogrom of Russians in the non-Russian republics unless the military intervenes. Alksnis wants the General Staff to install a Committee of National Salvation (i.e., a junta of reactionary and other notables – he has nominated the liberal Leningrad mayor, Anatoly Sobchak, as chairman!).[58] This would be the failed Baltic scenario of Minister of Defence Yazov writ large with a liberal veneer – and would pre-empt the call of some democrats for a coalition government of the centre-left.

The imperial idea is more frankly upheld by a celebrated reactionary writer, Alexander Prokhanov, a Slavophile who gives conditional support to the Bolsheviks as the contemporary upholders of Tsarist conquests. Prokhanov is widely known as the Soviet Kipling and 'the nightingale of the General Staff'. He warns about the dangers of a Soviet Union no longer held together by Army or Party and he predicts mass strikes and civil war in the wake of false, Western-inspired social reform. Civil strife will bring about more Chernobyls, and unauthorized missile launches will create a world disaster, provoking Western military intervention and spawning a new German empire in the East![59] (Alksnis also prophesies nuclear disaster.)

Will the Soviet Union become a Lebanon or a Sri Lanka on a vast scale? Collapsing empires, as we have noted, are said to be fraught with potential for fratricide *and* external armed intervention. Must the Soviet Union witness a replay of the Russian Civil War?

9.   CONFLICT RESOLUTION FOR A DECAYING EMPIRE

What can be done to limit, reconcile or creatively channel the erupting and colliding nationalisms – many of them in conflict with collapsing supranationalism – in the Soviet Union? What kinds of constitutional restructuring would be most desirable among those that are achievable; and how can they be achieved? What techniques, fora, processes and interested outside (non-Soviet) parties are available for creative conflict resolution in the Soviet ethnic maelstrom?

On the face of it, the most obvious peaceful way out of the current Soviet impasse would be a grand compromise between the Centre and the republics – and thus between the two main civilian contenders for power at the Centre, Gorbachev and Yeltsin: the voice of the more civilized tendencies of the apparatus, and the voice of the Russian people. The Moscow liberals reiterate that there can be no effective reform from the Centre while it is preoccupied with holding the Union together by intimidation and force; and there can be no effective reform from below while the republics and the nationalities organized below the republic level are hamstrung by the Centre's refusal to tolerate parliamentary self-determination and capitalist (free market) renovation. From a purely economic point of view, given the failure of the Gorbachev reforms (and their timidity has been staggering),[60] the only hope for the economy would seem to be resolute decentralization and privatization going well beyond Lenin's New Economic Policy of 1921, which followed the Civil War: the hope this time would be to avert another one. Integration or reintegration of the economy would have to await a production recovery to furnish something worth integrating. The Centre seems to lack the ideas or authority to direct economic revival, and, indeed, Gorbachev himself has been a prime target of massive strikes in the mining industry, which are sinking the economy to new depths. His continuing leadership is now a factor behind the accelerating economic collapse.

The appeal of a Gorbachev-Yeltsin rapprochement, even at the eleventh hour, is that it could serve the dual purpose of ensuring Western aid (the Gorbachev factor) while preempting an exclusive Army/KGB/Interior Ministry political ascendancy or coup attempt. (Gorbachev could still presumably carry with him much of the party and government apparatus, and even some of the military and police, in any new *entente* with liberal and democratic Russia.)[61] Although this rapprochement seemed unlikely after the last attempt at a '500 Days package' agreeable to both men in July 1990, in the end Gorbachev may have few alternatives politically or economically as his public support evaporates and he is increasingly crowded by the Left and Right. Yeltsin may be his only barricade against outright military takeover. As for the piecemeal solution of the many and diverse conflicts being played out at the present time, a range of fora and techniques is in use, and there has been considerable interest in the importation of Western social science approaches and techniques for conflict resolution.[62] (The Soviet President has apparently read the Roger Fisher and William Ury book, *Getting to Yes*, in translation.)[63] Gorbachev has negotiated directly with the presidents of dissident republics; he has repeatedly sent delegates for face-to-face negotiations in the Baltic capitals, and he has used the Federation Council as a sounding board on nationality issues. In their turn, the republic governments have used their official diplomatic representatives in Moscow (the Lithuanian representative has been especially prominent) to seek understandings with the Centre and avert unfavourable developments.

As for inter- and intra-republican conflict, there was a concerted mediation effort by the Baltic Council in the Azeri-Armenian dispute early in 1990, when delegations from the Caucasus travelled to Riga; but it bore no fruit.[64] The Soviet authorities have of course practiced a kind of armed mediation in Azerbaijan, in the Gagauz territory of Moldova, in Southern Ossetia and elsewhere – but these efforts have usually seemed tainted by divide and rule tactics. In early 1991 Soviet military and police activity in defence of the South Ossetians seemed to be a preliminary manoeuvre for crushing Georgian independence, recently declared. These forceful interventions have not been accompanied by creative initiatives to effect durable resolution of conflict. The lack of such initiatives, often after five years of ethnic strife, is striking.

The main source of effective, if informal, mediation at the present time is the President of the Russian Republic, whose political line has been to defend the republics against the Centre, but also to go along reluctantly with Gorbachev's efforts to renew the federation, as in the March 1991 referendum. After winning a popular election for the Russian Presidency, Yeltsin could have the authority to actually begin a process of genuine deconstruction and permanent conflict resolution. No doubt other sources of mediation and adjudication should develop – and to some extent are developing – within Soviet society. Paul Goble has urged the need for a higher court specializing in federal and nationality issues, together with a good dose of constitutional regularity and legitimation (by the Centre) of treaty relationships between the republics (Goble, 1989, p.14).

As for research capacity on nationality conflict, it is probably growing. Apart from the widespread interest in conflict resolution science mentioned earlier, several institutes of the Soviet Academy of Sciences are showing commendable capacity to upgrade skills and re-tool intellectually even where their own interest in domestic nationality issues is more pragmatic than logical. For instance, both the Institute of International Economic and Political Studies (formerly the Institute of Economics of the World Socialist System – there hasn't been time to change the visiting cards!) under Professor Oleg Bogomolov and the Institute of World Economy and International Relations (IMEMO) under Academician Mirsky have grasped the nationality nettle with a research emphasis on peaceful conflict resolution.[65] Since systematic and sensitive study of armed conflict

within and between states – how to avert it and how to con-
structively intervene in it – is now reaching critical mass
in Scandinavia and elsewhere (Touval and Zartman, 1985;
Zartman, 1989; Burton, 1990; Wallensteen, 1991; Wiberg, 1991;)
the time is ripe for close collaboration between Soviet, Western
and Third World scholars to face the intellectual challenge of
resolving Soviet nationality conflict peacefully.

The impact of external (non-Soviet) actors could become
decisive in the future. Although Western leaders generally, and
George Bush in particular, have been strikingly solicitous of
Gorbachev in facing his sea of internal troubles, opinion has
begun to shift in Washington towards favouring the nationalists.
Likewise, once Bonn has negotiated the extrication of Soviet
occupation forces from the former DDR, Chancellor Kohl may be
less concerned about Gorbachev's short-term political interests.
The Kohl-Mitterand initiative of 1990 in seeking a settlement
of the Lithuanian independence crisis showed that Western
involvement is possible in a mediating capacity; and there is a
strong juridical basis for it, in that many states have not
recognized the annexation of the Baltic states and because,
under Stalin's bizarre constitutional dispensation of 1936, all
Soviet republics are entitled to a foreign ministry, diplomatic
representation abroad and a seat in the UN (although only
Belorussia and the Ukraine have the latter) – as well as enjoying a right of secession. It would be a simple but momentous
step for the Western powers generally to follow Iceland in
recognizing an independent Lithuania as a first step, or in any
case to allow the Baltic republics and others free rein to pursue
their diplomatic and trade-seeking initiatives in the West.

There is a thickening of relations with the Scandinavian
countries in progress as new consulates are opened in the Baltic
capitals; semi-diplomatic information offices emerge in the
Scandinavian capitals; Estonian economic migrants appear in
Finland, and the Baltic diaspora from Scandinavia – and from
the rest of the world as well – begins to play an active role
on the ground in support of the cultural and information effort
underpinning Baltic independence. Various outsiders are also
offering free (but solicited) advice – legal/diplomatic, commer-
cial/educational, agrarian/technical and so on – about the independence prospect. In view of the massive amounts of aid potentially available from US, Japanese, German and European
Community sources for a Soviet state *in extremis* economically,

the Western powers could find themselves playing a major role in the end game of the Soviet empire.

In any case, whoever manages to begin the process of genuine renovation of Soviet imperial structures will be doing all of us a large favour. In the Caucasus and Central Asia there is certainly ample scope for foreign intervention in Soviet civil strife; while if the policy drift continues in Moscow and the Right prevails, the Cold War could be at least partially revived in Europe, and the final withdrawal of Soviet troops from the former Warsaw Pact countries could even be at risk, together with (perhaps) Polish independence. There is so much hanging on the creative deconstruction of the USSR – and Moscow's authority has become so weak – that the time has arrived for the world at large to show intimate and practical concern in the Soviet crisis.

For their part, it seems to me, the Soviet leadership should unambiguously concede a *practical* right of secession to those republics which wish to leave the Union (deconstruction scenario). Likewise, the republics should concede enhanced autonomy – or the right to opt for 'republican transfer' – to those many national groupings with so-called territorial formations who are clamouring for it (Nagorno-Karabakh, for instance). Thereafter, it may be possible to sustain, rebuild or creatively transform those inter-republic and inter-region economic and strategic links which are of most urgent practical importance. Whether some sort of political federation or confederation of the former Soviet republics will *then* be possible can be sorted out at leisure in comparative tranquillity. Any prolonged attempt to sustain the Union forcibly would gravely prejudice the chances of long term inter-republic cooperation, and would be ultimately futile in any case. This is the disintegration scenario – vast bloodshed, almost by definition and comprehensive disaster very likely.[66]

NOTES:

1. In late 1990 Gorbachev combined the government roles of State President (elected by the USSR Congress of People's Deputies); Chairman of the Presidential Council (until its dissolution on Christmas Day); Chairman of the Federation Council (consisting of the Presidents of the 15 Soviet republics, plus others), and Chairman of the Security Council (consisting of the Defence and Interior Ministers, KGB Chairman, Vice-President, Prime Minister and two personal appointees). He is also, of course, General Secretary of the Communist Party of the Soviet Union.

2. The *nomenklatura*: a list of hundreds of thousands of high-level party and government positions kept exclusively in the gift of the Communist Party's personnel department.

3. According to Anatoly Sobchak, reform mayor of Leningrad, 'The communists are still in control in the communes', despite repeal of Article 6 of the 1977 Constitution which legitimized the 'vanguard' role of the party in society. *Financial Times*, 10 April 1991, p.2

4. According to *Moscow News* pollster Yuri Levada ('The Big Niet', *MN*, No.9, 7 July 1990), 75% of a sample taken in mid-1990 had a 'positive attitude' towards 'growing criticism of the USSR government', while the Moscow poll agency, Data, put Gorbachev's support at 16% of the electorate in April 1991. Bruce Clark, 'Resignation Threat Becomes Riskier Ploy for Gorbachev', *The Times*, 26 April 1991. See also Clemens (1991).

5. On the fears of the *vozrozhdentsi* (believers in Russian renaissance), see Dunlop (1983), Ch.10. See also Brzezinski (1989-90) and Tucker (1991). On fertility among Russian women, see *Current Digest of the Soviet Press*, 43, 1, 6 February 1991, p.2

6. Roman Solchanyk, 'The Ukrainian Road to Independence', *Report on the USSR*, 3,1, 4 January 1991, and 'Ukraine: Student Strike Ousts Premier', *Current Digest of the Soviet Press*, 42, 41, November 14, 1990, p. 17. See also 'Ferment in the Western Ukraine: An Interview with Rosyslav Bratun', *Report on the USSR*, 2,18, 4 May 1990.

7. Yeltsin revealed the agreement to negotiate an alternative treaty of federation between four republics in the aftermath of the military crackdown in Vilnius. *The Australian*, 16 January 1991

8. In August 1990, for instance, Azerbaijan was barring Armenian road access to Karabakh in the southern sector of its border with Armenia, and preventing gas supply to Armenia through its northern pipeline. Armenian militias, for their part, were blockading or attacking Azeri border villages in Azerbaijan proper and in the Azerbaijani autonomous enclave of Nakhichevan, which is wedged between Armenia and Iran. 'New Armenian Attacks on Azerbaijan', *Report on the USSR* (translating *Izvestia*, 22 August 1990), 42, 34, 26 September 1990

9. On the bloody Soviet military and police operation in Baku of 19-20 January 1990, see 'January in Baku', *Moscow News*, No.33, 27 August 1990 and 'January in Baku', *Moscow News*, No.37, 30 September 1990 – where *Shchit* (Shield), the union of military dissidents, offers the results of its investigation.

10. Do Russians Want to Flee?' *Moscow News*, 3 February 1991, p.11. According to a survey by the Soviet Centre for Public Opinion and Market Research, 36% of Russians in Latvia, and 24% of Russians in Estonia, regard themselves as citizens of their republics rather than the USSR. (The figure is 7% in Kirghizia and 17% in Western Ukraine.) *ibid*. About half of Latvia's Russians were born in the republic.

11. Hennou Rajandi, Estonian Institute, *Interview*, Tallinn, 19 June 1990. See also Taagepera (1989)

12. Under the law on secession, a would-be independent republic must secure 75 per cent support at a referendum (twice), fully compensate the Centre for property to be taken over and secure the consent of the Congress of People's Deputies. *Moscow News*, No.6, 10 February 1991, p.4. In the Latvian referendum held on March 3, 1991, a week in advance of the Centre's referendum on renewing the Union (which was boycotted by Latvia of course), 87% of Latvians took part, and 74% of those voted for 'the democratic and independent statehood of the Republic of Latvia'. Soviet armed forces personnel were not entitled to vote; but Riga's voting population, which is only 37% ethnic Latvian, answered 'yes' – 61%, 'no' – 37%. *Latvian Information Bulletin*, Legation of Latvia, 4325 Seventeenth Street N.W., Washington, D.C., No. 29, April, 1991, p.1

13. Ergzali Ger, 'Lithuania: One Year of Independence within USSR', *Moscow News*, No.12, 24 March 1991. Latvia's Supreme Council (formerly Supreme Soviet), for its part, ordered a ban on the provision of supplies and services to Soviet military forces in November 1990 (*Report on the USSR*, 2 January 1991, p.50.)

14. For a profile of Estonia's military-industrial tsar and Interfront (International Front of the Workers of the Estonian SSR) leader, Vladimir Yarovoi, see *Report on the USSR*, 42, 7, February 7, 1990, p.28. Interfront headquarters in Estonia are at the All-Union *Dvigatel* enterprise, which produces a wide variety of components for military weapon systems.

15. Natalya Davidova, 'Estonia's Militia: Declaration of Independence', *Moscow News*, No.32, 20 August 1990, p.5. The agreement between Interior Minister Bakatin and Estonian Prime Minister Edgar Savisaar to transfer control over the militia from the Centre to Estonia included guarantees of the rights of non-Estonians.

16. In the view of liberal Supreme Soviet Deputy, Galina Starovoitova, popular non-violent resistance was decisively complemented by the intervention of Boris Yeltsin (who flew to Tallinn) and 'world public opinion' in averting what she calls a 'Baltic putsch'. 'The Mysterious "Third Force"', *Moscow News*, No.7, 7 February 1991. (Starovoitova is Yeltsin's chief adviser on nationality affairs.) Yeltsin's 'Open Letter to the Peoples of the Baltics' was published in *Rossiskaya Gazeta*, 19 January 1991: it revealed his agreement with the Baltic Presidents to promulgate laws guaranteeing Russian rights among Baltic peoples and *vice versa*, and to post RSFSR representatives in the Baltic states. Len Karpinsky, 'All Ethnic Groups Face Common Peril', *Moscow News*, No.5, 3 February 1991. p.11

17. The Slav proportion of Kirghizia fell by 4% between the 1979 and 1989 census. See Sophie Quinn-Judge, 'Retreat from Empire', *Far Eastern Economic Review*, 25 October 1990, p.24. A 'massive Russian exodus from your republic sometime soon' was regarded as likely by 71% of the Russians in Kirghizia and 79% of those in Tajikistan late in 1990. 'Do Russians Want to Flee?' *Moscow News*, No.5, 1991, p.11

18. See Kamilov chapter. For historical background on the Soviet presence in Central Asia see also Bennigsen (1985).

19. On National Day, 2 December 1990, President Ion Iliescu of Romania called for 'the unification of Bessarabia with the country' in order to restore 'Great Romania'. 'Call for Return of Soviet Moldova', *Sydney Morning Herald*, 3 December 1990. There has, however, been some coolness in relations between Kishinev and Bucharest, despite the opening of the joint border, educational exchanges, the re-Romanizing of Romanian script in Moldova and other evidence of fraternity.

20. Following elections in November 1990 won by Zviad Gamsakhurdia's anti-communist Round Table Party, Georgia's Supreme Soviet made the declaration of independence on 9 April 1991, second anniversary of the night Soviet troops killed 21 nationalist demonstrators in Tbilisi. *Financial Times*, 10 April 1991.

21. James Critchlow, 'Will Central Asia Become a Greater Uzbekistan?' *Report on the USSR*, 2, 57, 14 September 1990.

22. Yeltsin travelled to the Far East as Russian President, visiting Tataria, Bashkiria and other centres for the assertion of sovereignty on the way to Vladivostok in August 1990. 'Rights are not handed down from the Centre, but are voluntarily handed over from the bottom', he told the Tatars. 'Yeltsin inspires confidence', a Tatar leader told *Moscow News* (No.33, 27 August 1990, p.5)

23. On the plight of the peoples affected by the oil fields of the West Siberian plain, see Petra Campbell, 'Doomed Deer Herders of the Soviet Amazon', *Sydney Morning Herald*, 12 January 1991. See also 'Restore Rights to the People the Land Belongs To', Interview with Vladimir Sangi, President of the Association of Peoples of the North, *Izvestia*, 12 July 1990, p.3. Translated in *Current Digest of the Soviet Press*, 42, 29 (1990), p.20

24. 'A Map of Unrest in the USSR', *Moscow News*, No.11, 17 March 1991, p.8. *MN* lists the 'main territorial-ethnic claims and conflicts' at some length; but it is clear that (a) several of the 76 separate 'claims and conflicts' listed are in fact multiple (e.g., number 36 – 7 sub-items – and number 53), while others involve double-counting (e.g., 40, 41); and (b) many of the conflicts are not (yet) in fact 'mortal'. Nevertheless Moscow News' list appears to be the first attempt at comprehensiveness.

25. On the need to take over the local secret police establishment, see 'Getting Rid of the KGB', An Interview with Tiit Madisson, *Estonian Life*, April/May 1990, p.E7. On the sacking of 17 top foreign ministry officials thought to be KGB by new foreign minster Lennart Meri, see *Estonian Life*, April/May 1990, p.F1.

26. 'The Last Communist', Interview with Kalju Komissarov, *Estonian Life*, April/May 1990, p.E7. Somewhat confusingly, in Soviet parlance 'the militia' are regular and militarized (for internal security reasons) police under the control of the All-Union Ministry of the Interior. I am using the term 'militia' here to refer to those regular and irregular quasi-military forces which have arisen spontaneously or been created deliberately to support the pro-independence movement in individual Soviet republics.

27. For a reference to the Estonian *Kaitseliit*, see 'Congress of Estonia Meets in Tallinn', *Estonian Life*, March 1990, p.4. An archive on the Forest Brotherhood resistance is being established by the young oral historian, Maat Laar. *Interview*, Tallinn, 22 June 1990.

28. 'Yeltsin "Losing Reason" over Russian army plans', *The Australian*, 17 January 1991. At this time of threatened crackdown in the Baltic republics Yeltsin also called on Russian troops in the Baltics to disobey orders for firing on civilians. Whether Yeltsin has serious influence inside the armed forces remains to be seen.

29. Dainis Ivans (Chairman of the Latvian Popular Front and Vice President of the Supreme Council of Latvia), *Interview*, Riga, 25 June 1990.

30. Estonian Prime Minster Edgar Savisaar argued that the Soviet Congress of People's Deputies has in effect recognized Estonia's status as an annexed territory by publishing the secret protocols of the Hitler-Stalin pact, which paved the way for Soviet occupation of the Baltic states. An Estonian commission under Popular Front auspices has prepared a compensation'ledger' dating back to the Treaty of Tartu (1920) in which the Soviet government recognized Estonian independence. *Izvestia*, 1 February 1990

31. For the full text of Gorbachev's draft union treaty see *Current Digest of the Soviet Press*, 42, 47, 26 December 1990 (translated from *Izvestia*, 24 November 1990). A *Moscow News* columnist promptly criticised the draft treaty for failing to specify who would be parties to it. (Would it be existing republics only – or also autonomous republics who have declared themselves republics?) Rein Mullerson also objected that the treaty would go into effect immediately with no minimum number of signatories indicated. He argued that the draft failed to envisage any radical break with the *status quo*. 'More About Nations' Right to Self-Determination', *Moscow News* No.11, 17 March 1991

32. *Time*, 25 March 25 1991, p.16

33. *ibid.*, and 'The Referendum Scorecard', The *Economist*, 23 March 1991

34. Not all of this activity is under the close control of the ruling Popular Front governments in the dissident republics. In Tallinn, for instance, under the leadership of Tunne Kelam of the Estonian National Independence Party and others, a purist wing of the independence movement coexists uneasily with the Popular Front. The purists have mobilized hundreds of thousands around the project of registering all those with a claim to Estonian identity, both at home and in the diaspora, as citizens of a reconstituted Estonian nation. On this basis elections have been held for a Congress of Estonia, which in turn has elected a Council of Estonia, whose members continue to meet regularly in Tallinn and monitor the work of the Soviet-tainted (in Tunne Kelam's eyes) but Popular Front-controlled (and

still popular) Supreme Council. For the purists, it is psychologically, politically and juridically important to preserve continuity with the republic extinguished by Stalin's legions in 1940: there can be no question of 'renewing' a union which was never consented to in the first place; and there are deep reservations about political cooperation with ex-communists in the Popular Front (Tunne Kelam, *Interview*, Tallinn, 22 June 1990). See also *Bylaws of the Congress of Estonia*, Tallinn, 11 March 1990, and 'Congress of Estonia Meets in Tallinn', *Estonian Life*, March 1990, p.E3. There is, thus, a situation of 'triple power' in Estonia – Soviet power (expressed through the Interfront and Party establishment), Popular Front power (projected officially through the reformed Soviet parliament and ministries), and the anti-establishment power ('a plague on both your houses') of the independence parties. (Nevertheless there is a considerable overlap of membership between the Congress of Estonia and the Supreme Council.)

35. The Baltic republics have, in addition to meetings of Presidents – and of Popular Front leaders (the Baltic Council) – regular meetings of groups of ministers; of parliamentarians, and also of non-government organizations. A Baltic common market is projected for 1993. Nils Muiznieks, 'The Evolution of Baltic Cooperation', *Report on the USSR*, 6 July 1990, p.18

36. The five Presidents of the Central Asian republics met in Alma Ata during June 1990, and resolved on action to promote economic cooperation and to save the Aral Sea (65 per cent dry by now, and shrinking). The Presidents protested Moscow's decision not to divert Siberian rivers southwards into Central Asia as planned under Brezhnev. (The Soviet green movement killed this plan.) *Report on the USSR*, 13 July 1990, pp.18-19. Central Asian economic cooperation was, however, still at risk from bans on the export of listed consumer goods in the individual republics. *Report on the USSR*, 2 January 1991, p.30

37. Alexander Solzhenitsyn, 'How Should We Rebuild Russia?' *Literaturnaya Gazeta*, 18 September 1990 (cited in Sophie Quinn-Judge, 'Retreat from Empire', *Far Eastern Economic Review*, 25 October 1990). Solzhenitsyn also, however, thoughtfully suggested that in giving up the Central Asian underbelly Russia should keep just a little prime belly fat – the nearer parts of Kazakhstan so heavily colonized by Russians. This suggestion prompted street demonstrations in Alma Ata, capital of Kazakhstan. See *Report on the USSR*, 2 January 1991, p.2

38. 'Big Offensive on Democracy, Warns Yeltsin', *The Australian*, 16 January 1991. Of course at that point neither side possessed regular armed forces!

39. The Politburo of the Communist Party also now includes all republican first secretaries as a matter of right; but it apparently meets infrequently as a result, and power has shifted to the Party Secretariat.

40. See Ann Sheehy, 'The Draft Union Treaty: Preliminary Assessment', *Report on the USSR*, 2, 51, 21 December 1990, p.4

41. The Supreme Soviet – consisting of a Soviet of the Union ('lower house') and a Soviet of Nationalities ('upper house') – is elected by the Congress of People's Deputies, whose other responsibilities include constitutional change and the election of the President until democratic elections for the Presidency are held in 1993. Most members of the popularly elected Congress of

Deputies (and the Supreme Soviet) are still *nomenklatura* party and government officials, whose unrepresentativeness (and unpopularity) is increasingly apparent from the record of opinion polls, political strikes and mass
demonstrations against their leading defender and champion, Mikhail
Gorbachev.

42. The list is based on a conversation with Dr. Valve Kirsipuu of the Institute of Philosophy, Sociology and Law, Estonian Academy of Sciences,
Tallinn, 19 June 1990. According to her, Estonia's outstanding economic
grievances include the burning of 95% of valuable oil shale production for
power generation (instead of reserving it for the chemical industry); the
export of 97% of All-Union enterprise production out of Estonia, and distribution of 70% of all enterprise profits by the Centre.

43. A favourite Moscow joke compares Gorbachev's economic reforms to a
switch from driving on the right to driving on the left – in stages. Economic
perestroika has also been likened to leaping across an abyss – in two steps.

44. Peter Torday, 'Chaos Besets Soviet Market Reforms', *The Independent*,
4 April 1991.

45. *The Times*, 4 April 1991

46. From November 1990 the Ukrainian government will be paying up to
70% of individual wages in the republic with coupons valid for the purchase
of scarce commodities – a preliminary measure before the proposed introduction of a separate Ukrainian currency. For the view that Ukrainian economic sovereignty is likely to be not only difficult but costly, see J. Tedstrom,
'Economic Costs and Benefits of Independence for Ukraine', *Report on the
USSR*, 2, 49, 7 December 1990. Tedstrom, however, fails to take adequate
account of accelerating decline in the all-union economy as a whole, including centrally organized inter-republic trade; and he neglects the possibility
that a soft currency economic bloc, including the Ukraine and Russia most
notably, could emerge from the breakup of the USSR. Independence, in
other words, should not be equated with autarchy.

47. *Sydney Morning Herald*, 12 January 12 1991

48. Georgi Arbatov, Seminar on Soviet Foreign Policy and the Soviet Domestic Crisis, University of Sydney, 21 January 1991. See also 'Debate, Position,
Forecast: Even a Market Won't Save Us', *Izvestia*, January 10, 1991, translated in *Current Digest of the Soviet Press*, 43, 2, 13 February 1991, p.15.
(For the text of the Union Budget for 1991, see pp.18-19, and for Marshal
Akhromeyev's reply to Arbatov, see p.16. Akhromeyev is Gorbachev's principal military adviser). Some new (Soviet) estimates of Soviet military spending before the cuts of 1989-90 range up to 25% of GNP. Arbatov argues that
the military is still crippling the economy with its 96 billion ruble vote for
1991 (35% of budget outlays) – up from 71 billion rubles in 1990, and
including a 70-75% rise in expenditure on weapons purchase, military
construction and military research. (According to Arbatov, prices are forecast to increase by only 43-45%) If Arbatov's interpretation is correct, we
have here a striking illustration of Gorbachev's shift to the Right since 1989.
(Arbatov is Director of the Institute for the USA and Canada, Soviet Academy of Sciences.)

49. Open Letter to Gorbachev, *Komsomolskaya Pravda*, 23 January 1991, cited in Kux (1991), p.7. Shatalin envisaged an 'anti-crisis committee' representing a consensus among nationalities, parties and other groups.

50. In April 1991 Yeltsin was already bolstering Gorbachev's attempts to defuse the strikes and demonstrations threatening to engulf the Slav republics in return for a promise of fresh elections to a new federal parliament. *The Times*, 26 April 26 1991; *The Sunday Times*, 28 April 1991.

51. Of course Type D coalition-makers might reach past the republics to the autonomous republics and lower.

52. Pyotr Patrushev prefers the image of the *apparatchiki* on the Right as anaerobic bacteria, allergic to the lethal (for them) oxygen of *glasnost*.

53. Many, perhaps most, of the techniques and tactics of non-violent resistance categorised in Sharp (1973) have come into play in the Soviet Union, including strikes, economic boycotts, 'enterprise liberation' and 'official' tax revenue withholding; street demonstrations, hunger strikes, 'flag wars', human chains of solidarity and 'human wall' defence of sovereignty; conscription resistance and soldiers' union activity against the military high command; 'wars of laws', referendums and counter-referendums, extra-legal elections and several varieties of 'parallel' people's power.

54. For a discussion of Soviet and Western conceptions of sovereignty, see Kux (1990), p. 28. Kux, however, is unreliable on conceptualizing the varieties of contemporary federalism – his categorization of Australia, Canada and the Federal Republic of Germany as 'federations with relatively little independence or unitary federal states' is incomprehensible (Kux, 1990, p. 8).

55. Solzhenitsyn's former Slavophile comrade, Igor Shafarevich, has warned darkly against the Balkanization of the Russian Federation. *Komsomolskaya Pravda*, 18 October 1990, p.2

56. Sheehy, 'The Draft Union Treaty', p.4. Gorbachev has been ambiguous about whether large autonomous republics in the RSFSR which have claimed full republic status – such as Tataria – will be granted it.

57. Arbatov, Seminar, Sydney, 21 January 21 1991

58. Teresa Cherfas, 'Iron Man', Interview with Victor Alksnis, *New Statesman*, 5 April 1991. The political brief of the 'Black Colonel' from Riga seems to include throwing dust in the eyes of credulous foreign observers.

59. Vera Tolz and Elizabeth Teague, 'Prokhanov Warns of Collapse of Soviet Empire', *Report on the USSR*, 2, 6, 9 February 1990. In early 1991 a disaster of the Soviet industrial economy seemed imminent when a coalminers' strike threatened widespread destruction of the country's coking ovens – and hence steel production capacity. 'Kremlin Faces Bankruptcy and Industrial Collapse', *The Guardian*, 11 April 1991.

60. In Patrushev's words, '*Democracy* in the USSR means a curious blend of *glasnost* with dictatorship: an ability to vent your views but not ability to carry out decisions through action. *Market economy* means inflated prices and profiteering with limited private ownership and no long-term incentives' (1990, p.22).

61. However, Patrushev (1990, p.22) rightly notes 'the fear of retribution felt by the old elite for the wrongs they have committed and the anger and frustration of the people'.

62. Patrushev (*Interview*, 10 August 1990)

63. Roger Fisher (Harvard Project on Negotiations), *Interview*, Sydney, 15 August 1988. William Zartman has also, apparently, been widely read in Moscow. (See Touval and Zartman, 1985, and Zartman, 1989.)

64. The Baltic Council, consisting of the leaders of Lithuania's Sajudis and the Latvian and Estonian Popular Fronts, sponsored the talks. *Izvestia*, 31 January 1990 (translated in *Current Digest of the Soviet Press*, 42, 5, February 1991). *Moscow News* also tried its hand at mediation in the Armenian-Azerbaijan conflict. 'Need to Avoid Bloodshed', *Moscow News*, no.38, 6 October 1990.

65. Of course, if the Soviet Union breaks up in the near future, many 'domestic' nationality issues will become international ones, thus vindicating those international relations specialists who have rushed into the study of ethnic conflict!

66. I would like to thank all those who granted intereviews for this research, and the University of Sydney for providing leave and financial support. Juhan Lubek and Tiia Raudmaa (in Tallinn); Elise and Kenneth Boulding (in Boulder); John Groom (in Canterbury); Kjell-Åke Nordquist and Peter Wallensteen (in Uppsala); Kumar Rupesinghe (in Oslo), and Graeme Gill and Isobel Horton (in Sydney) are gratefully remembered for their human, infrastructural, critical and/or word processing assistance in the genesis of the work.

REFERENCES:

Anderson, Benedict, 1985. *Imagined Communities: Reflections on the Origin and Spread of Nationalism*, Verso, London.

Bennigsen, Alexandre, 1985. 'Soviet Muslims and the Muslim World' in Wimbush.

Brzezinski, Zbigniew, 1989-90. 'Post Communist Nationalism', *Foreign Affairs*, vol. 68, no. 5, Winter.

Burton, John, 1990. *Conflict: Resolution and Provention*, London: Macmillan.

Clemens, Walter C., 1991. *Can the United States Cooperate with an Empire in Decline?* Paper presented at the International Studies Association Annual Conference, Vancouver, March 20.

Dunlop, John B., 1983. *The Faces of Contemporary Russian Nationalism*, Princeton: Princeton University Press.

Ezhegodnik: Bolshoi Sovetskoi Entsiklopedii, 1990 [Yearbook: Great Soviet Encyclopedia], Moskva.

Goble, Paul, 1989. 'Ethnic Politics in the USSR', *Problems of Communism*, vol. 38, no. 4, July.

Kux, Stephan, 1990. *Soviet Federalism: A Comparative Perspective*, Occasional Paper No. 18, New York: Institute for East – West Security Studies.

Kux, Stephan, 1991. *Decline and Reemergence of Soviet Federalism*, Research Institute for Political Science, University of Zürich, March.

Lindgren, Karin, ed., 1991. *States in Armed Conflict, 1989*, Department of Peace and Conflict Research, Uppsala: Uppsala University.

Patrushev, Pyotr, 1991. 'Introducing Conflict Resolution into the USSR', *Conflict Resolution Notes* (Conflict Resolution Centre International, 710 Hamilton Ave., Pittsburgh, PA, USA) vol. 8, no. 3, January.

Sharp, Gene, 1973. *The Politics of Non-Violent Action*, Boston: Porter Sergeant.

Stavenhagen, Rudolfo, 1989. *Ethnic Conflicts and their Impact on International Society*, Paper prepared for the Colloque sur les Tendances Actuelles dans l'Etude des Conflicts Internationaux, University of Lausanne, December 8-9.

Taagepera, Rein, 1989. 'Estonia's Road to Independence', *Problems of Communism*, vol. 38, no. 6, November.

Touval, Saadia and Zartman, I. William, eds. (1985). *Mediation in Theory and Practice*, Boulder: Westview Press.

Tucker, Robert C., 1991. 'What Time Is It In Soviet History? Czars and Commiczars', *The New Republic*, January 21.

Wallensteen, Peter, 1991. 'Third Parties in Conflict Resolution' in Lindgren (1991).

Wiberg, Haakan, 1991. 'Reflections on Major Armed Conflicts in 1989' in Lindgren (1991).

Wimbush, S. Enders, ed., 1985. *Soviet Nationalities in Strategic Perspective*, London: Croom Helm.

Zartman, I. William, 1989. *Ripe for Resolution: Conflict and Intervention in Africa*, New York: Oxford University Press.

Epigraph Interviews:

Professor Yuri Levada, Director, All-Union Center for Public Opinion, Institute of Sociological Research, USSR Academy of Sciences, Moscow, June 28, 1990.

Dr. Peeter Vares, Deputy Director, Department of Political Science, Estonian Academy of Sciences, Tallinn, June 20, 1990.

(Paul Goble's remark can be found in Goble, 1989, p.13)

FIGURE 1: THE SOVIET FEDERATION

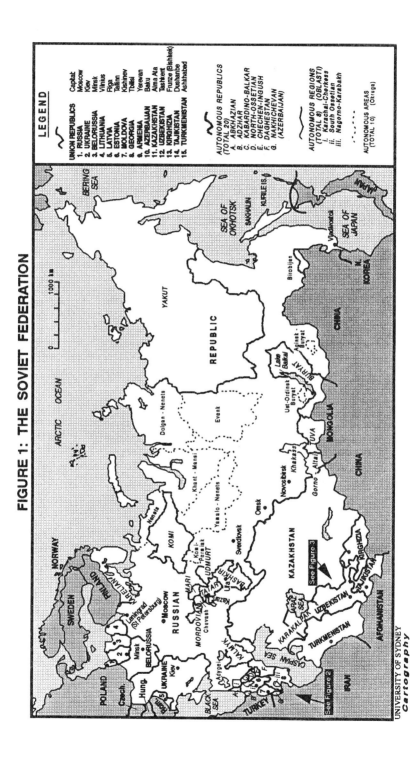

LEGEND

UNION REPUBLICS — Capital
1. RUSSIA — Moscow
2. UKRAINE — Kiev
3. BELORUSSIA — Minsk
4. LITHUANIA — Vilnius
5. LATVIA — Riga
6. ESTONIA — Tallin
7. MOLDOVA — Kishnev
8. GEORGIA — Tbilsi
9. ARMENIA — Yerevan
10. AZERBAIJAN — Baku
11. KAZAKHSTAN — Alma Ata
12. UZBEKISTAN — Tashkent
13. KIRGHIZIA — Frunze (Bishkek)
14. TAJIKISTAN — Dushanbe
15. TURKMENISTAN — Ashkhabad

AUTONOMOUS REPUBLICS
(TOTAL 20)
A. ABKHAZIAN
B. ADZHAR
C. KABARDINO-BALKAR
D. NORTH-OSSETIAN
E. CHECHEN-INGUSH
F. DAGHESTAN
G. NAKHICHEVAN (AZERBAIJAN)

AUTONOMOUS REGIONS
(TOTAL 8) (Karachai-Chorkess OBLASTI)
i. Karachai-Chorkess
ii. South Ossetian
iii. Nagorno-Karabakh

AUTONOMOUS AREAS
(TOTAL 10) (Okruga)

UNIVERSITY OF SYDNEY
Cartography

2

Inventions and Manifestations of Ethno-Nationalism in and after the Soviet Union

Valery A. Tishkov

1. INTRODUCTION

A striking feature of the entwining of ethnic nationalism and academic writings in recent decades is how often East European studies have been dominated by political considerations. The topic has been approached more as a political than as an intellectual problem; there has been a tendency to support the social engineering designs of Communist rulers and official ideology, rather than break significant new ground. These approaches served as a basis for elaborations of 'imagined communities' as proclaimed by the propagandists of existing regimes in 'socialist nations'. This was true for the USSR where all major ethnic groups (not only the largest one, the Russians, but also dozens of cultural minorities and Siberian indigenous groups) were granted this status; it was true for Yugoslavia with its republican 'nations' including the Macedonians; it was true for the Czechs and the Slovaks as well as for the Eastern Germans, who were treated as a new ethnic entity – 'the German socialist nation'. For at least half a century, the ethno-nation became a basic public category in this part of the world with its eclectic Stalinist definition combining territory, common economic ties, language and culturally constituted collective mentality dominating all spheres including anthropological studies.

Even today, despite radical societal changes and ideological liberalization, no serious re-evaluation or theoretical break-through has taken place in the Soviet social sciences regarding an interpretation of the nationality issues and ethnic unrest which have brought the former Soviet Union to an end. The vision of ethnicity remains heavily primordialistic, based on a politicized and scholastic academic theory of 'ethnos' which does not represent any serious separation from the so-called Marxist-Leninist theory of the national question.[1] For decades, social scientists in the Soviet Union studied ethnic groups as basic social entities, as 'ethno-social organisms' with their characteristic attributes of territory, language, culture and identity. An enormous amount of intellectual energy went into the study of ethnogenesis and ethnic history of the Soviet Union's peoples. With the enthusiastic participation of scholars in various academies, archaeological, physical anthropological, ethnographic and historical writings provided dominant groups in particular regions with 'pedigrees' back to upper-palaeolithic historical roots, cultural heroes, and pride as 'indigenous nations' with their 'own' territories and with their 'own' states.

This vision of ethnicity was closely tied into the official ideology and politics of ethno-nationalism dominant in the Soviet state – with ethnic groups forming pseudo-federal administrative units or Republics. The scholarly taxonomic classification of 'types of ethnic entities' (tribe, *narodnost* and nation) – which yielded such theoretical inventions as ESO (ethno-social organiz- ation) and ETHNIKOS (people of the same nationality living outside their 'own' state territories) – justified and served the purpose of an administrative statehood granted to what I call 'titular nationalities' – i.e. those whose names gave titles to republics.[2]

Ethno-nationalism, both as a theoretical paradigm and as political practice, dominated Soviet academic studies, which in turn fed politicians, intellectuals and the 'common man' with definitions and arguments in everyday language. To a very considerable extent, this Soviet theory constructed social realities and enforced scholarly definitions on political acti- vists as well as on the programmatic context of mass public movements during the time of perestroika. This complex dia- logue between science and praxis was not on the agenda for anthropological research in this country, leaving rather little space for arguments and explanations limited by positivistic methodologies one might use in studying ethno-nationalism. Unexpected for most Soviet and Western specialists, the outburst of nationalist sentiments and ethnic conflicts in the Soviet Union put them in a difficult situation. It suddenly became necessary to re-evaluate previous postulates. The new situation demonstrated the inadequacy of much of what had been previously published on ethnic issues. What responses were given to these challenges?

Recent academic writings in the West on the ethnic situation in the Soviet Union also seem to possess features related to the political allegiance of the scholars involved. For Western writers, most of whom are political scientists, the prevailing approaches are often motivated by a reflex to fight Communism and totalitarianism and by an euphoria of Liberal victory over the Soviet system. Nationalism, ethnic unrest and the dismembering of the Soviet Union are seen as a logical outcome of a this longagonizing, illegitimate empire – as a manifestation of democratization and the right to self-determination.[3] The main point of dispute within this group centres on their own status concerns – who in the past was the first to say this or who was lucky enough to predict the recent course of events. As a result, true ethnographic research is still scarce, partly because of existing political limitations and partly because of apparent lack of interest. Ethnographic research on the problem has dealt with a few groups only, and these have usually not been the most vocal and conflicting battlefields.

Among Soviet specialists, the major watershed runs along two lines which are not theoretical or methodological, but, political and ethnic. For 'periphery' scholars in the Republics, ethnocentric interpretations dominate, indirectly controlled by nationalistic forces and power institutions. Any approaches and opinions differing from the publicly accepted unilateral position may be proclaimed as 'subversive', as being expressed by 'enemies of the nation' and 'agents of the Kremlin.[4] The prevailing themes of the writings of these scholars are: elaborating lists of grievances against others, justifications for state, territorial, political, and cultural rights of titular nationalities, and a search for external enemies (mainly in Moscow or in neighbouring republics) as responsible for ethnic conflicts.[5] Historic-ethnographic in-group descriptions, without serious interest in the significance of ethnic interactions, within and outside the region, remain the most striking features of this Soviet 'peripheral' anthropology.

By contrast, scholarship in the 'centre' (mainly Moscow and St. Petersburg) is more academically oriented and less influenced by personal ethnic sentiments – although there are cases of openly expressed pro-Russian concerns, or sympathies for the minority and underprivileged groups studied.[6] Within this group which stands methodologically on the same side of positivistic primordialism there are at least two major divisions. They offer different explanations to questions of nationality, problems of ethnic conflict and prospects for the future. One group shares the views of the radical democrats who criticize the nationalities' policy of the previous regime. Blame is also focused on conservative Communist plots that seek to obstruct the 'historically unavoidable impetus' of each ethnic group to acquire its own statehood as a basis for keeping its culture and identity and for improving socio-economic conditions. (Koroteeva, Perepelkin, Shkaratan, 1988; Perepelkin, Shkaratan, 1989; Krupnik, 1990; Pain, Popov, 1990.) The other group is of a more pro-centre, anti-nationalistic orientation. It questions the ethnic principles of state organization, especially the sudden and uncontrolled process of devolution of power in favour of ethnic elites in the Republics. They assert that this has led to violations of individual rights and suppression of minorities, which in turn has stimulated violent ethnic confrontations. (Guboglo, 1989; Cheshko, 1989; Bromley, 1989; Yamskov, 1991.) Both groups explain events in terms of materialistic, economic, and social class analyses, or in terms of a simplistic, culturally based, 'we-they' dichotomy. Promising new developments in the West – such as post-modernist interpretations of ethnicity as a constructed phenomenon and recent approaches to the origins of ethnic conflicts based on social psychology, group behaviour, and elite-based theories of conflict remain unexplored by students of Soviet ethnicity. These approaches are frequently branded as sophisticated masquerades for chauvinistic, undemocratic and empire-saving approaches to the subject of ethnicity. But the most evident weakness of contemporary Soviet ethnography lies in its lack of strong empirical research based on sophisticated technique and observations to measure ongoing realities. Quite often this is substituted by old-fashioned sociological surveys or by enlightened journalism.

2. The Historical Contexts and the Modern Turn to Ethno-nationalism

If we explore the contexts within which ethno-nationalism developed in Europe, especially Eastern Europe, we can note an important pattern. The collapse of absolutist monarchies and colonial empires in Eastern Europe gave people an idea of enormous myth-making and political potential: the nation as a kind of mediating substance through which a civil society acquires the right to sovereignty and delegates political power. This idea encouraged those who aspired to build democratic civil societies to create national movements and sovereign states based on certain culturally dominant elements. These movements became the basis for ethnic (or ethno-) nationalism, which treats nations as a form of cultural grouping. There is a tendency for the nation state to become an ethnic state, in this regard, accepting its ethnicity as the legitimate basis for the functioning of the state, its economy and cultural institutions.

Ethno-nationalism was extremely popular among European Social-Democrats in the 19th and early 20th centuries. It helped in dismembering the Ottoman and Austria-Hungarian empires as well as in forming a new political map of Eastern Europe after World War I. Ironically, once Eastern European nationalists had acquired independence for their own nations, they discovered that it was impossible to realize the idea of ethno-nationalism in relation to the nation state (one ethnic group – one state). The boundaries between new states included minorities, who felt endangered by the new dominant groups and their political elites. New national leaders started pursuing towards minorities the same policy of intolerance as they had suffered from old imperial rulers. Weakened by internal and interstate conflicts, these political entities became an easy prey for the bloody designs of Hitler and Stalin that precipitated World War II.[7]

In the vast, multi-ethnic entity known as the Russian Empire, in place of the unifying idea of the nation, the feudal, eclectic formula of 'orthodoxy, autocracy and rootedness' prevailed until the beginning of the 20th century. Indeed, the term 'all-Russian' (or 'Rossian') is derivative from the title of the state, and denoted a citizen of the Empire irrespective of ethnic origin (Karamzin, 1990). Imperial laws were based on a notion of 'one nation' which included ethnic Russians, Ukrainians, and

Byelorussians, as well as the peoples of the Volga-Urals region which had formed part of the Empire since the 16th century. All these subjects acted according to one set of laws and regulations. The peoples of the more recently acquired periphery were treated as *inorodzi* ('aliens') for whom there were special regulations and by-laws. The dichotomy between two notions 'Rossian' and 'Russian' emphasizes an important distinction between imperial state and ethnic group which has been in existence for a long time in intellectual discourse, including among well known pre-revolutionary writers and political figures. Outstanding thinkers like Piotr Struve (1990) understood the nation as 'a spiritual unity, constructed and supported by common culture and by common national identity.' The complex, contradictory process of Russian nation-building prior to the Revolution of 1917 also included powerful and rapidly growing national identities movements among non-Russian groups of the Empire. By the last decade of the 19th century, Georgia's intellectuals, for example (not without the influence of Marxism) had provided considerable input into the making of the Georgian nation and the establishment of an independent republic in 1918 (Suny, 1988a). The same path was followed by a few other major groups on the ethnic periphery of the Russian Empire.

During the Revolution of 1917, Lenin and the Bolsheviks (unlike their political opponents, who stood for a 'one and undivided' Russia) used the slogan of the right to self-determination as a tremendously effective political weapon in winning the non-Russian regions to their side. This slogan was not simply a hypocritic political ploy. Rather it involved both a tactical response to existing political realities and a utopian belief in building a new world based on 'proletarian and class solidarity'. On the basis of this assertion, the peoples of Poland, Finland and the Baltic region successfully established separate states in the early liberal years of Soviet power. Elsewhere, as in the Caucasus, however, the Red Army resisted such territorial changes. During the Civil War, the nationalities policy of the Soviet state was often a decisive factor in rewinning territories of the country, under the loyalty of new authorities, by granting autonomous status to major non-Russian regions of the Russian Republic.

This was done even though nationalism was still little more than an elite credo, shared by a set of relatively isolated urban intellectuals. It hardly touched the bulk of the ethnic populations of the Russian empire, made up mostly of peasants who continued to identify with either their region or their religion (Suny, 1988b). In some regions, ethnic identities were so weak and overruled by clans or regional loyalties, as in Central Asia, that it was impossible to give any referent ethnic marker to a new republic or autonomous formation (such as Turkestan in the Russian Federation or the Bukhara and Khoresmian republics). In a few cases the ethnic mosaic was so complex that the self-determining unit chose to describe itself in non-ethnic terms (such as the Republic of Mountainous Peoples or Dagestan in the Caucasus). Nonetheless, ethno-nationalism became the basis on which socialist federalism was constructed. The principle of national (read: ethnic) statehood was enshrined as the foundation of Soviet federalism. A socialist federated state was considered to be composed of ethno-political administrative units, in which each 'indigenous socialist nation' had its own 'statehood' – as opposed to 'bourgeois federalism', where the constituent parts were held to be primarily economic-regional formations (Constitution of the USSR, 1982). All Soviet constitutions embodied the principle of a right to self-determination for ethno-nations, up to and including the right to secession.

It should be stressed that such a 'brave' social experiment could become possible only under conditions of an early emerged totalitarianism. This developed within the context of one-party rule and strict centralization enforced from Moscow, beginning with the first years of industrialization. It became a formalistic declaration, a philological reality, one that did not involve actual responsibilities or effective procedures for its realization. Even at the formal level, I should add, however, this principle applied only to certain categories of ethnic groups – those with Union Republic status. The others were arranged along a hierarchical ladder of relative autonomy, down to a level that made no provision for any administrative structure whatsoever. Additionally, among the peoples of the Soviet Union, there were those who were deprived of territories they had occupied, as well as those who suffered border 'adjustments' and/or changes in administrative organization.

Given the devastations brought by the Soviet regime to practically all ethnic groups of the country, it might seem easy to explain the cause of the current ethno-nationalism explosion by noting a long list of grievances. Indeed, we also contributed to this widely accepted explanation in previous publications

(Tishkov, 1991a). But exploring the issue further leads to a more subtle dynamics. Of concern is not only how a few years of perestroika revealed among Soviet citizens deep dissatisfactions and discontent with the existing social order. Of concern is also why this dissatisfaction became channelled into ethno-nationalism? Ronald Suny is right in saying the 'process of nation-building under Soviet rule was facilitated considerably by early Bolshevik policies. In particular, the party's commitment to Lenin's notion of national self-determination and its establishment of a pseudo-federal administrative system, the first in the world with territorial units based on ethnicity, to consolidate, rather than erode, ethnic and national cohesion' (Suny, 1989, pp. 503-528). This observation could be supplemented by Zbigniew Brzezinski's remark, that despite its having proclaimed itself to be a doctrine of internationalism, Communism in fact intensified popular nationalist passions and fused with and even reinforced intolerant nationalism. 'It produced a political culture imbued with intolerance, self-righteousness, rejection of social compromise and a massive inclination to ward self-glorifying oversimplification. Nationalism was thereby nurtured, rather than diluted, in the Communist experience' (Brzezinski, 1989/90, p. 2).

With the policy of 'nativization' that started in the 1920s an immense effort was put into training native cadres of professionals and educators, developing local languages and schooling, and into establishing professional high culture institutions (literature, theatre, science, cinema, publishing, etc.). Prestigious manifestations of 'the flourishing socialist nations' were sponsored and encouraged by the political centre in Moscow even in times of political repression. After 50 years of 'nativization' policy, the proportion of national intelligentsia and the rate of specialists with university diplomas had become fairly equal; in fact, for a few groups (e.g. Armenians and Georgians) it was higher comparing with the Russians.

This officially generated ethno-nationalism produced local elites in the Republics who, it turns out, were quite vocal and inclined to wasteful status displays in support of themselves. In the weakly modernized Republics of the USSR, such elites frequently degenerated into feudal-clan relations or produced organized criminal-mafia structures, neither of which tolerated any kind of opposition. Their energies tended to be directed toward establishing the priority claims of their group against those of neighbouring peoples for territory, cultural heroes and/or cultural legacies. And they displayed definite signs of local chauvinism – pretensions not only of inflated status but aspirations to assimilate the small, sparsely populated enclaves of ethnically different peoples living in the Republic. In some Soviet union republics and most of the autonomous regions, indigenous elites felt that the most disturbing challenge to their authority came from Russian-speaking populations,[8] who comprise a majority of the country especially in urban centres.

That kind of historical background cannot be ignored by specialists seeking for answers to the rise of ethno-nationalism. The Soviet situation is complex. It cannot be explained merely as a reflection of the world-wide trend toward ethnic revival and the growth of modern post-industrial nationalism, although these factors have undoubtedly had some influence. Nor can it be explained as the cumulative, long-suppressed discontent with historical injustices or with the low level of social and cultural conditions. In the final analysis, the strongest and most highly organized national movements have *not* arisen in the most backward regions of the country nor among the most socially downtrodden ethnic groups. Nor is the situation the result of 'errors' in the implementation of Soviet nationalities policy and 'deviations' from Leninist principle – a simplistic explanation suggested by many authors and politicians. I suggest that we must also focus on the inability of the political order to create even the most rudimentary civil institutions that would allow for effective local self-government or the creation of political and social structures through which citizens and groups, including ethnic groups, could defend and realize their interests and rights. As soon as the once omnipotent and all-encompassing power of the party apparatus weakened and official ideology collapsed, the fatal inability of the hierarchy of state structures to regulate and govern social affairs became obvious. For millions of Soviet citizens, aroused to political activism and facing a lack of truly effective forms for realizing their demands, the appeal of ethnic group loyalty and of the nationalist idea became the sole and most understandable basis for collective action and the expression of protest regarding conditions of social despair and profound political disillusionment. Ethno-nationalism became prominent as an alternative to a strong, centralized state with ineffective representation at the local level. It evoked romantic, emotional images for a new form of solidarity without necessarily resolving the problems of democratic representation on the local level. If and how these can be resolved under ethno-nationalism remains to be seen.

3. THE POWER OF ETHNO-NATIONALISM AND THE ROLE OF
INTELLECTUALS

Many Western anthropologists share the vision of nations as
'imagined communities', as cultural artifacts constructed by
intellectuals (writers, historians, anthropologists, etc.). But none
of post-modern interpretations have been tested on Soviet
realities as well as other influential theories.[9] My modest
attempts to write about the nation as a constructed idea, rather
than as an obvious reality, met with total misunderstanding and
repugnance even though past and current Soviet realities tend to
confirm the thesis (Bromley, 1989b; CPSU, 1990). After decades
of literary and practical nation-building, ethno-nationalism has
become entwined in a wide spectrum of public ideologies and
political mentalities and has won considerable social support.
Perestroika greatly facilitated the process. Activists of more than
a dozen ethnic groups – beginning with strong cultural minorities and small Northern peoples – started to speak about their
own 'nations'. Demands for recognition as separate 'ethnos' and
'nations' have been formulated by Gagauz in Moldavia, by
Karpato-Russians in Ukraine, by Siberian Tatars, and by those
native groups of the North where local authorities proclaimed
their own autonomous Republics. Elsewhere leaders are still
fighting to gain state status for their groups (such as the Far
Eastern groups of the Amur River).[10] Disproportionately large
ethnic elites – used to living under uncompetitive and complementary conditions awarded to them by the centre – challenged
their subordinate status by demanding full sovereignty (or
independence) for the purpose of a 'national revival' and the
building of a 'national state'. The new political climate allowed
intellectuals to push aside relatively easily the old party
and state apparatus thereby gaining political power in most
regions of the country. A vacuum of professional politicians,
among reformers and nationalists, allowed a number of intelligentsia with Ph.Ds and academic backgrounds mainly in social
sciences and humanities to take prominent leadership positions.
    The new political leaders and activists within the national-
ities movement relied on the high literacy and reading habits of
the populace to further the mystique and sense of collective
loyalty. They used the considerable data accumulated in local
academies on language, literature, historical, and archaeological
reconstructions of traditional culture as 'a source for inventing

ethnic (national) myths' (Gittelman, 1991, p. 34). The shaman-
istic effects and emotional appeal of the new leaders' presen-
tations first in mass public meetings and then through TV
broadcasting of parliamentary debates became a great mobilizing
force. The physical and emotional distance between academic
debates, public discourse, and political and militant actions
practically disappeared. An article in a newspaper or in a
scholarly journal could become the reason for a public meeting or
a protest demonstration. A speech in a parliament and a letter
by Gamsakhurdia to the Abkhazian leader Ardzinba on ancient
Georgian stone inscriptions at Sukhumi Bridge caused bloody
clashes between Georgians and Abkhazians at that locale.In its
turn the militant opposition to Georgia's President, led by
university professors and outstanding cultural figures and using
the Georgian Academy of Sciences building as a headquarters for
the Temporal Military Council, was able to mobilize armed
fighters and public support to overthrow 'leader of a nation' who
had been practically unanimously elected by the people only six
months before. Seen from this perspective, the modern ideology
of ethno-nationalism is not so much a reflection of social praxis.
Rather, the social praxis of ethno-nationalism was shaped by
ideological discourse and academic postulates. Soviet ethno-
nationalism was and still is both a result of and a reaction
to etatization and hierarchical structuring of ethnicity, when
citizens of the country were classified and divided into 'nations',
'narodnosts' and 'national groups' depending on voluntaristically
and arbitrarily formed statuses and borders of administrative
units.

It is not easy to write this in today's highly politicized
academic climate. But the above analysis suggests that inter-
ethnic strife and conflicts, not to mention the disintegration of
the USSR, derive not only from a failed Communist social
experiment, but equally from the 'progress' achieved in developing the Soviet 'socialist nations' as republics. Contemporary
political folklore and even many academics in the Soviet
(Dis)union and abroad are not yet ready to accept this conclusion. Hence, it should best be viewed as a subject for
additional research and testing. We need to explore ethno-
nationalism in public Soviet discourse as a form of poetic
therapy, as a form of healing for the deep trauma experienced by
the Soviet people on individual and collective levels. Ethno-
nationalism represents a means for regaining lost pride and

'personal worth' using Horowitz's (1985) perspective. Quite often this poetization breaks with reality. It appeals to a memory of ethos for this or that community and calls people to act in accord with this ethos. Under certain social and political conditions, poetization can mobilize immense constructive, creative potentials of ethnicity. It can also cause the emergence of a world-spreading Kalashnikov culture – a culture of intolerance and of destruction exercised by the machine-gun as an argument in achieving 'national goals'. Both perspectives are evident in the modern politics of the Soviet (Dis)union. Their joint future remains to be written – in relation to the on-going tensions between nationalist ideologies and multi-ethnic polities now dominating former Soviet Union politics.

What kind of role can intellectuals have in this historical drama full of militant realities? An answer was given by M.Foucault:

> *The intellectual no longer has to play the role of an advisor. The project, tactics and goals to be adopted are a matter for those who do the fighting. What the intellectual can do is to provide instruments of analysis, and at present this is the historian's essential role. What's effectively needed is a ramified, penetrative perception of the present, one that makes it possible to locate lines of weakness, strong points, positions where the instances of power have secured and implanted themselves by a system of organization dating back 150 years. In other words, a topological and geological survey of the battlefield – that is the intellectual's role. But as for saying, 'Here is what you must do!', certainly not. (Foucault, 1980, p. 62.)*

But again that is not the Soviet case. Generated by primordialistic visions of ethnicity and by historical-materialistic mentality of social engineering in accordance with unilinear realization of 'historical law' Soviet political and academic rhetoric did not change much after the collapse of the Union and its ideology. A belief in Lenin's principles and 'theory' as a reference of authority was easily replaced by arguments of sacral and providentialistic character. Demoralized by his ouster from the process he personally had initiated, Mikhail Gorbachev started to speak about ethnic groups in a slightly changed manner: 'Peoples are returning back to a process of self-awareness, to a search of their own roots. And each people – small and big – is a God's creation, and nobody has the right to deprive any people, especially a small one, to study and understand itself' (*Literary Gazette*, 4 December 1991).

Moreover, this thesis was prompted by numerous emotional statements on a part of writers and scholars. A member of the all-Union parliament, Belorussian writer Basil Bykov (*Komsomolskaya Pravda*, 19 June 1991) wrote on 'the sacred and God-given right of nations to self-determination'. Ukrainian writer Boris Oleinyk (also a member of the former all-Union Parliament) called nations 'eternal categories like the Sun and the Moon' (CPSU, 1990). In this he echoed the social scientist's vocabulary. We may note how historian Elena Guskova (*Moscow News*, 17 September 1991), writing on the case of Yugoslavia, drew a conclusion about the universal historical trend for the peoples 'first to disintegrate and to define themselves and only then to integrate'. Or, for example, consider professional ethnographer Galina Starovoitova (*Soviet Karabakh*, 22 August 1989), who during her spectacular political career frequently wrote and spoke publicly about 'growing interest among people to such eternal values as family and nation'. Here, the latter one is understood as a type of ethnic entity, the 'ethno-nation' as presented by professional academics as 'a basis for civil society'.

Soviet anthropology remains strongly political, making a sense of identity and a belief in the ethno-nation 'real' – but no more than a sense and a belief. What is 'true reality' is based on this construction's political practice and the mass actions of its recruits. The results speak for themselves: a million refugees and a few thousands killed among the rank and file.

4. THE END OF THE SOVIET UNION

What, then, awaits the former Soviet Union after six years of *perestroika*? What will be the fate of its population of 289 million, composed of more than 130 different ethnic groups? The legally constituted authorities were powerless to halt the violence or the large-scale dislocation of populations. Frequently the sole brake on violence was fear of reprisals by the opposing side. The authorities themselves – including the MVD and the KGB – were also ethnically engaged, and frequently sympathized with the national movements. In 1989 criminal charges were brought against 350 persons for participation in inter-ethnic conflicts, and in the early part of 1990 there were an additional 100 cases; but it was impossible for those responsible for law enforcement to fully investigate and prosecute each one.

This has caused gloomy prognoses concerning the inevitable and rapid collapse of the Soviet empire. Zbigniew Brzezinski has predicted the 'Balkanization' of Eastern Europe, the 'Lebanonization' of the USSR and the transformation of 'the existing Soviet bloc into an arena of the most severe national conflicts on earth' (Brzezinski, 1989/90, p. 1). Yuri Afanasiev, in an issue of *Time* magazine focused on 'Soviet de-unionization', expressed the view that 'the USSR is neither a country nor a state. The Eurasian territory so designated on maps is a whole world of worlds, made up of different cultures and civilizations... and the USSR as a country has no future' (*Time*, 12 March 1990, p. 52).

Different scenarios have been presented in Soviet academic and public discourse in recent years. *One variant* envisioned the future Soviet Union as a union of autonomous states. Within a number of these states, particularly the Russian Republic, provision would be made for regional self- government. Until spring 1991, this scheme probably had more adherents than any other, although its proponents differed widely as to specifics. For the ruling Centre, for many party and government leaders at the republic and autonomous republic level, and for Mikhail Gorbachev most of all, a renewed union was envisaged within the framework of the long-prevailing concept of a federal state structure. However, this was designed to be a federation 'filled with new contents' and created on the basis of a new treaty. Indeed, a new union treaty was one of the Centre's most serious concessions: as recently as 1989 the Communist Party Central Committee's platform on 'The Party's National Policy in Light of the Current Situation' maintained that the choice made in 1922 was immutable, and limited itself to a cliché about the 'openness of the treaty'.

But this concession came far too late. Consultations between an all-union delegation and representatives from the republics at the Kremlin in July and August 1990 proved to be fruitless, and several of the republics took recourse in parallel republic-to-republic negotiations. The formula 'fifteen plus one' (the republics plus the Centre) frightened many of the participants in this historical drama. As I could observe personally during the series of meetings, the delegates from the republics at that time wanted to see the centre transformed into a kind of switchboard for horizonal inter-republican ties – a part of the infrastructure to ensure their effective mutual cooperation.

The most succinct account of the position of the political Centre on this question was set forth in the draft platform for the 28th Party Congress approved by the Central Committee plenum in February 1990, entitled 'Towards a Humane, Democratic Socialism'. In the section entitled 'Towards a New Federation' both the fate of *perestroika* and the future of the country were directly linked to inter-ethnic relations. However, the causes of ethnic conflict were identified as lying in the 'distortion of the Leninist nationalities policy', while 'the main way out of the difficulties[!] that have arisen in this area' was conceived in terms of realizing various economic and political reforms and the principle of federalism.

The ideological basis of the platform remained 'the principle of self-determination in a revitalized Soviet federation', which presupposed the 'freedom of nation-state formations (read: 'ethno-states') to choose their own ways of life, institutions and symbols of statehood'. At the same time, the document stated: 'we are resolutely opposed to separatist slogans and movements that lead to the destruction of the large-scale, multinational democratic state', and to the loss of all that was 'great and worthy that was introduced into the life of our country by the October Revolution', including the 'sense of being an equal participant in a great world power.' *(Pravda*, 13 February 1990).

In his arguments in favour of a revitalized federation, Gorbachev emotionally conceded that 'we do not yet live under the conditions of a real federation'. Critical in Gorbachev's position was his insistence on preserving the Union as 15 'national states' with the existing hierarchy of nation-state formations, and guarantees of the rights and opportunities for development of the so-called 'non-indigenous' populations and national groups within the republics. This formula did not propose any radical change for the Russian Republic – firstly, because it did not acknowledge the concept of self-determination for civil-territorial communities (regional self-determination); and, secondly, because self-determination of the Russians on an ethnic basis would be impossible – as, indeed, it also is for the majority of other groups.

Although before the August putch the Centre had great bureaucratic and economic power, it could not realize its ostensible programme. The central bureaucratic apparatus and other powerful institutions, fearful of losing Union-wide power and subject to the inertia of imperial thinking, blocked the redistribution and decentralization of power in even the most innocuous spheres of life, despite the spectre of imminent disintegration. Even education, and culture – the prerogative of state or provincial institutions in every federal system in the world – remained subordinated to the central authorities in the USSR.

The confrontation in the spring of 1990 between the President of the USSR and the Lithuanian leadership reinforced the old great-power syndrome, provoking a resurrection of what only recently had been dismissed as outdated ideological clichés. In a speech to the 21st All-Union Congress of the Komsomol, Gorbachev referred to the territory of Lithuania as 'this coastal frontier which Russia gained over the ages'. In another speech he declared 'the demon of nationalism' to be 'terrible in all its manifestations', and suggested that 'the common goal of the younger generation' should be 'the total renewal and development of the friendship of our peoples' (*Pravda*, 11-12 April 1990). The Referendum of 17 March 1991 in nine republics brought a solid argument for Gorbachev's position (76% said 'yes' to the 'remodelled Union'). But steps by conservative forces against new Union Treaty and for restoration of status quo followed after and buried this alternative.

The *second variant* for restructuring the Union was proposed by the Baltic republics and then by Georgia and Moldova. It called for the establishment of independent or fully sovereign republics, to be associated within a single union on the model of the UN or the European Community. Two-three years ago, this perspective was considered as realistic and possible only for the Baltic region, which by 1991 had come closest to the realization of the goal of independence, at least at the level of policy, state symbols and international recognition.

Implementation of this variant did not in fact result in the restructuring or reform of the federation: rather it replaced it with an entirely new, as yet largely hypothetical, association of independent states. All the legal groundwork necessary to implement this variant was already in place; moreover, it gains legitimacy from the fact that it was based primarily on the right to self-determination common to all democracies and widely acknowledged around the world. But there are very important factors that have not been taken sufficiently into account by either of the opposing sides.

The right to self-determination, as validated in numerous international legal documents and achieved in historical practice, has generally been understood *not* as the right of nations *qua* distinct ethnic communities, but as a right inherent in civil associations or in a 'people' – using this term in the sense of shared citizenship.

In other words, self-determination does not apply to the Estonians or to the Lithuanians, nor to the Georgians, but to the *people* of Estonia, the *people* of Lithuania and the *people* of Georgia. These are not one and the same, although as a rule the majority, and in some cases even the overwhelming majority, of the population of these governmental entities will be composed of representatives of the titular nationality.

Self-determination on strictly ethnic lines was impossible in the past, and it is impossible today. The Soviet Union was no exception to this rule. Only the forcible, mass resettlement of millions of citizens could alter this state of affairs, but recourse to such a distasteful expedient would also leave the problem of what to do with the millions of people of mixed ancestry belonging to ethnically mixed families.

It would appear that the proponents of secession are now coming to realize both the danger and the dead-end logic of a narrowly-construed, ethnically-based interpretation of 'the right of nations to self-determination' as they approach their avowed goal. The basic phraseology of the leaders of national movements in these republics has changed over the past two or three years. There is much less talk now of the 'national statehood' or the self-determination of Kazakhs, Ukrainians or Lithuanians. Instead there is more talk of the self-determination of the *peoples* of these republics – a term which encompasses not only members of the 'indigenous nations' but indeed the citizens of all nationalities who live in these republics. On the 11 March 1990, V. Landsbergis announced that it was the people of Lithuania – including *all* citizens of the republic – who had proclaimed their independence. Later on he defined 'nation' as a multi-ethnic entity (*Izvestia*, 7 May 1991). The same position is taken by President Nazarbayev in Kazakhstan.

An analysis of the sovereign declarations of a number of republics, enthusiastically approved by their respective Supreme Soviets or Councils during the summer of 1990, confirms the persistence of this contradiction. The authors of most of these texts could not avoid, and in some cases did not attempt to avoid, the inherent contradiction between the civil and the ethnic versions of sovereignty. In several instances they explicitly used *both* in defining the sovereign political community. The Ukrainian and the Kazakh declarations, for example, refer to the sovereign group as the 'people of the Ukraine' and the 'people of Kazakhstan' as well as the 'Ukrainian nation' and the 'Kazakh nation' in an ethnic sense. In the declaration of the Russian Federation the relevant references are to the 'multi-ethnic people of Russia' and 'the peoples of Russia'.

In Russia, a difficult dialogue between civic democracy, human rights approaches, on the one hand, and ethno-nationalism as ideological paradigm and political practice, on the other, was finally outpowered by the latter one. Under condition of socio-economic crisis, weak democratic traditions and slow process of reforms, ethno-nationalism demonstrated its great mobilizing potential, its therapeutic effects in healing the lost pride and historical injustices felt by practically all ethnic groups after decades of the failed social experiment. When the centre committed suicide in August 1991 and the Democratic Russia won the victory, the imminent reaction in other republics was not a move towards democratization, but to finalize cecession and dismembering the Soviet Union. This move on the part of republican leaders was supported by majorities of titular groups and caused serious concern among the so-called Russian-speaking population and other ethnic minorities as well.

For several republics this proclaimed independence was a long pursued political goal and even an accompanied reality (as it was for three Baltic states). For the others it was rather a powerful argument in ongoing political bargain around reconstructing some kind of a new union. But common for all 15 states that have proclaimed their independence was the multi-ethnic character of their population (except Armenia) and the challenges of inter-ethnic tensions and violence. Now each republic finds itself confronted with rising numerous ethnic identities, mini-nationalism and autonomy sentiments among groups who may have kept silent before.

These new states need now to work out their own 'national-ities policy' to replace the anti-Centre aggressive nationalistic stand. Otherwise there is a real possibility of repeated escalation of disintegrationistic processes at the intra-republic level. How-ever, the inertia of ethno-nationalism remains strong among the dominant groups' elites. Even the politicians with the democratic and cosmopolitan reputation like Shevardnadze, could not be able to overcome nationalist stands. After his return to Georgia, there was a step aside of intolerable Georgian nationalism: Georgia was proclaimed as a 'national state of Georgians and Abkhazians', but not of Ossetians, Adzaris or Meskhetian Turks! The new authorities also decided to keep a procedure of official registration of ethnic origins for the citizens of Georgia (*Izvestia*, 25 April 1992). As a result, the situation in the new states has become aggravated after independence by border disputes between republics and by issues of self-determination for minorities and regional citizenships.

There is no longer a Centre-Periphery dimension in profiling inter-ethnic relations and conflicts. There is no longer the political substance (Kremlin and Communist rulers) who used to be blamed for conflicts by nationalists and by radical democrats, and blamed for disintegration of the great power by patriots and conservatives. But their new situation does not serve to ease tensions or lower ethnic violence. All major conflicts with manifested ethnic parameters are still there. Moreover, new places of militant activities appeared after the August putch, especially in Northern Caucasus, Crimea and Southern Russia.

Meanwhile, a *third alternative* could be recognized on the horizon of Commonwealth of Independent States' politics at this moment, at least for the Russian federation – still one of the largest political entities in the world. Three-day barricades around the Russian Parliament and Yeltsin's heroic resistance to the old guards demonstrated a new kind of identity for the people of Russia with newly acquired state symbols, popular rituals and sacralizations, and with a new multi-ethnic demo-cratic leadership (Tishkov, 1991b). On the basis of this all-Russian identity and political solidarity these leaders are attempting to build a new, 'normal' (based on the regional principle) federation within the limits of the largest republic, where ethnic Russians comprise a little over 80% of the popu-lation and lacking strong pressures for ethno-national self-determination.

This approach formed the basis of a draft of new constitution proposed to the Russian Parliament in October 1991. By this project the former autonomous republics will acquire full sovereignty as subjects of the federation but their status will be equal to the status of 'lands', also subjects of federation, formed on regional principle. Representatives of the republics protested strongly against this draft as potentially diminishing their exclusive status as of 'national states.' In some republics, independentist platforms became very strong in the recent political discourse, especially in Chechen and Tatar Republics. Ethnonationalism dominates local ideology, slogans and partizan aspirations. Nationalistic feelings are growing stronger in the non-Slavic republics of Russia, representing a serious challenge for democratic leaders bent on radical reforms and loyal to an integrated Russia. Will they be able to overcome centrifugal tendencies and to avoid further tensions between local ethnic leaders and the democrats in Moscow and in other large industrial centres?

The forces of nationalism in Russia are not so strong and politically elaborated as in the former union republics, but there is a sizable reservoir for discontent and for the mobilization of 20 million non-Slavic inhabitants this republic. All these groups have their own educated elites, prestigious strata of intellectuals, state and former party functioners who used to live in an atmosphere of potlatching and ethno-political privileges. They now feel insecure and uncompetitive in the universalistic type of democratization which gives priority to individual rights over ethnic privileges. Some of these feelings are more than justifiable, especially among small indigenous peoples of the North: after experiencing long period of diminished status and living in a fragile environment with a heavy reliance on traditional ways of subsistence, these groups cannot survive culturally and politically without consociational type of democracy combined with representational arrangements. Such groups need special protective legislation, affirmative programmes, exclusive rights for territories and resources, etc. On the other hand, these principles cannot be used as a basis for the whole Russian federative structure without generating new forms of ethnic inequality and competition.

The Soviet Empire has now fallen apart as a result of nationalities movements and conflicting ethnicity. A major lesson here involves recognizing not only former deformations and the more recent political plots and miscalculations of nationality policy, but also the disintegrating nature of the politics of constructing ethnicity and of using ethno-nationalism as a basis of state and political order. Paradoxically, the Soviet Union has died not only because of the intolerable crimes of the political regime, but also because of its undeniable achievements in 'socialist nation-building' – based on the Leninist-Stalinist theory of the nation, enthusiastically elaborated by generations of social scientists and implemented by generations of politicians and intellectuals in the Centre and Peripheries.

NOTES:

1. For the most comprehensive text, see Walker Connor (1984). For a critical analysis of Soviet academic writings on ethnicity, see Peter Skalnik, (1986; 1988). Also an overview of Soviet contributions for special issue 'Ethnicity in the USSR' of the journal 'Theory and Society', vol. 20, 1991, written by John Comaroff. For a more complimentary analysis, see Theodor Shanin (1989).

2. This kind of vocabulary was used by Soviet authors during the last two decades in their treatment of so-called 'ethnic processes'. For an English translation, see Yulian Bromley (1988); Viktor Kozlov (1988); Yulian Bromley and Viktor Kozlov (1989).

3. Since 1986, at least a dozen books and over a hundred scholarly articles were published by Western anthropologists and political scientists on Soviet nationalities issues. See, for example, Bohdan Nahaylo and Victor Swoboda (1990); Graham Smith (1990); Alexander Motyl (1990); Lubomyr Hajda and Mark Bessinger (1990).

4. There were many stories of moral persecution and even physical assaults of a number of intellectuals in Baltic republics, Moldova, Ukraine, Armenia, Georgia, Kazakhstan widely covered in local and central press for the last two-three years.

5. Most of this literature in local languages but there are also many brochures and articles written in Russian, for example on Trans-caucasus issues: Miminoshvili and Pandjikidze (1990); Barsegyan (1989); Arutyunyan (1990); Galoyan (1988; 1989).

6. See, Kozlov (1990; 1991). As to pro-minority statements, see articles in *Sovetskaya Ethnografia* (1989, no. 5), especially a discussion on a status of the Pamir's peoples in Tadjikistan.

7. The best anthropological and historical analysis of this period of transformation and the epogy of nationalism was done by Gellner (1989) and Hobsbawn (1990).

8. The widely used and politicized category *Russian-speaking population* is actually misleading for several reasons. Firstly, a substantial number of people among titular groups is also Russian-speaking. Secondly, some nonetitular minorities in the republics do have less command of the Russian language than titular groups. Finally, small indigenous groups and demographically dispersed minorities are predominantly Russian-speaking but retain their cultural characteristics and ethnic identity.

9. Some of these attempts to broaden the theoretical scope in explanations of Soviet ethno-nationalism, see Dutter (1990). A discussion 'Social Science Theory and Soviet Nationalities', especially Jerry F. Hough's article (1990).

10. As a Director of the Institute I had received for the last three years at least a dozen of those requests, or petitions, including the most recent one from the Cossacks – an example if emerging identity based more on historical and political tradition than on cultural characteristics.

REFERENCES

Arutyunyan, V.B., 1990. *Events in Nagorno-Karabakh*, Yerevan: Academy of Sciences Press (in Russian).

Barsegyan, Hikar, 1989. *The Truth is Precious...To the Problem of the Nagorno-Karabakh*, Yerevan: Znanie (in Russian).

Bromley, Yulian, 1988. *Theoretical Ethnography*, Moscow: Nauka.

Bromley, Yulian, 1989a. 'National Problems under the Conditions of Perestroika', *Problemi Istorii*, no. 1 (in Russian).

Bromley, Yulian, 1989b. 'On the Terminological Aspects of Nationalities Problems', *Sovetskaya Ethnografia*, no. 6 (in Russian).

Bromley, Yulian & Viktor Kozlov, 1989. 'The Theory of Ethnos and Ethnic Processes in Soviet Social Sciences, *Comparative Studies in Society and History*, vol. 31, no. 3, July.

Brzezinski, Zbigniew, 1989. 'Post-Communist Nationalism', *Foreign Affairs*, 68, 5, Winter.

Comaroff, John, 1991. 'Humanity, Ethnicity, Nationality: Conceptual and Comparative Perspectives on the USSR', *Theory and Society*, vol. 20.

Connor, Walker, 1984. *The National Question in Marxist-Leninist Theory and Strategy*, Princeton: Princeton University Press.

Constitution of the USSR, 1982. Political-Legal Commentary, Moscow (in Russian).

CPSU, 1990. 28th Congress of the CPSU. Session on National Politics of CPSU, *Bulletin for Delegates of the Congress*, Moscow (in Russian).

Cheshko, S.V., 1989. 'Economic Sovereignty and the Economic Question', *Kommunist*, no. 2 (in Russian).

Dutter, Lee E., 1990. 'Theoretical Perspectives on Ethnic Political Behaviour in the Soviet Union', *Journal of Conflict Resolution*, vol. 34, no. 2, pp. 311-34.

Foucault, Michel, 1980. *Power/Knowledge. Selected Interviews and Other Writings 1972-1977*, New York: Pantheon Books.

Galoyan, G.A., ed., 1989. The Truth about Nagorno-Karabakh: Documents and Materials, Yerevan: Academy of Sciences Press (in Russian).

Galoyan, G.A., ed., 1988. *Nagorno-Karabakh. A Historical Essay*, Yerevan: Academy of Sciences Press (in Russian).

Gellner, E., 1983. *Nations and Nationalism*, Oxford: Blackwell.

Gittelman, Zvi, 1991. 'Formation of Jewish Culture and Identity in the USSR: The State as a Social Engineer', *Sovetskaya Ethnografia*, no. 1 (in Russian).

Guboglo, M.N., 1989. 'National Groups and Minorities in a System of Inter-ethnic Relations in the USSR', *Sovetskaya Ethnografia*, no. 1 (in Russian).

Hajda, Lubomyr & Mark Beissinger, eds, 1990. *The Nationalities Factor in Soviet Politics and Society*, Boulder: Westview Press.

Hobsbawn, Eric J., 1990. *Nations and Nationalism since 1780. Programme, Myth, Reality*, Cambridge: Cambridge University Press.

Horowitz, Donald L., 1985. *Ethnic Groups in Conflict*, Berkeley: University of California Press.

Hough, Jerry F., 1990. 'The Logic of Collective Action and the Pattern of Revolutionary Behaviour', *Journal of Soviet Nationalities*, vol. 1, no. 2.

Karamzin, N.M., 1990. Speech delivered at the grand meeting of the Imperial All-Russian Academy, *Literary Criticism from 1800 to the 1820s*, Moscow: Nauka (in Russian).

Koroteeva, V.V., L.S. Perepelkin, & O.I. Shkaratan, 1988. 'From Bureaucratic Centralism to Economic Integration of Sovereign Republics', *Kommunist*, no. 15 (in Russian).

Kozlov, Viktor, 1988. *The Peoples of the Soviet Union*, London: Hutchinson; Bloomington: Indiana University Press.

Kozlov, Viktor, 1990. 'National Question: Paradigm Theory and Practice', *Istoria SSSR*, no. 1 (in Russian).

Kozlov, Viktor, 1991. '"Imperial Nation" or Unpriviliged Nationality?' *Moskwa*, no.1 (in Russian).

Krupnik, I.I., 1990. 'National Question in the USSR: In Search of Explanations', *Sovetskaya Ethnografia*, no. 4 (in Russian).

Miminoshvili, Roman & Guram Pandjikidze, 1990. *The Truth about Abkhazia*, Tbilisi: Merani (in Russian).

Motyl, Alexander, 1990. *Sovietology, Rationality, Nationality Coming to Grips with Nationalism in the USSR*, New York: Colombia University Press.

Nahaylo, Bohdan & Viktor Swoboda, 1990. Soviet Disunion. *A History of Nationalities Problems in the USSR*, London: Hamish Hamilton.

Pain, E.A. & A.A. Popov, 1990. 'Interethnic Conflicts in the USSR: Approaches to Studies and to Practical Solutions', *Sovetskaya Ethnografia*, no. 1 (in Russian).

Perepelkin, L.S. & O.I. Shkaratan, 1989. 'Economic Sovereignty and Ways for Development of the Peoples', *Sovetskaya Ethnografia*, no. 4 (in Russian).

Shanin, Theodor, 1989. 'Ethnicity in the Soviet Union: Analytical Perceptions and Political Strategies', *Comparative Studies in Society and History*, vol. 31, no. 3, July.

Skalnik, Peter, 1986. 'Towards an Understanding of Soviet Etnos Theory', *South African Journal of Ethnology*, vol. 9, pp. 157-66.

Skalnik, Peter, 1988. 'Union Sovietique – Afrique du Sud: Les "Théories" de l'etnos', *Cahiers d'Etudes Africaines*, vol. 110, no. 28, pp. 157-76.

Smith, Graham, ed., 1990. *The Nationalities Question in the Soviet Union*, London: Longman.

Struve, Piotr, 1990. *Essays on the Russian Revolution*, Moscow: Mysl (in Russian).

Suny, Ronald G., 1988a. *The Making of the Georgian Nation*, Bloomington, Indiana University Press.

Suny, Ronald G., 1988b. Nationalism and Class as Factors in the Revolution of 1917' *CSST Working Paper*, no. 9, University of Michigan, Ann Arbor.

Suny, Ronald G., 1989. 'Nationalism and Ethnic Unrest in the Soviet Union', *World Policy Journal*, Summer, pp. 503-528.

Tishkov, Valery A., 1990a. 'Assembly of Nations or a Union Parliament', *Sovetskaya Etnografia*, no. 1.

Tishkov, Valery A., 1990b. 'Ethnicity and Power in the Republics of the USSR', *Journal of Soviet Nationalities*, vol. 1, no. 3.

Tishkov, Valery A., 1991a. 'The Soviet Empire before and after Perestroika', *Theory and Society*, vol. 20, pp. 603-29.

Tishkov, Valery A., 1991b. 'The Suicide of Centre and the End of the Union. Political Anthropology of the Putch', *Sovetskaya Ethnografia*, no. 6 (in Russian).

Yamskov, A.N., 1991. 'Interethnic Conflicts in the Trans-caucasus: Causes and Tendencies', *Polis*, no. 2 (in Russian).

FIGURE 2: TRANSCAUCASIA AND SOUTH WESTERN RUSSIA

FIGURE 3: CENTRAL ASIA

3

Inter-Ethnic Tension in the USSR: A Socio-Psychological Perspective

Galina Soldatova

1. INTRODUCTION

Regions where social tension has become transformed into inter-ethnic tension present acute problems for the USSR today. Inter-ethnic tension as a mass psychological state takes root and develops when ethnic groups begin to reflect on their unfavorable living conditions and resist destructive pressures or find new ways of adapting. Consequently, inter-ethnic tension is not only a psychological backdrop to inter-ethnic conflict: it can also help mobilize an ethnic group's inner psychological resources to protect group interests, as well as activating protective mechanisms.

The uniqueness of the history, culture, socio-economic development, territory and climate peculiar to any ethnic group will determine its psychology, and also the peculiarities of inter-ethnic tension, in any given region. Nevertheless, general mechanisms are also at work. What, then, are the socio-psychological prerequisites and development mechanisms behind inter-ethnic tension? What is the critical level of tension that, once surmounted, may generate aggression and violence? In order to address these problems we must pinpoint common factors behind the development of inter-ethnic tension in all 'alarming' regions of the USSR, and then identify psychological indices that make it possible to investigate ethnic conflict fruitfully.

2. BACKGROUND TO INTER-ETHNIC TENSION

Despite the variety of forms of inter-ethnic conflict in the USSR, there is a shared basis for the development of inter-ethnic tension in the failures of Soviet economy and society. Beyond this, inter-ethnic tension derives from three sources: (a) inter-ethnic communications; (b) ethnic culture, and (c) the history of relations among peoples.Each ethnos shares representations, beliefs, opinions and attitudes that respond to the current inter-ethnic policy of the state. Each also has ethnocultural peculiarities – perceptual schemes and behavioral models, ingroup and outgroup images – that shape inter-ethnic communication and determine inter-cultural compatibility. Research on these socio-psychological phenomena is carried out in the USSR using ethno-sociological, ethnographical and socio-psychological methods and techniques. The contradiction between the unitary state and the national formations formally proclaimed by the Constitution has led to deformations in the development of ethnic cultures and to over-centralization in the regulation of inter-ethnic relations, which have aggravated relations between the various peoples of the country.

3. INTER-ETHNIC COMMUNICATION

In accordance with the political and administrative structure of the Soviet state, communication between different peoples as political, economic and social subjects has almost always been mediated by union, republican, regional and area administrative-command centres, and has thus, because of Soviet economic, social, and ecological problems, acquired a negative character in ethnic self-awareness. Today, the relation of national units towards the various centres of power suffers from a crisis of credibility. The Karabakh conflict provides a vivid demonstration of the distrust felt towards the Union Centre as a political arbitrator in inter-ethnic conflicts. The various stages in the development of this conflict were accompanied by demonstrations and meetings protesting against the decisions of the Centre which involved both Armenians and Azerbaijanis. All agree that they (the locals) 'give' much more than they 'get', and that the centre occupy a privileged position.

Besides, the complex multilevel national administrative system of power and subordination arouses feelings of injustice and deprivation in smaller peoples because of their extreme economic, political and social dependence. The over-centralized system of power-subordination has generated the following psychological consequences: firstly, the hierarchy of ethnic minorities and majorities has led to Union central power being identified with the power of Russians; republican central power with the power of the various 'titular' indigenous nations, and so on. Inter-ethnic relations are thus marred by distrust, intolerance and phobias. The contrast 'indigenous vs. Russian-speaking' has become standard in inter-ethnic relations. An obvious result of this has been an outflux of Russians from the Baltic republics, Moldova, Azerbaijan, the Tuva ASSR, etc.

One psychological consequence of social tension is an active search for social protection and stability: one's 'own' social niche and 'own' human surroundings. Ethnic groups with firm cultural and territorial boundaries become the most obvious reference groups among big social groupings. In the absence of a stable and ramified system of social units in Soviet society, the social status of ethnic groups as reference formations rises even higher. The growing need for ethnic identification has been reflected in the rapid rise of ethnic self-awareness and centripetal tendencies registered by ethnosociologists since the 1970s. These processes lead toward growing consolidation of ethnic communities and inter-ethnic polarization which provides a socio-psychological basis for social tension to be transformed into inter-ethnic tension. Ethnoses strive for national independence, self-determination and self-government: hence the various resolutions and declarations adopted not only by the Supreme Soviets and Councils of the union republics, but also by the autonomous republics and regions (Abkhazia, Bashkiria, Chukotka, Yamalo-Nenetski AR, etc.), as well as by peoples with no separate administrative or state system (the Gagauz people of Moldova).

4. ETHNIC CULTURE

Socialization in any healthy ethnic culture will give the bearers of the culture respect for other cultures despite preference for one's own. However, the official ideology and national policy of the USSR over several decades have adversely affected the natural development of ethnic cultures. On the one hand, the successive alienation of whole generations from their generic ethno-cultural values – the natural basis of human morals – has deformed national character and depersonalized individuals and whole peoples. On the other hand, for a very long time Soviet society has been bringing up individuals in the spirit of struggle rather than finding compromises. The habit of struggling in every sphere of life (to raise labor productivity, harvest crops, etc.) has spread into the sphere of inter-ethnic relations. The long-developing discrepancy between the declared principles of Soviet 'internationalist' inter-ethnic relations and the natural moral and cultural preferences of peoples, on the one hand, and deeply-rooted militant tendencies in everyday life and in official circles, on the other hand, could not but generate deformations in perceptual schemata and behavioral patterns among nationalities. Today this finds expression in an unwillingness to seek compromises and make mutual concessions in inter-ethnic conflicts, as well as in psychological barriers against inter-ethnic reconciliation and in the growth of inter-ethnic intolerance.

In one way or another, these processes have affected all social groups. The Soviet intelligentsia of the first and the second generations was affected most seriously, not only in small ethnic groups, but also on the scale of union republics. In many regions of the country, the intelligentsia constitutes a massive stratum of ethno-cultural marginals alienated from society and from their own cultural roots (language, arts, traditions, etc.). In regions where the indigenous language has not been accorded official status, these special groups among the urban population show a dramatic lack of proficiency in their native tongue. Nor should this come as a surprise, for there are practically no national secondary schools in Belorussia, in the autonomous republics of the Caucasus or in Chuvashia, Bashkiria, etc. In higher educational establishments native languages have been studied mainly in specialized faculties. This point is difficult to quantify, since with the growth of national self-awareness many people would deny their incompetence in their native language. However, according to an estimate made by Kazakh researchers, approximately 40% of the Kazakhs (the fourth largest ethnic group in the USSR) are either totally incompetent or have very superficial knowledge of the Kazakh language (*Literaturnaya Gazeta*, No. 13, March 1989.)

This alienation from native cultures was accompanied by socialization into the so-called 'socialist culture' that had no authentic spiritual or moral messages – a poor substitute for deeper ethno-cultural values, and a shaky foundation for the community of peoples. B. Bakhtin was correct in noting that the soil of ideological monologism could not nourish interacting minds. This is the most important reason why the socialist culture has failed at the crucial turning-point of the country's history. The rapid growth of ethnic self-awareness, typical of all social groups in the Soviet Union, is particularly painful and contradictory in ethno-cultural marginal areas, which have become a sort of inter-cultural space. Feeling themselves infringed upon and unprotected, and fearing psychological and cultural assimilation, the peoples of these areas are becoming a source of anxiety and aggression. Their aspiration towards national renaissance is combined with a search for scapegoats for their personal and national failures. Thus ethno-cultural marginals often become leading intellectuals in republican national movements, transforming social tension into inter-ethnic tension.

5.   HISTORY OF INTER-ETHNIC RELATIONS.

Every inter-ethnic conflict has its pre-history. The ethnic historical memory preserves chronicles of events in inter-ethnic relations, and images of other peoples as revealed in this history. Most vividly preserved are the emotionally coloured events, such as national disasters, tragedies and crimes and moments of national grandeur. Sometimes the crimes loom so large that they become a prism through which all other inter-ethnic events are perceived. The affronted national dignity of several peoples who were forcibly deported in the 1940s (Meskhetian Turks, Crimean Tatars, Ingush, Germans, etc.); the robbery of ethnic cultures in the 1950s, when national language education was severely reduced in the schools (Belorussia, Kazakhstan, national regions of the North, etc.); another wave of 'pacification' of peoples in the 1970s and 1980s (North Caucasus, Kazakhstan, Georgia) – all this forms the basis for distrust, raises sensitivity to any injustice and leads towards national self-isolation.

Large-scale public meetings on these issues hasten the transformation of social into inter-ethnic tension. These meetings constitute a powerful cognitive reinforcement of the emotional assessment of inter-ethnic relations. As examples we can note the meetings held in Lithuania in the summer of 1989: Vilnius,

13 June – Memorial Day of the Victims of Deportation; Kaunas, 23 June – The Overthrow of the Soviet Occupation Administration in 1941; Telshai, 24 June – Memorial Day of Anti-Soviet Insurrection Victims Killed in the Raikiis Woods; Vilnius, 12 July – Anniversary of the Treaty between the USSR and Lithuania; Vilnius, 20 July – Anniversary of the Molotov-Ribbentrop Pact. A vivid representation of historical memory is the recent establishment of a new national celebration – Independence Day – in the Baltic Republics, in Georgia, Armenia and Moldova. The creation of militarized formations of defenders of the Motherland (*fidianes* in Armenia, *aizsargs* in Latvia, *carabineers* in Moldova) also appears to be a reincarnation of historical traditions, and an objective result of national consolidation and the activation of protective mechanisms by ethnic communities.

6. SOCIO-PSYCHOLOGICAL SOURCES OF INTER-ETHNIC TENSION

Historical-ethnographic, sociological and socio-psychological analysis of inter-ethnic relations shows that, besides regional specificity, there are common sources reinforcing inter-ethnic tension in 'alarming' republics. (See Arutunyan et al., 1984; Krupnik, 1990, pp. 3-16; Tardt, 1903.) To identify the most important socio-psychological sources of inter-ethnic tension, material from the official and unofficial press as well as documents and material from national movements in several republics, provide a database. Here we limit ourselves to 1989, because the vectors of development of national processes in most regions of the USSR were determined during that year. We shall focus mainly on Moldova, which until recently was considered a successful polyethnic republic. Precisely in 1989 this republic came to rank among the most tense regions in the country.

Sociological research conducted by Moldavian scientists in 1987 found that 59% of respondents from 15 regions of the republic had encountered disrespectful statements about their nationality, national traditions or language – 18% of them 'often'. Further, 44% replied that they had heard negative statements about ethnic outgroups, 8% of them 'often' (*Sovetskaia Moldavia*, 23 June 1988.) Despite the banner headline, 'We – internationalists', which was run in the central newspaper of the republic, *Sovetskaia Moldavia*, until April 1989, negative reports about relations between Moldavian and Russian-speaking people began to appear in the official press as early as in the first half of 1988, against a backdrop of optimistic articles devoted to 'inviolable friendship of the peoples' (*Sovetskaia Moldavia*, 2 March & 8 April 1988.)

Development of inter-ethnic tension is determined by external as well as internal sources, including official and unofficial information on the development of inter-ethnic conflicts elsewhere. The Armenian tragedy of Nagorno-Karabakh and Sumgait was widely reported in the Moldavian press, and there was regular contact and exchange of information between the Popular Front of Moldavia (as it then was) and the Baltic Popular Fronts, where the struggle for sovereignty was further advanced – an example and inspiration for Moldavians. Incidentally, the first Moldavian publication in the Roman alphabet (in 60,000 copies) was prepared on Baltic territory. Contacts between the Popular Front of Moldova and national movements of the Ukraine and Georgia have also developed. On the other hand, the Intermovement of Russian-speaking peoples in Moldova has linked up with the Baltic Intermovements, and the Popular Front of Azerbaijan has lent support to the secessionist Turkic-speaking population in Moldova – the Gagauz. And, from January 1990, events in Romania became an important external source of intra-ethnic consolidation and emotional arousal within Moldova.

Among the internal sources of the growth of inter-ethnic tension we should note the actions of higher authorities of national units, on the one hand, and all forms of mass interaction and communication, both organized and spontaneous, on the other – meetings, demonstrations, pickets, strikes and so on. Language laws were one powerful catalyst of tension in Moldova and in the Baltic republics.[1] 'On the Functioning of Languages on the Territory of the MSSR', a law published in August 1989, included several important provisions (the necessity of knowing two or three languages for officials, educators and leaders of public organizations: introduction of the Moldavian language as a language of clerical work in all enterprises within the republic, except for a limited list issued by the Council of Ministers where one could use Russian or another language) which were hardly acceptable for regions with a sizeable Russian-speaking population.[2]

As for 'national' meetings and occasions, group unity is reinforced by public use of national language and symbols and by folk songs and dances that enhance emotional ties and induce a 'We-They' dichotomy in gatherings characterized by high contactability and emotional superconductivity. In Kishinev from early March 1989 almost every Sunday saw sanctioned and unsanctioned meetings being conducted by the Popular Front of Moldova and other Moldavian public organizations and by the Russian-dominated Intermovement group, 'Unity'. Russian-speaking meetings were conducted also in Pridnestrovie; and, in the Comrat region, meetings were organized by the Gagauz (Christian Turkish) national movement. On the eve of the adoption of the language laws by the Supreme Soviet of the MSSR (28 April), a meeting in Kishinev attracted several hundred thousand Moldavians (the first 'great national meeting') from the capital and environs. The demands agreed on by this meeting have speeded the adoption of the language laws and influenced their content. At the same time a separate meeting with several thousand participants was being conducted by the Unity movement in Kishinev. These emotional meetings became a barrier to inter-ethnic understanding in the republic: they were striking and worrisome indicators of inter-ethnic polarization – and not only in Moldova.

'National' meetings are characterized by the mass psychology of crowds: responsibility for one's own behaviour is reduced; there is a displacement from the rational to the emotional, together with a sensation of shared common force and personal anonymity. Interaction between participants in mass actions is based on the mechanisms of emotional contamination, psychological suggestion and imitation – all of which determine the growth of inter-ethnic tension (Porshnev, 1966; Tardt, 1903). A high degree of socio-emotional unity already exists among participants, indicating an excessive level of group conformity. In this atmosphere, even participants whose attitudes and beliefs differ from the majority's may find themselves carried away by the prevailing negative emotional wave, which usually has an anxious or aggressive content which leaders can transform into an action vector.

Inter-ethnic tension correlates with frequent mass events. In Lithuania, for example, there were at least 40 meetings with several thousand participants each, in addition to memorial services, masses, hunger strikes and other mass symbolic actions, among them the 'Baltic Way', a physical link-up of peoples across the Baltics. In Georgia there were no less than 50 meetings, some attracting more than 500,000 people and lasting for hours on end – and even several days. In addition, there were mass public prayers, memorial manifestations and sit-down strikes. In Armenia there were more than 60 meetings that sometimes gathered several hundred thousand participants: the situation was later exacerbated by the psychological conse-quences of the arrival of great numbers of unfortunate refugees from Azerbaijan and others escaping the disastrous Armemian earthquake. In Moldova there were more than 40 meetings, often leading to mass violations of public order.

Striking is a non-violent organized form of mass action. A political strike accompanied by national demands can be seen as formalizing social-ethnic unity. The level of emotional involve-ment rises fast among strikers. The strike reflects a high level of inter-ethnic tension and serves to stimulate its development even further. In response to the language laws adopted by the Supreme Council of Moldova, a preventive two-hour strike was called in Pridnestrovie by the Tiraspol United Soviet of Working Collectives (later the Strike Committee) to protest against laws seen as discriminating against the Russian-speaking population of the republic. The demands of strikers were generally ignored by the supreme power of the republic: as a result, the strike was resumed not only in Tiraspol but elsewhere in the region. According to official figures, political strikes against the language laws have already involved more than 200 industrial enterprises, not only in Pridnestrovie but all over the republic. These strikes lasted for about one month, further consolidating ethnic division. Data from the first referendum in the USSR, conducted in Pridnestrovie during 1989, eloquently reflect these processes. In Tiraspol, for example, where 92.3% of electors took part in the referendum, 88.6% voted 'for the creation of Pridnestrovskaya Autonomous Soviet Republic' and only 2.1% against.

Rumors circulate swiftly in the system of informal communi-cations, also considerably stimulating the growth of inter-ethnic tension. As a rule, rumors are emotionally colored, inexact descriptions of real or fictitious events, reflecting general public sentiments and expectations, ethnic attitudes and stereotyped appraisals. Rumors reflecting possible inter-ethnic conflict situations became an everyday occurrence in 1989. The mass media have a great influence here: an information vacuum in the press, or information that distorts real events, will generally precipitate a new round of rumors. This was the case with rumors about the cruel slaughter of seven Moldavians 'in plain view of the militia' in Kishinev.

The growth of inter-ethnic tension leads to ethnic demarcation in industrial, working and scientific collectives and even penetrates into young people's environments. In Kishinev, 30 mixed schools (with 19,066 Moldavian and 28,570 other pupils) became explosively tense in 1989, and so measures were taken to divide them, starting with the most prestigious schools.[3]

After accumulating in the psychological sphere, the symptoms of ethnic polarization proceed into the social-political sphere. So two independent republics – the Gagauz and Pridnestrovskaia Moldavian Soviet Republics – were declared in August-September 1989. Their attempts to secede from Moldova, aggravating opposition between the indigenous population and other ethnic groups, came as a natural result of the intensive growth of inter-ethnic tension.

7. PERCEPTUAL ASPECTS OF INTER-ETHNIC TENSION

Let us now examine in more detail an important social-psychological aspect of inter-ethnic tension: social perception, a basic process in the development of communicative interaction. The study of its peculiarities and results (perceptual phenomena) is often a primary focus in the social-psychological study of the formation and development of inter-ethnic relations. Inter-ethnic tension is characterized by specific psychological threshold-states such as mass neurosis and frustration that generate fears of cultural assimilation and feelings of the necessity of ethnic consolidation. Typical of these states is a high level of emotional arousal producing such negative feelings as anxiety, emotional tension and concern, irritability, confusion and despair.

Some events from recent years can provide relevant examples of what occurs in conditions of great national shock. One outcome can be a state of mass psychosis. Even two months after the tragic and irreparable events in Georgia of April 1989, many people with obvious symptoms of war-gas poisoning were still going to the Tbilisi hospitals. In the opinion of the French specialists in toxicology who arrived in Tbilisi to render help to victims of poisoning, this was not physiological poisoning but in a great many cases psychological poisoning (*Express-khronika*, no. 33, 1989.)

Data from experimental psychology suggest that such states considerably influence the process of mass perception and the formation of perceptual images. Moreover, such states promote the broad generalization of negative emotions and widen the circle of irritants that produce negative reactions. For example, frustration, high levels of anxiety and high emotional arousal contribute to an increasing perception of menace and offensive features in neutral objects. They push judgments toward the negative pole. (See Postman and Bruner, 1948; Reykovski, 1979; Secord and Backman, 1964.) Furthermore, inter-ethnic perception is based on attributive psychological mechanisms which tend to enhance ingroup estimations, yielding more positive auto-stereotypes. Ingroup successes are thus explained by the innate virtues of the group, and ingroup failures by outer circumstances related to ethnical outgroups (see Hewstone & Jaspers, 1982; Stephan, 1977: 255-65).

As inter-ethnic polarization deepens, psychological mechanisms may operate in extreme ways. Here we may cite cases of so-called 'emotional perversion', as when in the Baltic Republics, the Caucasus, Moldova and elsewhere in the Soviet Union, former holidays were transformed into days of mourning; former 'liberators' become 'occupants' or 'colonizers', and 'brotherly peoples' become 'migrants' and 'strangers'. We may distinguish at least four results of these processes: (1) a search for scapegoats on the basis of ethnic criteria; (2) ingroup and personal failures are laid upon the 'aliens'; (3) the balance of positive emotions and estimations tilts towards the ingroup, with inter-ethnic differences dramatically exaggerated as the accuracy of inter-ethnic perceptions (stereotyped images, attitudes, representations) is drastically lowered; and (4) heterostereotypes are transformed into ethnic biases and prejudices and into discriminatory behaviour and action.

NOTES

1. Indigenous languages were recognized as state languages in all Baltic republics by May 1989.

2. In Pridnestrovie the Russian-speaking population makes up 90% of the total in some places.

3. One of the secondary special schools of music in Kishinev was divided into a republic school with Moldavian language and a city school with Russian language (*Sovetskaiya Moldavia*, 14 June 1989.)

REFERENCES

Arutunyan, Y.V., L. M. Drobizeva & A. A. Susokolov, 1984. *Etnosociologia: tseli, methody i nekotornie rezultati isseledovani*, Nauka, Moscow [Ethnosociology: goals, methods and some research results].

Hewstone, M. & J. Jaspers, 1982. 'Cross-cultural Interaction, Social Attribution and Inter-Group Relations', in Bochner, S., ed., *Cultures in Contact: Studies in Cross-Cultural Interaction*, Pergamon, Oxford.

Krupnik, I.I., 1990. 'Natsionalny vobros v SSSR: boiski obiashenii', *Sovetskaia ethnografia*, no. 4.

Porshnev, B.F., 1966. *Sotsialnaia psikologia i istoria* [Social psychology and history], Moscow

Postman, L., & J. Bruner, 1948. 'Perception under Stress', *Psychological Review*

Reykovski, J., 1979. *Experimentalnaia psikologia emotsii* [Experimental psychology of emotions], Progress, Moscow

Secord, P.F. & C. W. Backman, 1964. *Social Psychology*, McGraw Hill, New York

Stephan, W.G., 1977. 'Stereotyping: The Role of Ingroup-Outgroup Differences in Causal Attribution of Behavior', *Journal of Social Psychology*, 101.

Tardt, H., 1903. *Lichnost i tolpo* [Personality and crowd], St. Petersburg

4

Management of Inter-Ethnic Conflicts in the Soviet Union

Olga A. Vorkunova

1. INTRODUCTION

Political changes in the Soviet Union have been more profound and rapid during the last five years than any experts anticipated. We have witnessed a complex transition period bringing new challenges to the Soviet system. On the whole, developments have proceeded more peacefully than one might have expected. Rapid changes in political structure have contributed to national renaissance in the Soviet multi-ethnic state. At the same time, *perestroika* has been accompanied by social tension and local and internal conflicts. I shall in this chapter try to assess the possible methods of conflict resolution and management on the basis of developments in the Soviet Union during the most dramatic period of national conflicts, 1988-1990.

In the early 1990s the Soviet Union appears to be a world of conflict. National priorities are given higher attention than solidarity within the framework of the Union. In the context of the paralysis of Soviet power at the Centre and the periphery, local government is compelled to respond to national pressure groups. Central government mistakes stimulate separatist movements and fragmentation of the society. The Centre is losing its role as the consolidating factor to Russia which is taking over through direct agreements with the other republics. However, during the transition period towards a market economy it is likely that internal conflicts in the Soviet Union will continue to emerge and be more violent.

The promotion of equal national rights was one of the main demands in Lenin's nationality policy. Even in his early works, especially the draft programme of the Russian Social-Democratic Party, Lenin (Collected Works) stressed full equality of rights for all citizens regardless of race; full freedom for suppressed nations formely included in the Russian state, and cultural and political self-determination.

From the beginning of the Soviet state, the national question was at the centre of consideration. Theoretically autonomous administrative-territorial units corresponding to nationality were organised in the following way at four levels below the Centre: the republic, the autonomous republic; the autonomous region, and the autonomous national area – each with its own elected (theoretically democratic) parliamentary assembly or soviet. At the same time, some central institutions were established with full responsibility for national questions, such as the department for national minorities under the People's Commissariat of Nationality Affairs. Later on, local departments for national minorities were organised within the structure of district soviet presidiums, and officials for national minority affairs were appointed. This practice was based on the first Soviet Constitution, which declared – as the basis for federation of Soviet national republics and the main principle of union – the right of every nation's citizens to adopt independent decisions through their soviets and to freely decide whether to join the Soviet Union.

Among the systemic roots of national conflicts in the USSR have been social and demographic deformations and the dictatorship of central power. Long-term extensive economic development, unbalanced industrial policy and alienated rural development – these were among the reasons for future national conflict. Many villages were left without population, and overpopulated towns appeared. Moreover, almost 60 million citizens are now living outside 'their' national borders, away from their cultural and territorial home areas. The waves of migration have provoked demographic changes, creating new tension and conflict situations. The critical limit for migration has been passed in many regions. For example, during one generation the proportion of Estonians in the Estonian republic has decreased from 92% to 65%, and it is continuing to diminish. The main principle of inter-regional and inter-republican communication was economic, not human or cultural in character. Little attention was given to inter-regional dialogue.

Ecological problems were growing, too, thanks to the incompetent, 'voluntarist' policy of the Centre. For example, in the Fergana Valley in Central Asia, the population has not more than 0.2 hectares cultivated land per person, and other land is unfit. The situation in the Aral Sea area is still disastrous. Unbalanced regional development in the Soviet Union also contributed greatly to social inequality. For example, in Uzbekistan, 45% of the population is living below the poverty level, and more than one million are unemployed, yet the population growth in Uzbekistan is three times the average in the Soviet Union. Nations in the Soviet Union also became unequal as a result of deformations of Lenin's nationality policy. Most of the larger nations have the status of a republic or autonomous republic, but some have no territorial-administrative status. Moreover, some of the autonomous republics have the same economic, scientific and cultural potential as the smaller union republics, but because of their status there are few possibilities for development. This inequity is seen in the judicial, economic, social and cultural fields. Neither the 1977 Soviet Constitution nor the autonomous republics' constitutions contain articles dealing with minority group rights, or even with the obligations of the Union concerning national minorities.

Deformation of institutions in the Soviet Union has frequently been the cause of ethnic conflicts. Dictatorship and administrative fiat in the economic, social and spiritual fields; official indifference to human rights and people's needs; ignorance of public opinion and the actual social experience of the working class – these are the main sources of social trauma in the Soviet Union. The system of soviets merely duplicated the structure of the party apparatus, and gave no possibility for structural or functional initiatives and change in the regions. As a result, the system became incapable of making elementary adjustments. It is also important to note that, despite theoretical separation of powers and the establishment of the legislative, executive and judicial systems, in practice there was no separation. There was a fourth power, the Communist Party, which violated the principle of power separation stressed in the

Constitution. Party power often replaced the three others. The head of almost every important institution – factory, school, district or province – was nominated by higher authorities, ultimately the Party.

The hierarchy of power was constructed according to the pyramid principle. Party leaders could interfere even in the judicial field. They could recommend to the judges what kind of decision was preferable. As a result, many administrative institutions became ineffective and without initiative, just waiting for instructions. Yet the people who took important decisions were amateurs. The pyramid of rulers was interdependent and constituted a narrow group with its own interests and intense hierarchical loyalty. The underdevelopment, poverty and ineffectiveness of local administration and its lack of judicial background influenced the development of ethnic conflict.

2. TYPES OF NATIONAL CONFLICT

We can distinguish four types of national conflicts in the Soviet Union:

a) *Identity conflicts with the central government* (e.g., Baltic conflicts). This type of conflicts between the Centre and the republican governments involve demands from the national movements for sovereignty or secession from the Union. The Baltic republics consider full independence the best guarantee for security.

b) *Identity conflicts among various nationalities* (Nagorno-Karabakh – Armenians vs. Azeris; Andijan-Osh – Kirghiz vs. Uzbeks; Abkhazia – Georgians vs. Abkhazians). This type of conflict can be divided into two main kinds. First are identity conflicts provoked by the inability of local government to meet the expectations of the population in the republics. The organizers of the 'black economy' have also contributed to increasing inter-ethnic tension in such places as Alma Ata, the Fergana Valley, Andijan-Osh and Nagorno-Karabakh. Most of the conflicts of this type are in the Central Asian and Caucasian republics. Second are identity conflicts resulting from failure to resolve the issue of a new union treaty. The wave of sovereignty movements in the republics affects the autonomous units within them. Some of the republics are facing the same problems concerning their autonomous units as they have in relations with the central government. There are conflicts between the Russian nationality, which is identified with the Centre, and the indigenous nationalities not only in the non-Russian republics but in the 'autonomies' of the Russian Republic as well. In Moldova, the majority Moldavians are confronted by Russians and Ukrainians in the Pridnestrovskaya region and Turkish-speaking Christians in the Gagauzskaya region, who have declared sovereignty and secession from Moldova.

Identity conflicts among the various nationalities which challenge the stability of the republics and which involve battle-related casualties are especially dangerous. The new situation in the Soviet Union which was marked by the appearance of national conflicts in Nagorno-Karabakh and the Baltic republics developed in a dangerous way during 1988-90.

c)   *Identity conflicts based on demands for autonomy or self-determination* (Crimean Tatars; Meskhetian Turks; Soviet Germans).

d)   *Religion-based national conflicts* (Western Ukraine – Uniate Catholicism vs. Russian Orthodoxy).

3.   THE WAY OUT: CONFLICT MANAGEMENT

In the light of the complexity of the national question in the USSR the need for flexibility in response to different conflict situations is clear. There is no single instrument to resolve internal conflicts, and when employing conflict resolution one must consider the specific features of the national movements. In some regions the national movements play the role of political organisations alternative to the Communist Party. In a situation where a civic political culture is lacking, the national question becomes a convenient focus helping different forces to unite. The confrontation between Centre and periphery is seen as a struggle of nations for their sovereignty. While the doctrine of national autonomy has been reaffirmed by various Soviet organs, this has not been reflected in practice. The real question is how to reach civil consent. This is a problem which should be tackled pragmatically, taking into account the different contexts and possibilities in various republics and autonomies. But the national movements must also confront the manipulation of the national question by local governments and opposition groups. When national movements play the role of an alternative political force in society, some leaders are tempted to develop a national-bureaucratic apparatus, whose interests soon differ from the interests of the nation (Zhukovitskii, 1990). This phenomenon accords with the logic of bureaucratic systems. The conflict situation answers the interests of the new national leaders, because it strengthens their authority. On the other hand, conflict resolution can undermine extremism on the national question.

On December 1, 1988 the All-Union Supreme Soviet adopted a law entitled 'On Changes and Additions to the Constitution of the Soviet Union', the first attempt to use the Constitution as a mechanism for the solution of minority rights problems. According to the revised Article 116 of the 1977 Constitution, the Soviet of Nationalities ('upper' chamber of the Supreme Soviet) must promote national equality, and must weigh the interests of nations, populations and national groups in comparison with the common interest and the necessities of the Soviet multi-national state. The Centre and the republics must promote the rights of all nationalities and national groups, and create all the necessary conditions for their development, with ultimate authority on national questions belonging to the republics. The Platform of the Communist Party calls for an all-union law 'On the Guarantee of Rights to the People of the Soviet Union who are Living Outside their State-territorial Borders', and similar laws are needed for the republics.

Such guarantees must include the use of the native language in official institutions on the 'territories of compact living' of the national groups; the right to create and develop national cultural organisations and institutions of self-rule, and the right to ecological security. The most important point is to guarantee the representation of national groups at the different levels of legislative, executive and judicial power, and in authoritative economic and socio-cultural bodies. One of the root causes of national conflicts in the Soviet Union has been the structure of the unitarian state. The creation of a genuine federation is very important: there must be clear separation of powers in the Centre-periphery relationship, and strict guarantees for the sovereignty of the republics.

To resolve ethnic conflicts in the Soviet periphery the central power must strengthen local institutions. The Platform of the Communist Party rejects the unitarian model of state unity and proclaims the federative principle. It stresses the principle of consent; the creation of qualitatively new judicial conditions, and the possibility of different forms of federal relations emerging through democratic dialogue. It proposes acceptance of a multi-ethnic society and pluralism as a way of life. But it also concludes that free and equal federal republics must grant powers to the Union for common purposes. The Platform upholds the principle of self-determination, which means the freedom to choose forms of social organization, political institutions and symbols of state. It notes that the ideal for a federation is not unification, but unity in various forms. It proclaims the right of nations to leave the Union, but concludes that the Communist Party must be against separatist movements which can destroy the unity of a multi-ethnic democratic state (*Pravda*, 6 February 1990). The economic basis for federation is an integration process: agreements between enterprises within the republics and the formation of a genuine union market.

The USSR Supreme Soviet has been working on federal forms of devolution. The main problem is to determine the extent of devolution. The first set of laws was drafted for spring, 1990: the 'Law on the Separation of Powers Between the Union of Soviet Socialist Republics and the Subjects of the Federation' (April 26, 1990); the 'Law on Free National Development of the Citizens who Have no Territorial Dimension with Definite Geographically Contiguous Areas of Habitation', and the 'Law on the Languages of the Peoples Living in the Soviet Union' (April 24, 1990).

The main principle required for a legal solution of the national and ethnic conflicts in the Soviet Union is self-determination and real power for every national unit. Mikhail Gorbachev's new concept of a Union of Sovereign States was unveiled at a meeting of the Federation Council on June 13, 1990. This concept combines national interests with Soviet state principles: it is a mixture of federative and confederative principles, with foreign policy and defence policy and specific economic and financial questions reserved for the Centre (*Pravda*, 6 September and 3 November 1990). The old system of relations between the subjects of the federation hindered free trade among them and the establishment of a free market economy. The old union treaty was part of totalitarian system, and it undermined the *perestroika* process because central government was identified with Russia, yet this structure also had desperate consequences for Russia's own development. Russia became overwhelmed by economic, administrative and party hierarchies which had nothing to do with specifically Russian interests. At the same time, multi-ethnic Russia was and is in principle a federal union itself: it includes autonomous republics, *oblasti* and *okruga*, and the new federative order should ensure that the old structures become genuinely federal. Every republic should decide what kinds of powers will be devolved to regional authorities, on the one hand, and passed upwards to the central government, on the other.

The most important issue in achieving a new federation is the connection between the proposed union treaty and the Union Constitution. First Deputy Chairman of the Russia Supreme Soviet, R. Kazbulatov, has noted three possible alternatives: first, the union treaty will replace the constitution; second, the union constitution will be part of the union treaty; third, the union treaty will be included in the union constitution (*Argumenty i fakty*, No.28, 1990, p.2). According to Kazbulatov, the union treaty should replace the union constitution and become a universal constitutional act laying down the main principles and norms for a renewed Soviet Union. The union treaty should be established through dialogue between representatives from the republics and autonomies, experts and scholars. It should be a compromise attempting to accommodate different interests and demands.

The strength of the union treaty idea is that it enables the republics to act independently within an integrated union while delegating some powers to the Centre. The weakness is that it is taking a long time to create the union treaty, and some of the republics consider it an effort by the Centre to retain power over the republics. Still, the future union treaty can be regarded as a potential mediator of identity conflicts, and it can create the necessary conditions for peaceful conflict resolution.

Another possible path of conflict management is the creation of special inter-republican peace-keeping forces as an alternative to the Soviet army. The Nagorno-Karabakh state of emergency showed that the use of the army creates tension: it achieves only temporary conflict management, and is mainly useful to prevent civil war. Internal peace-keeping forces could use the model and practice of UN peace-keeping forces. The weakness of this form of peace-keeping is that some of the republics – Armenia, Azerbaijan, Moldova, the Ukraine and Georgia – regard inter-republican forces with mistrust and hostility.

Human rights education is also a part of complex conflict resolution. Human rights must be upheld as superior to the rights of the nation. The interdependence of national and human rights is an important tenet of a correct approach to conflict settlement; but it is difficult to resolve socio-economic deformations and underdevelopment simultaneously. Nevertheless, the individual right to development in accordance with the UN Declaration on the Right to Development must be upheld (Eide, 1989).

States should prevent violations of human rights, and agree with obligations to respect and fulfil human rights. The problem is then how to divide obligations between the central state and the sovereign republics. Another problem is how to make local government power, both executive and legislative, effective and competent. Here, democratic elections on a real multi-party basis could play the decisive role. New authorities elected by legal democratic procedures will have the advantage of the confidence of the civil population, and will be better able to fulfil expectations. But they may need the experience and expertise of the previous administrative power holders: otherwise, the new politicians could be helpless and continue to organize meetings and other forms of mass activity without substantial political effects.

Conflict management is especially complicated in the case of conflict across boundaries. It is difficult to sustain the negotiation process and in particular to develop monitoring machinery. Unfortunately, there are important gaps in the institutional and organizational development of the negotiation process in the USSR, as well as in scholarship. There is only one centre for education in this field: the laboratory on conflict negotiation in the Moscow Institute of International Relations.

4. CONCLUSIONS

The main systemic root of national conflict in the Soviet Union has been the dictatorship of the central power and the social and demographic deformations which have resulted from it, including waves of forced or 'unnatural' migration which have provoked new tension and conflict situations. Identity conflicts in the Soviet Union can be ethnic, national or religious – or a combination of social and authority conflict. Following the deformed national policy of the years since the 1930s, some nations now face the threat of losing their religious, ethnic or linguistic identities altogether. These nations should be considered as distinct ethnic groups with a traditional homeland of their own and entitled to equal treatment. They should be assured that they will not be discriminated against at any level. That can be a basis for political settlement. An effective response to the historical demands of the ethnic groups must be accomplished through acknowledgment of their legitimate right to develop their own identities.

Any proposal to settle ethnic issues in the USSR should spell out how it will be implemented, who would supervise it and with what authority. It is important to construct a new juridical context; but it is also necessary to promote practical mechanisms and guarantees for laws to work out. The first step in this direction must be the establishment of a government committee on national questions. It is also necessary to encourage research and establish data-bases for looking at trends towards potential conflicts in the future, and to devise a new and effective mechanism for correcting development strategies, with input from expert international scholars of an inter-disciplinary orientation. Thus there would be a multi-cultural dialogue of scholars knowledgeable about ethnic conflicts with the aim of forecasting and averting potential tragedies.

REFERENCES

Eide, Asbjørn, 1989. 'Realization of Social and Economic Rights and the Minimum Threshold Approach', *Human Rights Law Journal*, vol. 10, nos 1-2.

Lenin, V. I. *Collected Works*, vol. 10, p. 343; vol. 6, pp. 206-8.

Zhukovitskii, L., 1990. 'The Whims of National Soul', *Literaturnaia Gazeta*, 23 May.

Pravda, 6 February 1990.

Pravda, 6 September and 3 November 1990.

Argumenty i Fakty, no. 28, 1990, p.2.

5

National Minorities in Estonia

A. & M. Kirch

1. INTRODUCTION

The Baltic republics are generally treated as one geographical
and cultural region. The links between Estonia, Latvia and
Lithuania in the cultural sphere are close. In the field of economy the cooperation is perhaps less obvious, but the Baltic is
treated also by the Soviet Union as a single economic unit.

The social and ethnic structure of Estonia, like that of
Latvia and Lithuania, has experienced deep changes since 1940,
when Soviet annexation started. These changes can be characterized as 'sovietization' of the country. The Soviet political and
social system was forcibly imposed upon the Baltic, which had
developed a civil society during the period of independence, like
many other states in Europe.

Religion has been an important factor in the life and culture
of the Baltic region. Estonians and Latvians are mainly
Lutherans, while Lithuanians are Roman Catholics. Through the
centuries these Western churches have imbued the Balts with
differing views regarding authority, community, ethics and the
law, and have thus given them different concepts of culture.
Roman Catholic or Lutheran faith and tradition account for
many of the differences between the Baltic region and Russia.
Commitments to these religious beliefs have provided the people
of Estonia, Latvia and Lithuania with ties to Western Europe,
ties that no other Soviet republic has to the same degree except
Armenia and, to a lesser extent, the Ukraine (Vardys, 1990).
Thus, we can conclude that the Baltic republics are not typical

republics of the Soviet Union: they are Western by location, history, cultural ties, alphabet and orientation.

At the same time, however, there are some obvious differences between these three republics. First of all, for specific historical and political reasons they differ widely in national composition. The share of indigenous people in Lithuania is 80%, in Latvia 52% and in Estonia 61%. Accordingly, assimilation processes are quite different in each republic. As indicated by Taagepera (1990) Estonians and Russians keep apart, Lithuanians and Russians interact on a more equal basis and Latvians are more prone to assimilation than are the Russians in Latvia. The conclusion is that, whereas assimilation processes may be significant in Latvia, they are negligible in Lithuania and Estonia.

2.   HISTORICAL BACKGROUND OF THE NATIONAL PROBLEMS IN ESTONIA

In the 13th century the Baltic region, including the territory of the Estonian tribes, was conquered and occupied by Germans and by Danes. Later came the Swedes; then the Poles, and, finally, in the early 18th century, the area was taken over by the Russian Empire. During the period of feudalism, and up to 1918, the landlords in Estonia were local Germans, so-called Baltic-Germans, even though Estonia was governed first by Sweden and then by Russia. Therefore the Estonian national movement was mainly directed against Germans. Not until the end of the 19th century, as a result of Tsarist Russification politics, did the Estonian national movement assume also anti-Russian features.

The process of constructing Estonia was difficult. No sooner had the Estonian Republic been declared (on 24 February 1918) than the German occupation began. From the end of German occupation the period of peaceful development did not last long. In November 1918 a new war began, against Soviet Russia – known in Estonia as the War of Independence. As a result of this struggle, the Tartu peace treaty of 2 February 1920 was concluded, whereby Russia acknowledged the sovereignty of Estonia. Under the Treaty of Tartu, the whole population of Estonia had an opportunity to become citizens of the Estonian

Republic (claiming Estonian citizenship was voluntary). Estonia became a relatively homogeneous national state with several national minorities. The early 1920s brought to fruition the goal first enunciated during the national awakening: the creation of a modern, independent Estonian culture (Raun, 1987, pp. 133-137). An Estonian-language educational system and professional and cultural institutions directed by Estonians themselves marked the beginning of a new era in Estonian culture. Having finally achieved cultural autonomy for itself, Estonia took steps to guarantee the same for its ethnic minorities.

3. NATIONAL MINORITIES IN THE ESTONIAN REPUBLIC

In the early 1920s the rights of national minorities were a subject of juridical discussions, and in September 1923 the Estonian government issued a declaration on the protection of national minorities in Estonia which was also intended to fulfil of the demands of the League of Nations (Aun, 1951, p. 27). The Estonian Republic was a good testing ground for ideas concerning protection of the rights of national minorities. The Law on Cultural Self- Government, adopted by the Riigikogu (parliament) on 21 February 1925, was a practical approach to a problem which occupies an established place in theory. The adoption of such a law had been a special aim of dispersed national minorities since World War I. A liberal treatment of foreign minorities, as an essential feature of democratic government, and as a condition for a more permanent international peace, found its way into the new Estonian governmental system. Under the influence of liberal ideas and concepts, various laws and guarantees to protect national minorities were adopted by other governments throughout Europe.

The actual development of the Estonian minorities law was a progressive process. In addition to the measures generally employed for the protection of national minorities, in Estonia two more special rights were promised and guaranteed: the right to cultural and welfare autonomy of national minorities, and the right of any citizen to decide his nationality at his own discretion. This latter right, guaranteed by the Estonian Constitution of 1920, was unparalleled in contemporary constitutional law (Aun, 1951-53).

What were the national minorities in the Estonian Republic at the time? The 1922 census yields the following data: Estonians – 969,976, Russians – 91,109, Germans – 18,319, Swedes – 7,850, Jews – 4,566, other nationalities – 14,508. The total non-Estonian share was 12.4%. In Estonia cultural self-government of national minorities was instituted in 1925 and remained in operation until it was abolished by the Soviet government after the occupation of the Estonian Republic in 1940. The Law of 1925 stated that the national minorities entitled to create their own cultural self- government were the Germans, the Russians, the Swedes and other nationalities who lived within the boundaries of Estonia and whose numbers were not less than three thousand persons.

Such cultural self-government was financially based on:

• subsidies of the Estonian Government for elementary and secondary education;

• expenditures and other obligations of local self-governments towards elementary and secondary education;

• subsidies by state and local self-governments for the cultural development of the people;

• taxes of the self-government when imposed upon its members by the Cultural Council, and

• gifts, collections, donations, endowments and revenues from the property and undertakings of the self-government.

The Constitution of 1920 guaranteed access to the educational system for the national minorities in Estonia. For example in 1933/34 there were 103 Russian, 19 German, 18 Swedish, 5 Latvian, 3 Jewish and 2 Finnish elementary schools. Moreover, there were 22 minority secondary schools (6 Russian, 12 German, 2 Jewish, 1 Swedish, and 1 Latvian); 2 German trade schools, and 4 German advanced training schools (*Eesti Valitsusasutuste...*, 1935). On the one hand, the necessity of having a system of cultural self-government derived from the complicated domestic situation after the Brest-Litovsk peace treaty and the victorious War of Independence against Soviet Russia. On the other hand, the Estonians as a small nation could well understand the need of national minorities to develop their culture and maintain their identity.

The matters which definitely concerned each nationality included language, culture, customs, folkways, folklore and a common historical memory: no other nationality is sufficiently interested in these to be able to preserve or promote them. If the individuality of each nationality is to be respected, their promotion must be left to each national group itself. It should be noticed that the concept of 'national minorities' covered all nationalities, including Estonians, who were sometimes a minority within a majority population of another nationality. Under the Law of 1925 the Estonian government had the right to regulate the Cultural Self- Government of citizens of Estonian nationality in those administrative districts of local self-government where a national minority was in a majority – in the north-east and south-east regions, near the frontier.

As a policy, cultural autonomy was aimed at winning the loyalty of all minorities to the government of Estonia, to unite citizens in their common affairs and to make their country a real home for all citizens. The Estonian approach to the problem of national minorities meant in fact a differentiation between the state and the nationality (or nation) on a functional basis (Maddison, 1930, p. 3). The turning point for Estonian national development came with the year 1940, when the Estonian Republic was incorporated into the Soviet Union. From that time on, to interpret Estonian national development we must take into consideration the specific features of the changing situation in Soviet society in general. After 1940, the Estonian nation became a national minority within the Soviet Union.

4. THE NATIONAL SITUATION TODAY

To understand what has happened from the period after World War II until today we must begin with the national composition of the Estonian Republic. The 1934 census shows the following data: Estonians – 88%; Russians – 8%; other nationalities (Germans, Finns, Jews, Swedes, etc.) – 4%. The biggest losses among Estonian national minorities involved Swedes and Germans. The majority of Germans left Estonia in 1939-1941 on Hitler's call, while Swedes either escaped the effects of war (according to the treaty between Germany and Sweden) or suffered from repressions in 1944.

World War II was a heavy blow to the Estonian population. Between October 1939 and January 1945 the Estonian nation was reduced by 200,000 people, i.e., by 17.5% (Katus, 1990, p. 22). On the eve of war in June 1941, 10,157 people were forcibly and illegally deported by Soviet authorities to Siberia. The second mass deportation (20,702 people, according to official Soviet data) took place in 1949. However, most of the deported people returned to Estonia in the late 1950s (Laasi, 1988). After the World War (1945) the Soviet Union annexed some regions from eastern Estonia to the Russian Federation. These regions were inhabited by Russians and Estonians, and annexation reduced the Estonian population by 56,000 people, leaving Estonia a relatively homogeneous republic (97.3 % of the population were indigenous). Estonia had lost practically all its national minorities.

Immediately after World War II, however, a well-organized immigration stream started from the Soviet Union to the Baltic republics. This was a colonization process managed by Moscow. During the years 1945-1989 the total number of Estonians increased by 22%, but the number of non-Estonians in the same period grew 26 times. The natural increase among Estonians had not been great even during the Estonian Republic. In the Soviet period it was even lower. From 1961 to 1989, the natural increase in the entire population of Estonia was 160,770 people, but the Estonians among them were only 34,330 (i.e., 21.3 %). Today the population of the Estonian Republic is very heterogeneous (See Table 1). The largest group of non-Estonians is the Russians – they have grown from 20,000 (in 1945) to 474,800 (in 1989). If we add up all Slavic-language peoples (Russians, Ukrainians, Belorussians) we get a total of 551,000 Slavs, or 35% of the population of Estonia. They constitute 91.4% of all non-Estonians (Tables 1 and 2).

Assimilation processes in Estonia have been quite specific. Among non-Estonians the process of assimilation mostly involves assimilation with Russians, because the majority of non-Estonians are Slavs. Assimilation of Ukrainians, Belorussians and other peoples proceeds on the basis of the Russian language. Their education is mostly in Russian, which brings them close to their Russian cultural surroundings, endangering their national identity. The main principles of Soviet nationality policy have been unification and equalization, with no perceived need for cultural autonomy of small national groups.

Thus, the Russians have been in a strong situation as the only national minority with the opportunity for schooling children in their mother tongue. At the same time this school system has served as a channel of sovietization not only for Russians, but also for Ukrainians, Belorussians and other peoples who assimilate readily with Russians. Moreover, the unified school system has intensified the ideology of chauvinism (the so-called *derzhava* ideology). So Russians, Ukrainians and Belorussians, more than other national groups, took on the Soviet ideology and acknowledged the identity of a unified Soviet People. This process of sovietization led to the situation where the nation (ethnic unit) as a social subject in society gradually lost its salience. We must add that certain objective factors made possible a heavy immigration stream from the East: a relatively highly developed infrastructure; an advanced educational level of the indigenous population; a shortage of workers in industrial regions. But there was also a demographic policy specially directed from the Centre aimed at the formation of a nationally mixed population in every region of the Soviet Union.

Due to their concentration in industrial areas, the non-Estonians are living in a special, Russian-speaking social and cultural environment. Thus, there are some offices (for example railway and militia offices) and even localities (mainly in the North-east region) where it is impossible to communicate in Estonian, although it is possible to communicate in Russian almost anywhere in Estonia.

Table 1: *Population of Estonia by Nationality and Language, 1969-89*

	1959	1979	1989
Estonians	892,653	947,812	963,269
Russians	240,227	408,778	474,815
Ukrainians	15,769	36,044	48,273
Belorussians	10,930	23,461	27,711
Finns	16,699	17,753	16,662
Jews	5,436	4,966	4,613
Tatars	1,535	3,199	4,058
Germans	670	3,994	3,466
Latvians	2,888	3,963	3,135
Poles	2,256	2,897	3,008
Lithuanians	1,616	2,379	2,568
Others	6,112	9,280	14,124
Total	1,196,791	1,464,476	1,565,662

Source: Soviet Census data

5. A NEW AWAKENING

In the autumn of 1988 the first congress of the Estonian Popular
Front was held. This marked the beginning of a new stage – a
process of national awakening. From that time on the Estonians
saw an opportunity for the determination of national rights for
Estonians within the Soviet Union as well as for the national
minorities within the Estonian Republic. But the situation was
still ambiguous. The destruction of national ties and connections;
the altered demographic balance between Estonians and non-
Estonians; the restriction of cultural processes, etc. have led us
to a situation in which Estonians perceive a risk of being extinguished as an ethnic unit. In addition comes the urgent need to
change the fundamental structure of the economy and social life
in Estonia so as to develop a true civil society.

The Forum of Estonian Nations is the most prominent result
of the national awakening process in Estonia. In 1988 this
institution brought together fourteen national groups who are
interested in working out new principles for developing national
processes in Estonia. The first session of the Forum (September
1988) worked out a new ideology, expressed in two declarations:
firstly, a declaration on relations between Estonians and the
national minorities in Estonia; secondly, a declaration about
principles for the formation of cultural autonomies among
national minorities. The purpose of the Forum is formulated as:
democratization of national relations; the protection of national
identity, and checking the assimilation process.

The main hope for arresting assimilation lies in creating
national cultural organizations and societies. Every national
minority group may now have close connections with its mother
country and with its native culture. For the past two years the
cultural societies of national minorities have born witness to
this. Today there are about thirty cultural societies registered in
the Ministry of Culture, the more numerous and active ones
being Russian, Jewish, Latvian, Lithuanian, Armenian, Belorussian and Azerbaijani. The Jewish and Belorussian cultural
societies each publish a newspaper. After a 50 year break, there
is now a Jewish classical grammar school in Tallinn. The protection of the interests of Estonian minorities is quaranteed by the
Estonian Supreme Council law (adopted on 15 December 1989),
'On the National Rights of Estonian Citizens', the first in 50
years to provide real opportunities for national minorities to

pursue their cultural activities. This was the first step towards a contemporary law on cultural autonomies for national minorities in Estonia.

Creating national cultural units and organizations is fruitful because it opposes the denationalization and unification process which deepened during the so called stagnation period (approximately 1970-85). The Forum of Nations has shown that people who are interested in keeping their own national identity can understand better the aspirations of the indigenous people. The Russian-dominated social movements and groups which oppose the independence movement of the Estonian Republic (for example the Interfront) have pro-Soviet interests – to keep socialism as a system, to maintain the planned economy and collective ownership of property and so on. The interests of Russia and Russian culture are actually neglected.

6. NATIONAL CONFLICTS IN ESTONIA

What are the underlying reasons for the present conflicts and national problems in Estonia? Firstly, there is a political conflict between two actors – the Supreme Council and government of the Estonian Republic, on the one hand, and the central authorities of the Soviet Union on the other. Secondly, there is a social conflict between the indigenous people and some immigrant groups.

The underlying reason for political conflicts in Estonia (as also in the other Baltic Republics) is as follows : three independent Baltic states, members of the League of Nations, were forced in 1940 to become parts of a totalitarian state – the Stalinist Soviet Union, which sought to realize in the Baltic region a colonial economic and demographic policy. Violent changes of political system and social structure caused the subsequent antagonism and resistance of Estonians against the Soviet regime. The common destiny of the Baltic republics after their incorporation into the Soviet Union in 1940 raises similar problems today. One major reason for antagonism has been the so-called mechanical increase in the non-Estonian population, a total of half a million people. The basic channels for immigration were newly created industrial enterprises, especially in Tallinn and Northern Estonia (see Table 2).

Today we can say that the Estonian language, culture and traditions have disappeared from the North-east region of Estonia. According to the 1989 census, Narva is 96% non-Estonian and Kohtla-Järve 79%. Even in the capital city, Tallinn, more than half of all inhabitants are non-Estonians.

As we can see from Table 2, the process of diminishing the proportion of Estonians in the total population has been continuous – and it is a result of the nationality policy of the Soviet government. Until 1940 the Estonian Republic communicated with the nations of Western Europe (Germans, Finns, Swedes, etc.) and with the nations of the East (mainly with the Russians). After 1940 the international relations of Estonians extended mainly to the Slavic cultures. At the same time the indigenous Estonian population decreased from 88% (in 1934) to 61.5% (in 1989), while Russians, always the biggest minority, increased their share from 8% (in 1934) to 30% (in 1989). Today Estonia is no longer a national republic with some national minorities: the Estonian Republic comprises approximately three fifths native Estonians and two fifths nationally mixed minority population, overwhelmingly Slavic.

The unstable demographic situation and the uncontrolled immigration can be seen as a powerful factor in conflicts, not only between Estonians and non-Estonians, but also between native people generally and immigrants. Moreover the ethnic and cultural differences between Estonians and Slavs exacerbate the tension between these two groups. In Estonia the increasing proportion of immigrants has brought with it many social problems. A major issue concerns the unjust social welfare conditions which favour immigrants. Until 1989-1990 when some regulatory laws were adopted by the Supreme Council of Estonia, immigrants enjoyed real privileges, such as getting good housing quickly, while the native population needed to wait for years on end. Already in the early 1980s, 81% of Russians and other non-Estonians lived in flats with full comfort, obtained as a virtual gift from the state (free of charge, low rent). Of the Estonian population, only 54.5% lived in such housing (Drobizeva, 1981, p. 80). This tendency became even more visible towards the end of the 1980s.

Most recently, the main point of contention has been the election law, which requires a definite residence-time for the right to become a deputy of the Estonian Supreme Council. And now a new conflict issue is emerging: the problem of Estonian citizenship. Of the various projects concerning citizenship, the plan supported by the radical nationalists of the Congress of Estonia (see chapter by King, Note 34) proposes Estonian citizenship only for citizens of the former Estonian Republic and their direct descendants (children, grandchildren, etc.). The project supported by today's political power centre (the Popular Front and the majority of the Estonian population) proposes citizenship for all who were born in Estonia or have lived there for a certain, as yet unspecified, period. The recent plan for privatization of the economy proposes ten years' residence as a necessary condition to become the owner of privatized property.

Obviously, these plans do not satisfy many non-Estonians, who instead demand that citizenship be fixed on the basis of the status quo: that all the current population of Estonia may become its citizens. Most non-Estonians want to keep their status in Estonia.

Table 2: National Composition of Estonians and Slavs

	Urban Population			Rural Pop.	
	Total	*Tallinn*	*Kohtla-Järve, Narva*	Total	Total
Estonians					
1959	418,265	*169,697*	*29,765*	474,388	892,653
	61.9%	*60.2%*	*27.6%*	91.0%	74.6%
1970	506,418	*201,908*	*33,116*	418,739	925,157
	57.4%	*55.7%*	*21,0%*	88.2%	68.2%
1979	555,943	*222,218*	*29,971*	391,869	947,812
	54.7%	*51.9%*	*16.7%*	87.5%	64.7%
1989	572,547	*227,245*	*25,528*	390,734	963,281
	51.2%	*47.4%*	*12.9%*	87.4%	61.5%
Slavs (Russians, Ukrainians, Belorussians)					
1959	231,318	*101,554*	*64,845*	35,608	266,926
	34.2%	*36.1%*	*60.2%*	6.8%	22.3%
1970	340,356	*147,570*	*115,618*	41,082	387,926
	38.6%	*40.7%*	*73.5%*	8.7%	28.1%
1979	432,652	*197,914*	*140,662*	44,631	468,283
	41.7%	*46.2%*	*78.3%*	10.0%	31.2%
1989	504,474	*232,558*	*162,415*	46,342	550,816
	45.1%	*48.6%*	*82.3%*	10.4%	35.2%

Source: Census data and Aun, 1951-3

The best solution seems to be double citizenship – both Soviet and Estonian. If this becomes possible, a recent study has revealed, then 45% of respondents would definitely want Estonian citizenship, while 31% had some doubts but would be potential citizens. At the same time Russian specialists with higher education are rather more positive towards Estonian citizenship.

7. THE RUSSIAN PROBLEM

Confrontation between Estonians and Russians has persisted since the summer of 1988. What is the essence of the 'Russian problem' in Estonia? One basic issue is that some Russian groups (leaders of the Communist Party, directorial staff of military-oriented factories, officers in the military forces) stand to lose power in Estonian society. That is why they are ready to create a confrontation between nations: if they succeed, they can re-establish their power in society.

Other Russians are confused. They do not have such clear ambitions for power, but they feel suspicious about Estonians and the Estonian Republic. They have to reorganize their values and convictions and their attitudes towards social and economic organization: collective property will be in private hands; a market economy will replace the planned economy; the perspective of a happy future society seems to disappear. Many Russians have believed that socialism is a great attainment; but there are many Estonian Russians who look approvingly on the difficult and often dolorous rebirth of Estonian society.

We can conclude that non-Estonians are ready to stand up for their political and social interests – not only to keep their jobs and social status, but also to maintain certain social privileges in Estonia. Likewise, Estonians are acting in support of their national interests – to survive as an ethnic unit and to maintain their ethnic identity. These purposes are rather different: the non-Estonian population groups are worried about their individual futures in the republic, whereas Estonians are anxious about their common future, culture and language.

Recent sociological survey research (See Note 1) has shown that Estonians value living and working in their own linguistic and cultural surroundings. Although 74% of Estonians know the Russian language well enough to communicate easily (see Table 3), 80% of them prefer living and working among their own nationals. Among Russians, only 27% prefer a Russian majority in their working and living environment, although only 39% of them know the Estonian language to any significant degree. The Estonian Law of Language is directed towards changing this abnormal situation. Knowledge of Estonian (and Russian, and also other foreign languages) is set as a required professional skill for a number of jobs. A definite period – from one to four years – is given for this requirement to be met. However, non-Estonians who do not know the Estonian language and who regard Estonia as a part of Russia see the language law as a discriminatory act aimed against them.

For Estonians, not only the Estonian language but all of the national culture is a major consolidating factor. For the non-Estonians, especially for the sizeable group of Slavs, the cultural/ ethnic factor is less significant. For them, Soviet state unity is the highest value. Here we find a conflict between the Estonian nationalistic concept and exaggerated Russian enthusiasm for the glory of the great Soviet empire ('socialist commonwealth'). Analysis of many indicators has shown that the national identity of Russians who have left their native land is disturbed and dissolved by official Soviet ideology.[1]

Table 3: Knowledge of Estonian and Russian Language: Estonians and non-Estonians

	Estonians	Non-Estonians
Good everyday knowledge of the other language	74%	37%
Poor knowledge of the other language	22%	39%
No knowledge of the other language	5%	23%

Source: See note 1.

The majority of Russians have responded in another more recent survey conducted by us that they want to hold Soviet and Estonian citizenship simultaneously. Contemporary Russian attitudes towards the institutions wielding power in Estonia reveal their changed political views. We mentioned to our respondents six alternative political institutions which could wield power. The majority (71%) of Estonian Russians replied that the Supreme Council of Estonia had the right to decide the future of Estonia, while 17% thought that the President of the USSR had this right and 5% favoured the Central Committee of the CPSU. Half of the Russians of Estonia felt that they had no right to speak on this matter. Thus, the majority of Estonian Russians see the Supreme Council of Estonia as an authoritative legislative body, and they no longer consider the CPSU Central Committee important: a considerable transformation of attitudes indeed.

We also surveyed the attitudes of national minorities in the Estonian Republic towards the role of Cultural Self-Government (1918-1940). Fiftyseven percent of Estonians responded that this was a good historical experience; but only 14% of Russians had the same opinion, while 49% had heard nothing about this system at all. Attitudes towards the necessity of Cultural Self-Government for national minorities in Estonia today, however, are positive: 62% of Estonians and 71% of Russians support the idea. Nevertheless, different stereotypes of national historical memory are upheld by Estonians and Slavs.

Table 4: *Attitudes toward the Historical-National Development of Estonia. (Indices calculated by positive and negative answers on a 5-item scale)*

	Estonians	Russians
Period of Estonian Independence	+78	+18
Neighbourhood with Finland	+60	+33
Neighbourhood with Sweden	+60	+24
Neighbourhood with Latvia and Lithuania	+48	+16
Influence of Foreign Estonians	+41	-2
Influence of Germans and Baltic-Germans	+24	-8
Influence of Estonians living in the USSR	-13	+5
German Occupation (World War II)	-37	-45
Increasing Proportion of non-Estonians in Estonia	-45	-11
Neighbourhood with Russia	-56	+40
Influence of the Communist Party	-85	-17
Belonging to the Soviet Union	-90	+9

Source: See note 2.

From Table 4 we can clearly see that Estonians and Russians evaluate differently the factors which influenced the development of Estonian society during the past century. Not surprisingly, to Estonians the period of the independent republic was the most significant agent in Estonian's national evolution. By contrast, in the opinion of Russians Estonia progressed during the last century mainly thanks to its neighbours, especially Russia. Estonians, however, have strong negative attitudes towards all influences from Russia and the Soviet Union.[2]

But what about the future? In Table 5 we present some results from sociological research among Estonians and Estonian Russians about preferences for the future political status of Estonia. The overwhelming majority of Estonians (96%) now demand the status of a politically independent and separate state. The Russian community living in Estonia prefers a partially independent Estonian Republic. Only 26% of this population group are currently in favour of a fully independent Estonia.

However, these data indicate also that the proportion of Russians who support the idea of Estonian independence is continuously increasing. Nevertheless, relations between the two national groups are strained, and political tension may well lead to conflict in reality. The Russian (and the Russified Ukrainian and Belorussian) population of Estonia cannot change or adapt overnight because of essential differences in current attitudes and traditional value systems. The Slavs by and large understand civil society, the relationship between the individual and society and the proper structure of power in a different way from Estonians. Probably at least a generation (some 25 years) will be needed for their adaptation and integration.

Table 5: Preferences as to the Future Political Status of Estonian (%)

	Estonians				Non-Estonians			
	1989		1990		1989		1990	
	Apr	Sept	Jan	May	Apr	Sept	Jan	May
Maintenance of Status Quo	2	2	0	0	54	37	20	21
Estonia stays in a reformed Soviet Union (confederation)	39	31	15	2	25	47	52	46
Estonia becomes a Fully Independent State	56	31	15	2	25	47	52	46
Don't know/ No Answer	3	3	4	2	16	7	1	7

Source: Kirch, 1990, p. 55.

8. CONCLUSION

The contemporary inter-ethnic situation is unsatisfactory for Estonians and non-Estonians alike. This situation has taken shape during decades, and so time will also be needed for its improvement, which must be realized on the basis of the interests of both Estonians and non-Estonians. On the positive side, the sphere of common interests is very wide – the political and economic independence of Estonia is one such common interest, and the increasing support of non-Estonians shows it.

The interests of the Estonian people lie in securing a legal guarantee of their right to self-determination, including the right of governmental independence, real sovereignty and independent statehood. The national interests of the non-Estonian inhabitants of Estonia must be guaranteed on the basis of human rights in general. This means, on the one hand, that all citizens of Estonia, irrespective of their nationality, must be equal in their rights; and, on the other hand, that non-Estonians must enjoy the necessary conditions for their national life, language and culture to flourish. The best way of realizing this goal is through wide cultural autonomy for national minorities.

NOTES:

1. The research used in this section was carried out in March-April 1988 by the Sociological Centre of Estonian Radio. 960 people from all over Estonia were polled – 37% were from Tallinn; 34% from the countryside. The research was the first in this field of sociology in Estonia during *perestroika*.

2.The sociological data in this section were gathered in September and December 1990 by researchers of the Institute of Phisosphy, Sociology and Law of the Estonian Academy of Sciences and the consultancy EKE-ARIKO. (We are thankful to Ms. L. Lepane and Mr A. Altosaar for cooperation.) The research is representative for the population of Tallinn.

REFERENCES:

Aun, Karl, 1951. *Der Volkerrechtliche Schutz nationaler Minderheiten in Estland von 1917 bis 1940*, Hamburg.

Aun, Karl, 1951-53. 'The Cultural Autonomy of National Minorities in Estonia', in *Yearbook of the Estonian Learned Society in America*, vol. 2.

Drobizeva, Leokadia M., 1981. 'Dukhovnaia obstsnost narodov SSSR', Moscow.

Eesti NSV Keeleseadus AE Signalet, 1989. Tallinn

'Eesti Vabariigi maakondade, linnade ja alevite rahvastik 1989', 1990. *I. Statistika kogumik*, Tallinn.

Eesti Valitsusasutuste Tegevus Aastatel, 1918-1934 [Operations of the Estonian Government], 1935. Tallinn.

Katus, Kalev, 1990. 'Eesti demograafiline areng läbi sajandite', *Eesti edasivaates*, Metroo kolmas raamat, Tallinn.

Kirch, Aksel, 1990. 'Karta polititseski sil v Estonii' in *Sotsiologicheskii Isledovania*, no. 12.

Laasi, Evald, 1988. 'Veelkord lunkadest,' *Sirp ja Vasar*, 26 February.

Law on the Cultural Self-Government of National Minorities, 1925. *Riigi Teataja*, N 31/32, 21 February.

Loeber, D.A., Vardys, V.S. and Kitching, L., eds, 1990. *Regional Identity under Soviet Rule: the Case of the Baltic States*, Kiel – Hackettstown, New Jersey

Maddison, Eugen, 1930. *Die Nationalen Minderheiten Estlands und ihre Rechte*, Tallinn: Reval.

'Naselenie Estonskoi SSR': po dannym Vsesoijuznoi perepisi naselenia 1979 goda, 1982. *Statisticheski Sbornik*, vol.I, Tallinn.

Taagepera, Rein, 1990. 'Who Assimilates Whom? The World and the Baltic Region' in Loeber, *et al.*

Raun,Toivo U., 1987. *Estonia and the Estonians*, Hoover Press.

Vardys, V.Stanley, 1990. 'The Role of the Churches in the Maintenance of Regional and National Identity in the Baltic Republics'in Loeber, *et al.*

6

Causes of Inter-Ethnic Conflict in Latvia

M. Ustinova

1. INTRODUCTION

The course of the rapid national and socio-political development
taking place in Latvia, as well as in Estonia and Lithuania, is
being closely watched by the Soviet and the world public. Confer-
ences devoted to scholarly analysis and discussion of the Baltic
situation are held both in the USSR and abroad. High-level
politicians, scholars and practitioners in different fields
deliberate on ways to untangle the complex network of political,
national, socio-economic, legal, demographic, cultural and other
problems in the Baltic republics. This chapter offers an ethnographer's viewpoint on the causes of inter-ethnic conflicts in
Latvia.

Latvia's inter-ethnic conflict have the same roots as those in
Estonia, Lithuania and some other regions of the USSR. Today
the Soviet state finds itself in a deep crisis in practically all
fields of activity. This situation is due to deformations in the
socio-economic and political structure of the USSR, historically
aggravated by the despotism of Stalin, by 'voluntarist' experiments and by the irresponsible acceptance of deteriorating
conditions in the years of stagnation. The start of *perestroika*
after April 1985 was dictated by the urgent need to reshape the
entire system of socio-economic and political relations. In such a
polyethnic country as the USSR, this need inevitably affected

the national consciousness of people. Indeed, we could say that the national revival in the USSR expresses the same objective need as *perestroika* itself. The barbaric utilization of Latvia's natural resources; the irresponsible actions of all-union economic ministries that have stimulated large-scale migrations, cutting people off from their ecological niches and pushing them into alien socio-cultural environments; the absence of any real possibilities to influence decisions, and a national policy of unification which has resulted in Latvians finding themselves on the verge of becoming a national minority in Latvia – this is a far from complete inventory of the causes of inter-ethnic conflicts in the republic. In the following I would like to point out some specific historical conditions which may explain why the national movement in Latvia, as well as in Lithuania and Estonia, differs from related movements in other regions of the USSR.

Unlike the majority of regions in the USSR, the Baltic republics were incorporated into the Union at a late date. Current lifestyle and culture bear witness to many traditions from the times when these republics existed as sovereign Baltic states. Latvians, Lithuanians and Estonians have a highly developed national consciousness and historical memory, which has made them better prepared to accept the ideas and aims of *perestroika* than many other Soviet peoples. No doubt, this was stimulated by the higher level of socio-economic and cultural development of the Baltic republics, together with their historical experience of functioning democratic institutions and other characteristics of the European cultural tradition.

2. SOCIO-ETHNIC CHANGES AND CHALLENGES

What, then, can explain the rise of inter-ethnic contradictions and conflicts in a region where – to judge by folklore evidence – there had been no enmity towards other peoples? According to recent census data the share of Latvians in the national composition of Latvia's population has diminished from 62% (1959) to 52% (1989), while that of Estonians fell from 74.6% (1959) to 61.5% (1989) (Kozlov, 1982, pp. 117-122; Moors, 1990). Latvians constitute only 44% of the urban population; Estonians 52% ('On the results...,' 1989; Rebane, 1988). Before the eyes of the

present generation the capital of Latvia and its largest towns
(especially seaports) have become Russian-speaking, while the
language and cultural traditions of the native people have been
forced out of offices and away from the social and service
spheres. Latvians now comprise only 36.5% of Riga's population;
in the big industrial centre – Daugavpils – the figure is 13%
('On the results...,'1989).

Massive and ecologically incompetent industrialization of the
republic have resulted in dangerous conditions for human life.
Due to the scarce local labour resources, the expansion of industrial production in the Baltic republics was supported by workers
and engineering/technical personnel imported from other, mainly
East Slavic, republics. This trend led to social polarization
between peoples.[1] Simultaneously there was a polarization
within the political structure: the attempt to maintain the
leading role of the working class in the composition of the CPSU,
which consists mainly of members of the Russian-speaking
population, resulted in a lower percentage of the indigenous
people belonging to the Party: in 1988, only 40% of the members
of of the Communist Party of Latvia were Latvian (Vagris, 1989,
p. 11), and the Communist ideology has almost no resonance in
the mass consciousness of the Latvian people.

The Russian-speaking population living in Latvia, as in the
Baltic region as a whole, is ethnically heterogeneous. It consists
of three groups of East Slavic peoples, mainly Russians (34%),
but also Belorussians (4.5%) and Ukrainians (3.5%). These
groups, both as a whole and separately, are heterogeneous in
their adaptation to an alien ethnic environment. Some sections
have been residing in the area for ages; others have been there
since World War II. However, the great majority are recent
settlers from the period 1950-1980.

In Latvia the 'mechanical' increase of population from 1971
to 1988 alone was about 200,000, i.e., more than 11,000 yearly
(Council of Ministers, 1989). As a result of the 1951-1987 inflow,
the population of Estonia increased by 280,000 and the annual
average net migration inflow is 7,500 (Rebane, 1988). In terms
of social composition, most of the newly arrived settlers have
come from the working class, being engaged in big Moscow-
subordinated industrial enterprises located in the capital,
seaports and other urban centres. The unity of this Russian-
speaking population is determined more by socio-economic and
political demands than by national interests.

The inflow of this non-indigenous population into a quite alien ethno-cultural environment has taken place during a historically brief period, too short to ensure their adaptation to the local population. Indeed, for many of the recently arrived Russian-speaking settlers, the question of adaptation to local culture never arose. As a rule, the newcomers were concentrated at industrial enterprises with few indigenous people among the workers. Moreover, they settled in residential areas with the same ethnic homogeneity. Demographic studies have shown that inter-ethnic tension has been aggravated by their frequent moves and short periods of residence in any one location.

From the ethnographic viewpoint differences between peoples in culture, folk traditions, behaviour, value systems and orientation, psychology, etc. are also of great importance. To some of the established residents, the influx and spread of an alien culture, with a different language and norms of behaviour, seemed to herald the erosion of their own cultural values, as well as posing a threat to the continued existence of their entire cultural and linguistic ecology. The earlier East Slavic settlers, as well as the immediate post-war ones, have already adapted to the socio-cultural conditions of Latvia and the other Baltic republics, and are aware of the history and of the national interests of the native peoples. By contrast, the recent arrivals are unprepared for any comprehensive perception or objective appreciation of the revival of national consciousness among the peoples of the Baltic. Consequently most of the inter-ethnic conflicts have arisen between the indigenous peoples and the recently arrived Russian-speaking population. No doubt, mutual adaptation has also been impeded by the previous dominant ideological concept of 'internationalism', which placed ultimate value on the ability of people to speak the Russian language – a policy which rendered the Russian people a poor service.

3. RISE OF NATIONAL MOVEMENTS

When the national movements began to emerge, the Baltic peoples began to strive for the preservation, revival and refinement of their own ethno-cultural and historical identity, and for the restoration of real state sovereignty on their respective territories. The striving increased as shocking facts became known about recent political history and the historical role of certain politicians; about contemporary socio-economic conditions, and about the real danger of ecological catastrophe.

However, the national movement in Latvia started and grew without due consideration of attitudes at the highest levels of central state power or of the socio-political orientations of the Russian-speaking population. The national movement did not foresee the emergence of the problem of self-identification on the part of the Russian-speaking people in the new ideological situation of *perestroika*. Discussion of Latvian rights in the spheres of state language, citizenship, voting rights, etc. was accompanied by the first waves of indignation on the part of Russian-speaking people, who feared infringement of their human rights. The close ties between the recently arrived Russian-speakers and the central industrial and political structures can explain why individual human rights were stressed ideologically by Interfront, which ignored the right of nations to self-determination, as commonly accepted in international law and in the Constitution of the USSR. While the underlying conditions for inter-ethnic conflict had accumulated over the decades, the issue of people's versus human rights was fundamental from the very beginning of the national movements.

Another important cause of inter-ethnic tension in the period of *perestroika* was due to the fact that top level state and party agencies underestimated the determination of the national-democratic movements in the republics. This problem was aggravated by the slow preparation and adoption of laws, as well as by the ambiguity of these laws – the law on the economic independence of the Baltic republics, the law on secession of republics from the USSR, etc. Of course the pace of *perestroika* in the USSR as a whole was determined by differences in the levels of socio-economic, cultural and political development. Moscow's efforts to preserve the unity of the USSR while taking into consideration the wide diversity of national and socio-political interests in the country tended to lead to conservatism. As a result, many of the early initiatives of the Baltic republics[2], including Latvia, were initially condemned by the central mass media, which accused the Baltic movements of separatism and nationalism until these things became generally accepted by other republics as well. Rejection at the Centre left the Baltic peoples with a feeling of grievance; it affected their sense of social well-being; shook their confidence in *perestroika*, and thus intensifed their striving for state sovereignty.

Another cause of inter-nation dissension in the Baltic Sea area was the nationality doctrine in the USSR prior to 1985, which painted a pretty picture of consensus and peace in inter-nation relations, and acted as a brake on scholarly research on inter-nation and inter-ethnic conflict. The unitary state with its dogmatic ideology did not demand scientifically based approaches to the prevention or resolution of such conflicts. Lacking these methods, as well as any experience in applying them to nationality policy, scholars did not mitigate the incompetence of the Soviet leadership in dealing with problems of the peoples' history, culture, psychology and religion.

4. CONCLUSION

Despite the complicated political situation in Latvia, I would like to end on a note of optimism, based on the firm conviction that all the peoples living in Latvia – as well as in the other Baltic republics, and indeed everywhere else in the USSR – are striving for the same goal: for a life worthy of the dignity of the human being in general and for freedom of self-expression. In this sense human rights and the rights of peoples may be considered as equal in value, because human rights cannot be observed outside a context of satisfied national interests, and *vice versa*. The parliamentary and generally peaceful character of inter-nation conflicts in Latvia, Estonia and Lithuania; the construction of a new legal system; the domestic irreversibility of reconstruction processes – all of these factors lead me to hope that the contemporary revolution in the USSR will be crowned by achieving true inter-nation consensus.

NOTES:

1. The indigenous population of Latvia is engaged mostly in science, culture and agriculture; Latvians comprise only 38% of the industrial workforce, but in some branches as little as 9% – while they are 70% of the rural population (Chevachin, 1988). The share of Estonians in the total rural population is 86% (Rebane, 1988).

2. For example, on the priority right of the republics to use their own natural resources; on the priority of republican laws on their own territories; on the need to diversify state structures in the USSR, etc.

REFERENCES

'On the results of the All-Union Population Census of 1989 in the Latvian SSR' (1990). *Tsina*, 21 March

Chevachin, V., 1988. 'Unfavourable migration', *Tsina*, 10 December.

Council of Ministers and Council of Trade Unions of the Latvian SSR (1989), 'On measures aimed to brake the unfounded mechanical increase of the population and to regulate inflow processes in the Latvian SSR', Decision No. 46, *Tsina*, 16 February

Kozlov, V.I., 1982. *Nationalities in the USSR*. Moscow.

Moors, G., 1990. 'What are we in the Baltic region?', *Tsina*, 21 February

Rebane, J., 1988. 'The main features of national processes in the republic', *Communist of Estonia*, no. 6.

Vagris, J., 1989. 'Socio-political processes in the republic and a programme of action for the CPL', *Communist of Soviet Latvia*, no. 9.

7

The Azerbaijani Armenian Conflict: Possible Paths towards Resolution

V. Nadein-Raevski

1. INTRODUCTION

The Azerbaijani-Armenian conflict has become widely known as causing one of the first outbreaks of violence on the grounds of nationalism during the period of *perestroika*. Commentary and analysis in the USSR and in the world following the events in Nagorno-Karabakh and Baku differ greatly, however, in their scientific and political approach. Within the Soviet Union, analysis tends to focus on the socio-economic grounds for the conflict – an approach in line with official Marxist-Leninist doctrine. Central mass media have tried to show that the conflict is a result of the joint activities of corrupted state bureaucrats and leaders of 'underground' economic structures fighting against the reforms of *perestroika*. According to this interpretation the bureaucrats connected with the 'mafia' feel that power is slipping away from them, which means not only the loss of considerable profits, but also the beginning of legal actions against corrupt elements and possible future imprisonment of those involved in the 'underground'. Indeed, trials in Uzbekistan have showed that this process bears real danger for the mafia (although these trials were held in a manner reminiscent of the Stalin-Brezhnev era). In fact, dozens of groups, including hundreds of state prosecutors, have begun official investigations of corrupt elements in Azerbaijan.

The second prevailing tendency in the central mass media has been to focus on the social and economic problems of Azerbaijan which eventually led to a worsening of living conditions for the local population, and resulted in mass dissatisfaction among the people, including the 180,000 residents of Nagorno Karabakh. Party and government officials in Baku have been accused of being totally misguided and incompetent in finding solutions to economic problems.

The third tendency of analysis at the Centre has been to assert that 'violation of Lenin's nationality policy' in the Stalin-Brezhnev period was the main reason of mass for dissatisfaction of the local Armenian population in Azerbaijan.

2.   POLITICAL PARTIES IN AZERBAIJAN

The spectrum of political forces in the republic covers almost all possible varieties of political thought in the modern East. The Islamic trend is represented by three main parties: Islamic Society, headed by Muhammed Hatemi; *Toube*; and *Vahdat*. In several regions of Azerbaijan one can also note the activities of Hezbollah.

A pro-Turkish orientation is represented by *Dir Chalish*, whose leaders seek to promote a union with Turkey, and the *Gour Tolush* society which aims, under the banner of the *Musavat* party, to secede from the Soviet Union. The Independent Azerbaijan group is active in Baku, the capital of the republic. The leaders of this group propose leaving the Soviet Union in order to form an independent country through unification with Iranian Azerbaijan (*Resalat,* 28 February 1990).

But the largest and strongest political force in Azerbaijan is the Popular Front, organized in January of 1989 as the National Defence Organization. Headed by many popular political leaders of the republic, this organization was closely connected with the ruling Communist Party. But under the pressure of a mass movement inspired and organized by the Front, its leaders had to drop official ties with the Communist Party, beginning from 20 January 1990, and have started the process of capturing power independently in the main cities.

Azerbaijani newspapers and political leaders, differing in their political interests and ultimate purposes, have nevertheless agreed on at least one point: they consider the Armenian population of the republic to have no rights on the territory of Nagorno-Karabakh. According to the official Azerbaijani point of view, Armenians are newcomers to the area, while the Azeris are the native population. Numerous Azerbaijani scholars, following Turkish examples, have written dozens of 'scientific works' to prove this idea. They try to find direct and indirect evidence to underscore the fact that some Armenians were allowed to leave Persia and to move to the regions of historic Armenia, which by that time had a multi-ethnic population, including Armenians, Azeris, Kurds and others – both ancient Caucasian and new Turkic-speaking peoples. For example in March 1990 an Azerbaijanian literary magazine published a commentary on a book by the prominent Russian writer and diplomat, A. S. Griboyedov. The author paid special attention to a pair of letters devoted to Griboyedov's 'critical attitude' towards the 'policy of the Tsarist government on the question of resettlement of Persian Armenians on the territory of Azerbaijan and in particular in Nakhichevan and Karabakh.' (Yakubova, 1990, p. 126)

Modern Azerbaijani authors usually write nothing about the Armenians who inhabited this territory before the invasion of the waves of different Turkic tribes. They also do not mention that the 'newcoming Armenians' were moved to Persia precisely by these numerous invasions of Turkic nomads. But what is well known to European scholars is unknown to the mass audience of Azerbaijan. Oriented to the surrounding world only through the schemata of 'local science', which are very influential in the mass-media of this republic, the Azerbaijani population is not ready to perceive the problem of Azeri-Armenian relations in a broader context.

Another popular theory that serve as a foundation for modern Azeri nationalism is the Azerbaijani variant of the so-called 'Caucasian Albania' theory. According to this hypothesis, the ancient territory of Caucasian Albania covered all the modern territory of Azerbaijan and some other territories of the Caucasus long before the invasion of Turkic nomads. Part of this population was later 'Armenianized' and 'Christianized', while another part was 'Turkified' and 'Islamized'. The main propagators of this view are such Azerbaijanian authors as Z. Buniyatov, F. Mamedova, D. Ahundov and M. Seyidov, who follow theories of this type widely disseminated in Turkey. A scientific hypothesis, when it is simplified enough for easy understanding by a broad public, can prove a strong political weapon, convenient for popular political movements – especially nationalistic ones. The political situation in Azerbaijan gives a good example of mass support for such a politicized hypothesis.

The concrete political slogans that have been extracted out of this hypothesis are rather astonishing. Adherents insist that all the Karabakh population has common roots and that there are no Armenians in Karabakh; neither are there any Azeris. Both are 'Albanians' (or 'Albans' – to distinguish them from residents of modern Albania on the Balkan Peninsula). And so, if they are Albans, there is no need for any Nagorno-Karabakh Autonomous Region, which 'divides the nation' and leads to 'Armenian separatism.' That is how the slogan for the liquidation of Karabakh autonomy appeared in Azerbaijan and became a leading one for the nationalistic mass movement. Had it not been for the Armenian population of Karabakh – who see the differences between the two peoples, and whose national self-consciousness is an Armenian not an 'Albanian' one – the problem would have been easily solved through 'Azerbaijanification' and 'Islamization' of the local population, in favor of Azeri nationalism.

3.   ARMENIANS AND THE KARABAKH MOVEMENT

The basic ideas of the mass people's movement in Nagorno-Karabakh (*Artsah*, as it is called both in Armenia and Karabakh, according to the ancient Armenian name of this territory) differ considerably from the Azerbaijani interpretation. Armenian historians stress the ancient roots of the native Armenian population of this territory, basing their work on both ancient sources and modern Armenology. Many works have been devoted to the thorough study of the architecture and culture of Artsah. Armenian scholars have focused on the study of Armenian architecture and the cross stones (*hachkars*) that can be found all over the territory of *Artsah* (cf. Mkrtchan, 1989). On the other hand, Azeri scholars try to prove that these cross stones are not Armenian but of the pre-Christian Albanian period. (One can observe the results of this scholarship in Baku museums.) But for the local authorities in Azerbaijan all these scholarly discussions are too complex to understand: they prefer to destroy ancient churches and to convert the cross stones into building material.

One of the most important fields of historical research in Armenia is the absorption of Artsah by Soviet Azerbaijan. Armenian authors point to the continuity between the Azerbaijanian *Musavat* ('Equality') party policy and the policy of Soviet Azerbaijan and its leaders, N.Narimanov, Husseinov and others. They seek to prove that the main role in the 'annexation' of Karabakh was played by Stalin. Indeed, numerous documents released lately give them opportunity to prove that Armenian territory was used by the revolutionary leaders of Russia as a pay-off to Turkish revolutionary powers for 'the continuation of World Revolution in the East'. Thus Turkey received such parts of Western Armenia as Kars and Ardahan, while Azerbaijan received Karabakh and Nakhichevan – the detached autonomous republic which is wedged in between Armenia and Iran – belonging to Azerbaijan.

Public opinion in Armenia was always highly sensitive on the question of the genocide of Armenians in Turkey and Azerbaijan, and any reference to the problem of ancient Armenian territory causes an instant and sharp reaction among the local population. The idea of restoration of Armenian power over the 'territories of historic Armenia' is still quite popular among Armenians, and cannot be ignored by any political force in the republic. This is not a consequence of broad agitation – on the contrary, during the Stalin period, for the sake of 'Soviet-Turkish friendship', the territorial problem was not to be discussed in any context – except for a brief period after World War II, when acute problems arose in Soviet-Turkish relations and the territories of Turkish Armenia became one of them. Sharp polemics about these territories by Soviet representatives in the United Nations and in the Soviet mass media aroused hopes among Armenians for the restoration of their former rights. But normalization of Soviet-Turkish relations led to the rise of pessimism and dissatisfaction, because in almost every Armenian family one can find victims of the genocide that has claimed about two million lives in different periods of Turkish-Armenian relations. (Cf. Nersisyan, 1983, pp. iii-xvi.)

Before the October Revolution of 1917 Nagorno-Karabakh (Artsah), together with another Armenian territory, Zangezur, was a part of Elizabethpol province (*Elizavetpolskaia Gubernia*). Even at that time, relations between the two communities were strained. In 1905 and, later, in 1918-1920 there were massive attacks against the civilian Armenian population: in Baku –

30,000 Armenians were killed there (Hushudyan, 1989, p. 10); in the town of Shusha – 32,000 Armenians died there; and elsewhere in this region (Barsegov, 1989, p. 88). From 1917 until the final victory of Soviet power in Azerbaijan, the Musavat party government in Azerbaijan, friendly to Ottoman Turkey, used Turkish and later British military forces in trying to defeat the national liberation movement of Karabakh Armenians.

Armenian scholars write that this was achieved later with the help of a series of political and diplomatic maneuvers by N. Narimanov and Stalin, and deny that any Armenian government in the Soviet period accepted the annexation of Nagorno-Karabakh. Moreover, the officials in Soviet Armenia have several times raised the problem of Karabakh, appealing to the central government on the basis of the mass dissatisfaction of the Armenian population in this territory. But all these appeals were ignored, and their organizers repressed. And so at the beginning of *perestroika*, the Karabakh Armenians started a new campaign for territorial reunification with Armenia.

4. THE BEGINNING OF THE KARABAKH CONFLICT

Naturally both parties involved tend to lay the blame for the initiation of the conflict on the other side. Armenian sources state that the life of Karabakh Armenians was unbearable under the power of the Azerbaijanis, who tended to take from the region as much as possible while giving almost nothing in return. The Azerbaijanian side tries to prove that the Karabakh Armenians living under the power of Baku enjoyed a happy and prosperous life compared with other Azerbaijanian citizens.

According to the Azerbaijani view, the Armenian community of Azerbaijan had all the necessary opportunities for cultural development. By contrast, according to one Armenian authority:

> *The following comparisons are interesting – in Yerevan with 2,300 Azerbaijanis (1979) there are two Azerbaijani schools, an Azerbaijani theatre and an Azerbaijani faculty in the Armenian Pedagogical Institute named after H. Abovyan, while at the same time in Baku, with more than 200,000 Armenians, the Armenian theatre and Armenian Pedagogical Institute were closed, and, out of 76 Armenian schools in Baku during the pre-war period [before 1941], not a single one was left. (Glazami, 1990, p. 36)*

In a special 'Decision of the USSR Supreme Soviet Presidium concerning the Decisions of the Supreme Soviets of the Armenian SSR and the Azerbaijanian SSR on the Question of Nagorno-Karabakh', the following statement appeared:

> For a long period, many problems touching the national interests of the Armenian population were not being solved in the Autonomous Region, especially in the field of culture and education and in the field of cadres policy. The constitutional rights of the Autonomous Region were violated. (Izvestia, 20 July 1988)

The 'initial step' in this conflict was taken when the Karabakh Armenians appealed to the all-union powers in Moscow. In 1986-1987 they collected signatures for a petition in favour of reuniting Karabakh with Armenia. On 1 December 1987 a Karabakh delegation was received at the Central Committee of the CPSU, and in January 1988 another delegation was received in the Presidium of the USSR Supreme Soviet. In January-February 1988 numerous meetings in all the enterprises of the Autonomous Region 'unanimously adopted decisions to ask the higher powers to solve this problem positively' (Arutunyan, 1990, p. 32). Communist Party organizations of the Karabakh Region, predominantly Armenian except for those from Shusha and some Azerbaijani villages, joined in the campaign. On 12 February, several high officials of the republic were sent to the capital, Stepankert, to get the situation under control. At the same time special officials from Baku were obliged to control the everyday activities of local Communist Party secretaries, state prosecutors and militia (police) commanders (Aruktunyan, 1990, p. 33).

All these activities only aggravated the conflict because the republic chiefs used the language of rude pressure and threats, effective in the past but not sufficient for the present time. On the same day that the Karabakh mass meetings began, new threats followed from the Azerbaijanian 'patriots'. Further escalation of tension and the arrival of a division of the 'Inner Forces' (Soviet analogue of the Italian Carabinieri) on 13 February could not weaken the mass movement. Despite the high-ranking Regional Party and Soviet leaders who acted together with the authorities of the Republic, it was impossible to put a halt to mass demonstrations or to change the position of Armenian deputies in the Regional Soviet, who adopted a resolution in emergency session on 20 February asking the

Supreme Soviets of Azerbaijan, Armenia and the Soviet Union to transfer the NKAR from the Azerbaijanian SSR to the Armenian SSR. (*Sovietskii Karabakh*, 21 February 1988) On 21 February the Central Committee of the CPSU adopted a special decision 'About the Events in Nagorno-Karabakh'. On the same day, according to Armenian sources, the first attacks of Azerbaijanis against the Armenian population began in different regions of the Republic (Arutunyan, 1990, p. 38). According to Azerbaijanian sources the first meetings in Baku and Sumgait with the slogan 'NKAR is an integral part of Azerbaijan' began on 22-23 February (*Tragedia*, 1990, p. 1).

An immediate answer from Moscow to the Armenian appeals came with the dispatch to Baku on 22 February of two ruling Politburo members G.Razumovsky and P.Demichev – the latter was at that time the first deputy chairman of the USSR Supreme Soviet Presidium. The local party leader, Kevorkov, an annoying figure for the Karabakh Armenians, was dismissed, and G. Pogosyan appointed instead. Party leaders visiting Armenia used mass media to calm both sides, televising an appeal by the CPSU General Secretary, Mikhail Gorbachev. But the next day the Azerbaijani side launched the Sumgait violence, sparked off by a mass meeting in the Azerbaijanian city of Agdam. A crowd of several thousand Azerbaijanis had moved into the Armenian town of Askeran, attacking cars and buildings on the way. As a result, in a clash not far from the town of Askeran, several dozen Armenians were wounded and two young Azerbaijanis were shot (*Tragedia...*, 1990, p. 1) Armenian sources stress that one of these two first victims was shot by 'an Azerbaijanian militiaman' (*Sumgait...*, p. 11). The Azerbaijani side tends to avoid this fact.

The events in Askeran are considered by both sides to be the starting point for the Sumgait tragedy, which the Armenians see as a new act of genocide against the Armenian people, planned and organized by the Azerbaijanian state and Party leaders. In order to prove this, Armenians use the official documents from the trials of the participants in the pogroms, showing that the sharp iron rods used during the attacks had in fact been prepared beforehand in one of the city plants, that some Azeri militiamen took part in the actions against Armenians, while others did nothing to stop the mass vandalism, and that 'vodka and drugs were distributed free of charge' among the Azerbaijani demonstrators (*Sumgait...*, 1990, p. 13). Moreover, on the second day of action after another meeting held in the city centre, 'the First Secretary of the Sumgait City Party Committee Muslim-zade took the state flag of Azerbaijan and led a huge crowd after himself'. According to official figures, 27 Armenians were killed, 17 women raped and 276 soldiers were injured in trying to stop the 'pogroms'. The Armenian side considers the real figures to be even higher.

According the Azerbaijani side, 'The Sumgait events were organized by the Armenian extremists in order to blackmail the Azerbaijanian people and to make easier the annexation of NKAR' (*Sobitiya...*, 1989, p. 4). It is not only the Azerbaijanian mass media that takes part in this campaign, but also representatives of official scholarly institutes in the republic, in particular Academician Ziya Buniyatov of the Azerbaijanian Academy of Sciences; and corresponding member of the Academy, M. A. Ismailov, as well as many other scholars. Although their arguments are too weak to convince the majority of Soviet or world scholars, they accord with public opinion in the Republic because mass psychology there, heated by the continuing conflict, is ready to believe almost any argument about 'Armenian cruelty' and the correspondingly high moral quality of the Azerbaijani nation.

In the Armenian mass media, the main publications are not so crude; but mass self-awareness also tends to stress the cruelty of 'the neighbor', as Armenians usually call Azerbaijan. One can find many publications devoted to the history of the Armenian people and Armenian-Turkish relations, and the black pages of the genocide of Armenian people in the Ottoman Empire are often compared with modern events in Azerbaijan. The Armenian side tends to argue that recent events show continuity with the old Turkish policy. Over the past few years a new theme has appeared in Armenian publications. Armenian scholars have published a series of documents showing the process of transfer of some regions of the Russian Empire to Turkey, and the role of Bolshevik leaders in this process. The Armenian authors try to show that the proposal for such transfers made by Stalin and Narimanov was finally adopted by Lenin, whose name in connection with these events was taboo for years. The Armenian All-National Movement (AOD, as it is known in Russian) has taken up this issue in its struggle for an independent Armenia. In private talks the functionaries of the AOD stress that the Russian orientation of Armenians was an historical mistake, and that current circumstances make it essential for Armenia to find a new political and strategic line in the surrounding world. Some stress that it is necessary to do away with old territorial ambitions, to forget about 'ancient Armenian lands' and 'Ottoman genocide', and to seek friendly ties and even a union with Turkey, and in that way achieve a final normalization of Armenian-Azerbaijani relations. These ideas are not very popular with Armenians, but an anti-Moscow and anti-Gorbachev trend is gradually beginning to prevail in mass opinion. Anti-communism is gaining more and more new adherents because of mass disappointment with the Armenian-Russian union. Young people and war veterans, non-partisans and party members, stress that Armenians gave the Union more than 60 generals and 500,000 soldiers to fight the Nazi invasion, and yet when the Armenians needed protection in Sumgait, Baku, Gyandja and other cities of Azerbaijan they received neither protection nor help. On the other hand, despite the anti-Union tendency, the old pro-Russian forces have been trying to convince their opponents that this new AOD policy will prove a catastrophe for the Armenians. Their hopes are linked to the idea of union with the new democratic forces within the Russian Federation.

5.   CONFLICT ESCALATION

Step by step the Karabakh conflict escalated. New waves of refugees fled across the borders of the two republics. In Nagorno-Karabakh, Azeris expelled Armenians from schools, enterprises and offices, and attacked their houses in the ethnically mixed towns and villages on the territories where they had a majority of population. The Armenian side did the same. Both sides strove to show that their actions were only a counter to the actions of the other. Gradually all these activities became so widespread and devoid of any control (even by local nationalist leaders) that no observer can now mark the starting point or determine the guilty side or the victim side. The ordinary people of both nations became the victims, and leading nationalists from both communities were surely guilty.

As to the organization of mass deportations, we must note that the attacks in Azerbaijan against the Armenian population had a mass character. Crowds of hundreds or thousands of people attacked Armenians and those who tried to defend them. The victims were often wounded, and, without retaining any property, fled to Armenia, in turn causing new waves of deportations of Azeris from Armenian territory. Bearded young men were the organizers of deportations from Armenia. In private talks these 'bearded ones' claim that in the beginning of the conflict they deported Azeri families only after giving them an opportunity to sell their houses and other property. 'But when we saw severely beaten Armenians, together with raped women and girls, coming from Azerbaijan, we stopped giving the Azerbaijanis the opportunity to sell their houses.' Official documents published in Azerbaijanian confirm these facts (*Sobitiya...*, 1989, pp. 86-91).

The total number of deported Armenians was more than 300,000. The situation in Armenia was worsened by the disastrous earthquake of 7 December 1988, which killed tens of thousands of people, and left about half a million homeless. Armenian refugees from Azerbaijan were the urbanized residents: industrial workers, engineers, scientists, school teachers, civil servants, etc., who are not suited to a new life and work in the countryside. In conjunction with the victims of the earthquake they have created an immense problem of declassed masses in Armenia. In order to solve this problem, what the Armenian government needs is to have vast resources and a stable situation within the Republic and on its borders; but neither the old government of the Republic nor the new one have achieved these two essential conditions. Wide international and all-union help after the earthquake so vital for Armenia has still not been forthcoming.

In the USSR and abroad some hoped that this tremendous disaster would put an end to the conflict between the two Republics. But all hope was in vain. Although humanely oriented circles in Azerbaijan were sincerely shocked at the disaster and were ready to help by sending specialists and resources, certain active nationalists commemorated the disaster as a holiday. Of course the Armenians were insulted, and their nationalist circles refused to receive any help from Azerbaijan. More than that, the escalation of mutual attacks on the borders and in Karabakh continued, and the Azerbaijanis mounted a full blockade of railroads connecting Armenia with the outside world. An attempt at transit through Georgia could not compensate for the losses, for this channel had served to carry only 15% of the total transport of goods, and was thoroughly exploited by Georgia itself. Georgia had also received some materials through the Azerbaijanian railroad before the blockade, and was in no position to expand the transportation for Armenia through the mountainous regions. Besides, the border region between Georgia and Armenia is populated with Azeris, who attacked the trains and started a terror campaign against Armenian locomotive crews. Only when the crews were replaced by Georgian ones did the terror diminish. The border situation led to the paralysis of reconstruction works in the earthquake zones, and resulted in a further escalation of hatred against the Azeris, who were blamed now for inhumanity. Those in Armenia who were ready for a dialogue lost credit in the eyes of the public. The situation led to the strengthening of nationalistic circles in the political parties of the Republic (the total number of political parties in Armenia is more than 70 by now). The strongest political trend – AOD – moved to a more extreme position and began a campaign for the creation of 'Self-Defence Forces', now consisting of the existing groups of 'bearded ones' and some recently formed detachments.

The campaign to create such forces received a strong impulse after attacks carried out by the Azerbaijanian Popular Front military units against the border guard systems along all the border of Azerbaijan with Iran and Turkey. Widespread declarations by Azeris that they wanted only to restore relations with their relatives in Iran, whom they had not seen for 70 years, could not convince Armenians of the peaceful intentions of 'the neighbor'. Armenians were sure that the 'anti-border war' was organized to receive arms and help from Southern Azer-baijan to permit escalation of violence against Armenia. New waves of refugees from Azerbaijan, mass pogroms leading to total deportation of the Armenian population and the capture of young bearded Iranians by units of the Soviet Army seemed to prove this. As a result, numerous terrorist groups started a massive campaign for the seizure of armaments all over Armenia, while the central powers tried to control the situation in both republics.

According to Armenian sources, 157,000 Azeris have been deported from Armenia. The majority of these were country people not able to substitute for the lost urban Armenian popula-tion in Azerbaijan. Their qualifications do not correspond to positions in city enterprises; nor are they psychologically pre-pared for life in large cities. Moreover, these people did not feel guilty and could not understand why they were deported. That is why blame for the deportations was laid on all of the Armenians, including those in Azerbaijan; and it was not difficult to channel Azeri grievance into the anti-Armenian campaign. According to the Azerbaijani point of view, they were the main force used by the militant nationalists in the anti-Armenian pogroms.

Another problem also faced the Azerbaijanian authorities: the 40,000 Meskhetian Turks who had immigrated to Azerbaijan from Uzbekistan after the clashes in the Fergana Valley. The Meskhetians had been deprived of their property and had suffered heavy losses in the fierce inter-ethnic clashes with the Uzbek population. They proved a fertile ground for the anti-Armenian campaign.

6. ATTEMPTS AT CONFLICT REGULATION

In early March 1988, a group of scholars arrived in Nagorno-Karabakh to study the social and economic situation in the region. Research by commission members showed that the level of social and economic development of the region was poor. They offered a package of suggestions aimed at raising the standard of living and promoting the development of the region: this package included reunion with Armenia, or, if that were impossible, incorporating Nagorno-Karabakh in the Russian Federation. In any case it would be necessary to broaden the rights of the local authorities in the region. The commission proposed putting a halt to the anti-Armenian campaign in the Azerbaijanian mass media and strengthening the police forces in Karabakh (Arutunyan, 1990, p.58).

Some additional military units appeared in the region on 21 March, and the Presidium of the USSR Supreme Soviet adopted a special decision on Nagorno-Karabakh. The Azerbaijanian authorities reacted simultaneously: the *Krounk* Committee of Karabakh Armenians was officially dissolved, and demonstrations without official permission were forbidden. During the confrontation we can note many steps that aggravated the situation, causing new strikes, demonstrations and clashes. These were not only the result of 'emotional' decisions by the parties involved: oral declarations made by high-ranking Communist Party officials and published in the central press were considered to be unbalanced or provocative by one side or the other. (Those who defend a state-controlled press scarcely understand that even Soviet journalists have the right to express their own point of view.) These actions led to many new attacks, deportations and escalation of the information war. (On this point, see Arutunyan, 1990, esp. pp. 62, 90.) These were not only the result of 'emotional' decisions by the parties involved: oral declarations made by high-ranking Communist Party officials and published in the central press were considered to be unbalanced or provocative by one side or the other. Those who defend a state-controlled press scarcely understand that even Soviet journalists have the right to express their own point of view.

On 13 June 1988 the Presidium of the Supreme Soviet of the Azerbaijanian SSR declared the claims of the Karabakh Armenians 'unacceptable' on the ground that the status of Karabakh gives in practice providing the opportunity for all the nations and ethnic groups of Karabakh to satisfy 'all their economic, social and cultural necessities' (*Bakinskii Rabochii*, 14 June 1988). Later this decision was confirmed by a session of the Supreme Soviet of Azerbaijan. But on 15 June the Armenian Supreme Soviet gave 'its permission for the entry of Nagorno Karabakh Autonomous Region into the Armenian SSR', and asked the USSR parliament 'to examine and decide positively this issue' (*Communist* Yerevan, 16 June 1988). The leaders of the two republics had failed to solve the problem on the basis of mutual understanding. Thus further escalation of tension in the inter-republican confrontation became the official policy of both.

7. THE CENTRE IN ACTION

On the basis of the provisional Constitution of the USSR (Article 78: 'The territory of a Union Republic may not be altered without its consent'), the Presidium of the USSR Supreme Soviet refused to approve the decisions of the Armenian Parliament; while at the same time admitting that complex measures for the revival of the Karabakh territory were necessary (*Izvestia*, 20 July 1988). A special representative of the Central Committee of the CPSU and the Presidium of the Supreme Soviet, A.Volsky, was sent to Stepanakert to help in solving of the problem. Later, on 12 January 1989, a new body was formed: the Special Ruling Committee, headed by A.Volsky, was appointed (*Izvestia*, 15

January 1989). Understanding that the positions of both sides are totally opposed without any overlap for possible consensus, the Union authorities have sought resolution through partial satisfaction and partial punishment for both sides, corresponding to President Gorbachev's idea: 'neither any winners nor any defeated'. That would seem to be a proper way, if it could be accepted by both sides. Central rule from Moscow through the Special Ruling Committee partly satisfied the Armenian desire to do away with the 'Azeri oppression', while at the same leaving the region under the jurisdiction of Azerbaijan.

To achieve positive results, the Committee needed not only good intentions but proper conditions: time – for progress to be made in the social and economic development of the Region; strong support in the mass media of both republics to check massive nationalist propaganda; help from military units to stop acts of genocide in Azerbaijan and deportations in both republics; lifting of the disastrous transport blockade of Armenia, and mobilization of joint efforts by the Communist Party, the Popular Front leaders and other representatives from both sides to seek resolution of the conflict. However, none of these essential conditions existed in practice, and in the end this led to a crisis in the activities of the Committee. The Committee remained active for several months. However, its decisions, although useful for normalization of the situation, were blocked by both sides, each claiming that the Committee was acting in favor of the other side. Besides, the blockade of Armenia was not eliminated by the Centre, and that fact had not only irritated Armenians but provided the militant nationalists with an excellent opportunity to demonstrate that the policy of the Union was being conducted in favor of Azerbaijan.

When analyzing the problem we can perceive a common theme in the steps taken by the central powers: to preserve the existing power structure, and to use the local bureaucracy to achieve control over the rising nationalist movement. This policy was partly successful in Azerbaijan, where army units managed to get the situation under control and to dissolve the main detachments of the Popular Front. Moreover, elections in the Republic, organized in the autumn of 1990, gave the local Communist Party leaders the chance for revenge on the opposition and for gaining an absolute majority in the Parliament of the Republic and in the local Soviets. Former First Secretary of the Communist Party of Azerbaijan, Geydar Aliyev, was elected to the Supreme Soviet of his native Nakhichevan ASSR by an over-whelming majority of voters and became a real banner of the restoration process. In Nagorno-Karabakh, power remained in the hands of the military, who kept everyday life under strict control, thereby causing growing anger among local Armenians. In Armenia itself, the attempt to preserve power in the hands of the old guard failed after a dramatic political fight. The results of the elections to the Supreme Soviet of the Republic showed the growing unpopularity of the local Communist party leaders, who lost their majority in the Parliament. Thus the current political leadership of the Soviet Union failed to receive support in both republics, losing out to the conservative forces in Azerbaijan and to the non-communist movement in Armenia.

8.   POSSIBLE PATHS OF RESOLUTION

•   Presidential Rule should be established in both Republics. Although this may seem anti-democratic, it is difficult to calm both sides in any other way. Of course the Union parliament must guarantee the restoration of democratic institutions after the success of the regulation process.

•   The Committee appointed by the President must control the borders of the Republics in order to stop all terrorist actions.

•   Immediate measures must be undertaken to lift the railway blockade of Armenia and Georgia.

•   Because the mass media in both republics have been violat-ing the laws of the country and publishing inflammatory propa-ganda materials, insulting national feelings on the other side, the legal organs must apply existing laws to stop the propa-ganda war between the Republics.

•   Strong support is needed on the part of military units in both republics to stop acts of genocide in Azerbaijan and deport-ations in both republics. These units, not effective up until now, must be re-formed on a professional basis.

•   The leaders of different political parties and tendencies, including the Communist Party hierarchy, Popular Front leaders, religious leaders and other representatives from both sides, must be attracted to seek resolution of the conflict.

• Acts of genocide must receive humanitarian, political, and juridical condemnation on the basis of international and Soviet law. Perpetrators should be punished according to these laws.

• Both republics must return all deported population and guarantee their security, as well as compensate all those who prefer not to return for their material losses.

• Broad economic measures should be undertaken to enable progress in the social and economic development of the entire region of Armenia and Azerbaijan. Of course the results of any new measures will be highly dependent on the success of shifting the Union as a whole to a 'market economy'.

• The history of inter-republic relations must be presented free of ideological stereotypes, such as 'Revolutionary Turkey', 'Revolutionary Azerbaijan', 'Imperialistic Armenia', and so on.

• Historically the Russian Federation was the side that created the problem in the Eastern Caucasus. And now it must be the side to take an initiative towards solving the problem.

REFERENCES

Arutunyan, V.B., 'Sobitiya v Nagornom Karabakhe', *Khronika, Chast 1*, February 1988 – January 1989, Institute of History, Academy of Sciences of Armenian SSR, Yerevan, 1990.

Barsegov, Y. G., 1989. Pravo na samoopredeleniye – osnova demokraticheskogo resheniya mejnatsionalnih problem: k probleme Nagornogo Karabakha, Ayastan, Yerevan, p. 88.

'Genotsid Armyan v Osmanskoi Imperii', 1983. *Sbornik dokumentov i materialov.* (Ed. Nersisyan), Ayastan, Yerevan, 2nd ed.

Glazami nezaviaimih nablyudateley: Nagorny Karabakh i vokrug nego ..., 1990. (Sbornik materialov.) Sostavitely: S.T.Zolyan, G.K. Mirzo-yan. Yerevan State University Publishing House.

Hushudyan, L.A., 1989. Istina – yedinstvennii kriterii istoricheskoi nauki, (Prichini i tseli novogo etapa antiarmyanskoi, kampanii, razvernuvsheysya v Azerbaijane v svyazi s problemoi Nagornogo Karabakha.), Yerevan State University Publishing House.

In: Mkrtchan, Shagen, 1988. 'Istoriko-arkhitekturnie pamyatniki Nagornogo Karabakha', *Vtoroie izdaniie, Parberaken Yerevan.*

'Sobitiya vokrug NKAO v krivom zerkale falsifikatorov', 1989. *Sbornik materialov*, Academy of Sciences of Azerbaijanian SSR, Elm, Baku.

'Sumgait...Genotsid...Glasnost?', *Znaniye*, Armenian SSR, Yerevan, 1990, p. 11.

'Tragedia dlinnou v 2 goda', *Fotokhronika sobitii*, Azernesh, Baku, 1990.

Yakubova, M.(1990). 'Stiraya "beliye pyatna", Literaturny Azerbaijan. (Baku). no. 3.

8

Inter-Ethnic Conflict in the Trans-caucasus: A Case Study of Nagorno-Karabakh

Anatoly Yamskov

1. INTRODUCTION

This chapter reviews the economic, social, historical-cultural and political factors contributing to inter-ethnic conflicts in the Transcaucasus. Specific analysis of the present situation is a task for a separate study – which in today's rapidly changing situation, could become obsolete within months or even weeks. I shall therefore focus on identifying trends in the development of the conflicts and underlying causal factors. Some of the latter have already had their effects, while others continue to play a role or are likely to influence future development in the region. The Karabakh crisis is the most acute and complex of the Trans-caucasus conflicts, and was therefore selected to illustrate the conclusions proposed by the author.[1] Many aspects of this conflict have close analogues in other arenas of conflict in the USSR as well.

Inter-ethnic conflicts reflect the contradictory interests and aspirations of different ethnic groups, and have been accompanied by the formation of national movements seeking to defend these interests. National movements are almost always heterogeneous: within their ranks or affiliated with them there may be extremist groups who consciously employ or provoke 'spontaneous' violent actions; however, most participants in the Transcaucasus ethnic movements have striven to employ legal methods.

2. FOUR TYPES OF INTER-ETHNIC CONFLICT

We can distinguish between four types of inter-ethnic conflicts in the Transcaucasus on the basis of the goals which the protagonists put forward:

1) National-social conflicts, arising from movements demanding change in the existing socio-economic status of particular ethnic groups. These movements are often directed against ethnic groups which consititute a minority within the given territory.

2) National-cultural conflicts, arising from demands for the protection and restoration of a native language and ethnic culture. National movements of this type are generally directed against higher (republic-level) governmental organizations and, to some extent, against the dominant ethnic group within a republic.

3) Mass-based inter-ethnic conflicts resulting from demands for the revision (or preservation) of existing territorial boundaries and national state structures. Such movements are directed against opposing national movements, government organizations and the peoples of neighbouring union or autonomous republics.

4) National-political conflicts, arising from demands for total independence and secession from the USSR. National movements in this case are directed against the central (all-union) government and, to some extent, against the Russian people, with whom the central government is generally identified.

This four-part typology can be usefully applied to the situation in the Transcaucasus in the autumn of 1990 and later. Whereas the situation in Georgia most closely approximates a type 4 conflict situation, type 3 is clearly represented by the Armenian-Azerbaijani, Ossetian-Georgian, and Abkhazian-Georgian conflicts.

The various inter-ethnic conflicts within Georgia – in the southeast (Azerbaijani-Georgian) and the south (Armenian-Georgian) – can be regarded as type 2 at present; but any of them could potentially spill over into more dangerous conflicts of type 3. Type 2 conflict situations are also developing in central Georgia (Greco-Georgian), as well as in Azerbaijan – in the south (Talysh-Azerbaijani) and in the north (Tat-Azerbaijan and

Lezghin-Azerbaijan). However, due to the similarity of the cultures and religions of the peoples involved, excesses will be less likely to occur in these cases.

Type 1 conflict situations have not been particularly notable in the Transcaucasus, due to the abundance and acuteness of more serious conflicts. They have, however, characterized the relationships between Azerbaijanis and Armenians in the towns and rural areas of Azerbaijan (outside of Nagorno-Karabakh). This type of conflict has also been found in areas of Russian rural settlement in the Transcaucasus. Russians, unwilling to accept the preferential appointment of members of native nationalities to leadership posts and to prestigious and well-paid positions as specialists in agriculture, trade, public health, education, etc., are departing for Russia with increasing frequency. The situation becomes further aggravated once those Russians who remain find themselves in an absolute minority.

The types of inter-ethnic conflicts proposed here are essentially models which in practice do not exist in pure forms: in real world conflicts we see a close interweaving of the major features of these models. Nevertheless, the further development and refinement of such models can be useful in improving our methods of studying and predicting inter-ethnic relations. Events in the Transcaucasus demonstrate that, when large ethnic groups are involved, conflict situations of type 1 or 2 tend to intensify and acquire the characteristics of type 3 or even type 4. The Karabakh crisis can serve as an example: originally it was localized within Nagorno-Karabakh and represented an intermingling of features of conflict types 1 and 2. Once the conflict drew into its orbit the entire population of Armenia and Azerbaijan, however, it took on characteristics of type 3, and even began to gravitate towards a type 4 conflict.

3. MAJOR CAUSES OF CONFLICT

Analysis of the causes of the Karabakh conflict is the main task of this chapter. Out of the entire tangle of problems and contradictions which led to this conflict we can distinguish these major causes: economic, social, historical-cultural and political.

Economic causes include the real regional and, correspondingly, ethnic differences in the standard of living of the population. For example, according to statistics published in the newspaper *Bakinsky rabochii* (2 March 1988), an Armenian in Nagorno-Karabakh lives on average better than the general population of Azerbaijan. In Nagorno-Karabakh there are 26.3 registered motor vehicles per thousand people (in the republic as a whole – 17.5). In the rural areas of Karabakh, ordinary every-day domestic services were valued at 41.2 rubles per person per year (for the entire republic – 16.7 rubles); housing allotments in rural areas – 14.6 m^2 per person (for the entire republic – 9.2 m^2), etc. However, in Armenia the standard of living is significantly higher than in Azerbaijan, and also exceeds the standard of living in Nagorno-Karabakh. We may here note that infant mortality in Armenia is 23.6 per thousand (in Azerbaijan – 30.5 per thousand); consumer goods production stands at 1190 rubles per person per year (in Azerbaijan – 635 rubles), and commodity circulation in the rural areas per person was 405 rubles per year (in Azerbaijan – 278 rubles).

Knowing that the people live better in neighbouring Armenia, the Armenians of Nagorno-Karabakh tend to see their lower standard of living as a result of the policies of the republic government of Azerbaijan, which controls the development of the economy in the *oblast*. (Actually, the standard of living in the neighbouring mountainous areas of Azerbaijan is even lower than in Nagorno-Karabakh.) This dissatisfaction played an important role in the first stage of the conflict, although even then it was inflated out of proportion in the mass media and in the slogans of the Armenian Karabakh movement. The high-lighting of economic demands, as being the most readily under-standable for an initially politically passive population, was entirely predictable. Subsequently, as the inter-ethnic conflict intensified, the significance of such demands has decreased.

Similar economic causes can be seen operating in the Armenian districts of southern Georgia. These districts are less well supplied than the surrounding Georgian districts, and the Armenian people in these areas clearly have a lower standard of living than those in neighbouring Armenia.
These causes of inter-ethnic conflict could be eliminated by making national-territorial associations self-supporting.

As to *social causes* of conflict, two will be considered here. First, the established practice of designating managing cadre and leading specialists in the areas of production, trade, security organs, public health, etc. only 'from the top down', by the higher organizations in the republic, is a primary source of inter-ethnic conflict. This practice has meant that in areas populated by ethnic minorities leading posts are occupied primarily by members of the republic's dominant nationality. Under such conditions, any incompetence or corruption among leaders will be viewed by the population through the prism of inter-ethnic relations, which fundamentally exacerbates the situation. This was the situation in Nagorno-Karabakh, and it remains the case in the ethnic minority districts and particularly in the rural soviets of Georgia, Armenia and Azerbaijan. This cause can be eliminated by increasing the independence of production teams and the territorial self-government of the population, and also by expanding the training of managers from ethnic minority groups.

Secondly, a particularly important role in the formation of conflict situations has been played by the voluntary ethnic migrations of the 1950s-1980s. This involves not only the arrival of migrants of a nationality different from that of the local residents, but also uneven rates of emigration by various ethnic groups to the cities from agricultural districts with historically mixed ethnic compositions. When the traditional and accepted balance between ethnic groups then begins to change radically, the nationality which is threatened with the loss of its previously dominant position may initiate inter-ethnic conflict.

The Karabakh case presents a classic example of these processes. During the period 1959-1979 in practically all the districts of Nagorno-Karabakh, as well as in the neighbouring districts of Azerbaijan and Armenia which historically had a mixed Armenian-Azerbaijan population, the rural Azerbaijani population increased greatly, while the Armenian population remained constant or even fell. Large numbers of Armenians migrated to the city, while virtually no Azerbaijanis left the rural areas. Also, the Azerbaijanis have a higher overall rate of natural population growth, which also tends to increase their share in the population. This process was augmented by an influx of Azerbaijanis from neighbouring mountainous districts with high underemployment, who arrived to take the jobs formerly held by the now departed Armenians.

In the case of Nagorno-Karabakh, the size and share of Armenians in the total population decreased from 124,100 persons (94%) to 123,000 persons (76%) between 1921 and 1979, while the Azerbaijani population in the same period increased from 7,400 persons (6%) to 37,000 persons (23%). And between 1979 and 1987 the Azerbaijani population of Nagorno-Karabakh increased to 44,000 persons (24.5%), while the Armenian population increased to 133,000 persons (74%).

Likewise, in southeastern Georgia the number and share of Azerbaijanis in the local population has been constantly increasing. An additional source of conflict has been the arrival of Azerbaijanis experienced in animal husbandry to work on sheep farms in the wake of the migration of the local Georgian population away from their villages and rural districts to the cities. Meanwhile the Abkhazian-Georgian conflict in northwest Georgia was being exacerbated by the influx of Georgians into Abkhazia, a trend particularly strong during the late 1940s and the 1950s. This cause of inter-ethnic conflict can be relieved, in part at least, by giving local soviets the right of effective control over the development of their local economies. This would enable them to regulate indirectly the migration of populations, by creating or eliminating jobs.

Historical-cultural causes are extremely varied. First of all, inter-ethnic conflicts have in many cases been aggravated by ancient and fundamental differences in religion and world outlook among the principal peoples of the Transcaucasus – primarily between Christians (Armenians, Georgians) and Moslems (Azerbaijanis, Abkhazians, etc.). We must also note the varying degree of accommodation to modern urban culture, lifestyle and living standards – Armenians and Georgians are more Europeanized; Azerbaijanis less so. Thus, in values and behavioural patterns, many Armenians and Azerbaijanis differ even more strongly today than their ancestors did a century ago, inasmuch as they then belonged to traditional peasant societies with similar orientations toward life. The cultural-historical opposition between Azerbaijanis and the settled Christian peoples of the Transcaucasus is also aggravated by the circumstance that significant numbers of Azerbaijanis pursued a semi-nomadic existence right up to the 1920s.

Secondly, the entire history of the peoples of the Transcaucasus is filled with internecine warfare. An important component of the ethnogenesis of the Azerbaijanis was the nomadic Turks, whose destructive assaults against the settled peoples of the region have been and continue to be the subject of great deal of highly emotional writing by Armenian and Georgian popular historians and novelists. Today, in a situation of rapidly increasing national self-consciousness and growing attention to history, the victories and tragedies of past centuries have become the focus of discussion by broad masses of the people.

Thirdly, and perhaps most importantly, the repeated past migrations of the settled peoples and the regular seasonal wanderings of Turkish herdsmen have resulted in highly contradictory and confused conceptions as to what are the 'homelands' and ethnic territories of the populations of the Transcaucasus. During the first half of the 19th century, when most of the region became a part of Russia, it was characterized not by ethnically homogeneous states with ancient and stable frontiers, but rather by feudal/vassal states with unstable borders and ethnically mixed populations. Thus, in the centre and east of Georgia there were already numerous settlements of Ossetians, Armenians and nomadic Azerbaijanis, while in Southern Abkhazia there were settlements of Georgians. In the Moslem (Azerbaijani) khanates within the territory of present-day Armenia and in most of Azerbaijan (including the Karabakh Khanate) Armenians, Azerbaijanis, Tats and others lived in alternating settlements. After the area became incorporated into Russia, the massive migrations of the l9th century complicated the picture still further: Armenians migrating from Persia and Turkey mainly occupied the territory of today's Armenia, but they also settled in many districts of Azerbaijan, somewhat enlarged the Armenian population of Karabakh, settled in Southern Georgia and spread into Abkhazia. During this period Greeks settled in Georgia and Abkhazia, while Georgians continued to move into Abkhazia, and Russians settled in Eastern Georgia, Armenia and Azerbaijan. Indeed, by the beginning of the 20th century, the Russian population represented 10% or more of the total in some rural districts.

In the light of the Karabakh crisis, the historical dispersion of the Azerbaijanis is worthy of particular attention. In 1830 their ancestors, primarily Moslem 'Turks', comprised half the population of the 'Armenian *oblast*', the territory of the former Erevan and Nakhichevan Khanates (i.e., almost all of present-day Armenia and the Nakhichevan Autonomous Republic of Azerbaijan). In 1845 'Turk' nomads (Azerbaijanis) were twice as numerous as Armenians in the territory of the former Karabakh Khanate. Even after the separation of the mountainous districts populated by Armenians from this historical territory in the early 1920s and the formation of the Nagorno-Karabakh Autonomous Region, Azerbaijanis from the adjacent plains of the Karabakh steppe continued their summer migrations into the mountains, including those within Nagorno-Karabakh. (In the late 1890s, only about one thirtieth of the Azerbaijanis remained on the plains during the summer season.) The present-day population of the Azerbaijanian plains districts adjacent to Nagorno-Karabakh consists of the descendants of these semi-nomadic people who first settled there in the early 1930s. Even today, old residents can clearly remember their camps in the mountains. Therefore they, their children and grandchildren consider the land of Nagorno-Karabakh to be Azerbaijani.

Such historical sources of conflict cannot of course be eliminated. However, some reduction of cultural difference is probable in the future if the peoples of the Transcaucasus continue to acquire industrial world cultural traditions and the behavioral standards typical of urbanized society.

Political causes affecting the development of these conflicts are also widely varied. Some of them arose during the first years of Soviet power, when the borders of the union and autonomous republics and regions of the Transcaucasus were established through compromises between the competing claims of the local ethnoses and with an eye to established economic inter-connections. Due to the historical peculiarities attending the dispersal of the various peoples throughout the region, it proved impossible to prevent significant masses of the population from being transformed into ethnic minorities, particularly in districts near the borders. The decision to include Nagorno-Karabakh, populated by Armenians, within Azerbaijan was based on economic requirements: this territory, separated from Armenia by a mountain range, was economically and socially linked with the central districts of Azerbaijan and the city of Baku. This decision also took into consideration prospects for the future development of herding in this area of the republic. However, with the recent stormy growth of national self-consciousness and political activity among the population, the priority previously accorded to economic criteria in the determination of national and state demarcations has been brought into question.

Between 1930 and 1970, official policy involved utterly rejecting the essential elements of national-cultural autonomy, as well as the frequent implementation of practices which infringed on the rights of national minorities to develop their own native languages and cultures and communicate freely with the principal body of their peoples living in neighbouring republics. Under the slogan of the victory of the idea of 'internationalism', this policy actually prepared the soil for today's inter-ethnic conflicts. This is clearly seen in the case of Nagorno-Karabakh.

The political causes that aggravate inter-ethnic conflicts have continued to operate even in the most recent period. For one thing, democratization and *glasnost* have not only permitted the open discussion of conflict situations and the search for mutually acceptable solutions: they have also provided the possibility for the dissemination of extremely nationalistic (frequently even chauvinistic) propaganda and the tendentious selection of historical facts. Unfortunately, in this regard the national intelligentsia has played an essentially negative role. Secondly, the initial attempts of the central and local official media to hush up reports of the activities of national movements, or to distort their goals and discredit their participants, aroused the indignation of the local population, thereby strengthening the position of extremist forces within these movements and further aggravating the situation. Over the past year or two, the serious deterioration of the economic situation throughout the country, coupled with the passivity of the central and republic governments in the resolution of inter-ethnic conflicts, has caused a decline in the authority of all government. In consequence, a significant portion of the population of the Transcaucasus now sees in the national movements and their leaders the only political force capable of exercising power effectively in the republics.

4. THE WAY AHEAD

The total elimination of inter-ethnic conflicts in the Transcaucasus within the next few years seems practically impossible. In the future, the normalization of inter-ethnic relations throughout the region, and particularly in Nagorno-Karabakh, seems possible only within the framework of a government based on the rule of law and with popular acceptance of the right of every territorial population group (including national minorities in areas of compact settlement) to self-government and self-determination concerning national-state affiliation.

The present trend is towards increasing sovereignty and autonomy for the union republics of the Transcaucasus. Given the abundant contradictions between ethnic and republic boundaries in the region, success for this trend will preserve numerous sources of inter-ethnic conflict well into the future. Further, the more the idea of republic sovereignty – and the related concept of the inviolability of republic boundaries – enters into popular consciousness in the Transcaucasus and is reflected in legislation, the greater the danger that inter-ethnic conflicts will develop into inter-republican ones. The Azerbaijani economic blockades of Armenia and Nagorno-Karabakh – and armed border clashes involving loss of life – mean that an important step has already been taken in this unfortunate direction.

NOTE:

1. The sources of the factual data on which this study is based, and a more detailed presentation of the author's conclusions concerning the causes of the conflict in Nagorno-Karabakh, with an analysis of its population dynamics, ethnic composition and living standards, can be found in Yamskov (1990). The author has also relied heavily on personal impressions, since during 1983-1990 he spent nearly one year in Georgia (including Abkhazia), Armenia and Azerbaijan (including Nagorno-Karabakh and Nakhichevan), doing ethnographic field research in rural settlements.

REFERENCE

Yamskov, A., 1990. 'Nagorno-Karabakh: an analysis of the causes and proposed methods for resolution of an inter-ethnic conflict', in *National Processes in the USSR: Problems and Tendencies*, Moscow: Nauka.

9

Internal Conflicts in Soviet Central Asia: Causes and Consequences

Abdulaziz Kamilov

In recent years a number of internal conflicts have broken out in different parts of Soviet Central Asia, each with its own historical, socio-economic, religious and national origins. These conflicts have not only seriously destabilized the situation in the Central Asian region, they have also increased socio-political tension in the country as a whole.

The contradictions that generate conflicts usually exist at three levels: inside each of the republics; between the republics – subjects of the Soviet federation, and between the republics and the Centre, where the existing federal form fails to meet not only the interests of the republics but those of the Centre as well. This chapter will focus mainly on the causes and consequences of conflicts that have emerged inside the separate republics.

Underlying and aggravating all the present conflicts in the Soviet Union are the consequences of trying to solve inter-ethnic disputes by administrative-command methods. A dangerous tendency is becoming evident: with the growth of hotbeds of tension and an increase in the number of participants in inter-ethnic conflicts, violence and terror are being invoked more often as a method of resolving disputes.

Typical of the recent conflicts in the Central Asian region has been that hotbeds of tension appeared on the basis of contradictions between the indigenous population and other ethnic groups who have settled there. As an example we can cite Kazakhstan, December 1986: in protest against new appointments to the leadership of the republic, a group of inhabitants organized meetings in the capital, Alma-Ata. These meetings erupted into mass disturbance in which hooligans also took part. For the first time since *perestroika* began, a confrontation between the indigenous population and immigrant groups led to heavy casualties. Also in Central Asia, clashes took place in Novi-Uzen in late June 1989 between Kazakhs and people from the Transcaucasus, replicating skirmishes in Uzbekistan.

The nations of Central Asia have in common many religious and cultural features as a result of their common historical destiny and their great ethnic similarity. Almost all Uzbeks, Kazakhs, Turkmen, Tajiks and Kirghiz profess the Sunni Islam faith. Today representatives of more than 100 nationalities reside in Soviet Central Asia (see Tables 1 and 2.) Many of them originate from other parts of the Soviet Union, such as Russians, Ukrainians, Jews, Meskhetian Turks, Volga Germans and Crimean Tatars; while others have their roots in other countries, such as Greeks, Koreans, Arabs, Persians, Uigurs and Dungans, who are Chinese by birth. They have settled in this region for diverse reasons: for instance most Russians arrived after Turkestan became part of Russia in 1880, while Volga Germans, Crimean Tatars and Meskhetians were deported to the area from their native regions in 1940 on orders from Stalin, who saw them as potential enemies ready to fight against Soviet power. There are national minorities in almost all Central Asian republics. In most cases they are concentrated in one location, forming a kind of enclave both in the big cities and the rural areas. This is typical of the Crimean Tatars, Koreans, Meskhetian Turks and Greeks.

Russians and Ukrainians, however, are not concentrated in distinct regions. As for the Crimean Tatars and others, their desire to live in enclaves can be explained not only by their wish to preserve their cultures, language and communities, but also by the needs of collective defence.

Since the Revolution, the population of Soviet Central Asia has increased from 7 to almost 40 million; by the year 2000 the figure is expected to pass the 50 million mark. This creates an extremely complex demographic situation.

Table 1: *National Composition of the Population in the Central Asia Republics (1979 census data, in thousands)*

Uzbekistan (15,389)

Uzbeks 10,569 (68.7%)	Tajiks 595	Turks 49
Russians 1,666 (10.8%)	Koreans 163	Armenians 42
Karakalpaks 298	Kirghizes 142	Germans 40
Tatars 649	Ukrainians 114	Uigurs 29
Kazakhs 620	Jews 100	Bashkirs 26

Kazakhstan (14,684)

Kazakhs 5,289 (36.0%)	Belorussians 181	Greeks 50
Russians 5,991 (40.8%)	Uigurs 148	Bashkirs 32
Germans 900	Koreans 92	Mordvinians 31
Ukrainians 898	Azerbaijanis 73	Moldavians 30
Tatars 313	Poles 61	Turks 26
Uzbeks 263		

Kirghizia (3,523)

Kirghiz 1,687 (47.8%)	Tatars 72	Azerbaijanis 17
Russians 912 (25.9%)	Uigurs 30	Koreans 14
Uzbeks 426 (12.1%)	Kazakhs 27	Kurds 9
Ukrainians 109	Dungans 27	
Germans 101	Tajiks 23	

Tajikistan (3,806)

Tajiks 2,237 (58.8%)	Kirghiz 48	Turkmen 14
Uzbeks 873 (22.9%)	Germans 39	Koreans 11
Russians 395 (10.4%)	Ukrainians 36	Kazakhs 10
Tatars 80	Jews 15	Ossetians 8

Turkmenistan (2,765)

Turkmen 1,892 (68.4%)	Tatars 40	Belujes 19
Russians 349 (12.6%)	Ukrainians 37	Lezgines 8
Uzbeks 234	Armenians 27	Belorussians 5
Kazakhs 80	Azerbaijanis 24	Persians 5

Source: *Brook*, 1986.

Overpopulation in rural areas is aggravated by a low rate of outflow to towns. In planning the socio-economic development of the region, demographic problems were not sufficiently heeded, while the research work of foreign authors was sharply criticized and not taken into account.[1]

The overwhelming majority of the population of the region are rural dwellers. Moreover, it is in the agricultural areas that the greatest part of the population who are not engaged in labour is concentrated. To indicate the acuteness of the problem for Central Asian republics it is enough to mention the example given in the USSR Supreme Soviet in May 1990: out of six million unemployed in the country, one million resided in the territory of Uzbekistan. Most of the unemployed, euphemistically called 'redundant man-power' in the past, are young people. In the course of the last decade, the population in Uzbekistan has grown by seven million; and today, in every fourth family in the countryside, there are five or more children under the age of 18 (*Izvestia*, 17 June 1989).

Looking at the geography of recent conflicts in Ferghana, Kokand, Andizhan and Osh, we may note that they all broke out in the Ferghana Valley, which is situated on the territory of Uzbekistan, Kirghizia and Tajikistan. This is a very densely populated region where an average family of five has at most only one hectare of irrigated land, and, for much of the valley, even less – 0.3 hectares. In Osh, Kirghizia, a conflict occurred in June 1990 between the indigenous population and Uzbeks, sparked off by a decision of the local authorities to allocate plots of land only to native inhabitants. Within a few days, mass disturbances spread to a number of other towns. Participants at a meeting held in the Kirghiz capital, Frunze (now Bishkek), demanded the resignation of the leadership of the republic. In the ensuing clashes, more than a hundred people were killed and several hundred were wounded. There were at least five hundred acts of arson. A state of emergency was imposed in many areas.

The conflicts were inter-ethnic, but their roots went even deeper. Some analysts have seen the strained relations between Kirghiz and Uzbek communities in Osh as a classical Central Asian conflict. In the 19th century in the khanates of Kokand and Khiva there were over 20 such bloody inter-ethnic conflicts, usually ignited by claims concerning land, water and pasture. Local people lead a beggarly existence: in view of the high rate of unemployment, it is not hard to understand that people are seething with passion. A tiny spark is enough to set off a conflagration, as happened in Osh. 'It is sad and tragic that conflicts are settled with classical methods inherited from the Kokand and Khiva khanates: open confrontation with arson, pogroms and murders', as the Central Asia analyst, T. Pulatov, observed in June 1990 (*Moscow News*, No. 26, 1990).

Present-day Uzbekistan comprises twelve *oblasti* (regions). One of them is Andizhan, where disturbances took place in May 1990, during which nationalistic slogans were advanced, although they did not become the principal driving force. In this oblast unemployment amounts to 150,000 people, which is equal to the rate of unemployment in East Germany (*Pravda*, 3 May 1990). The high birth rate is accompanied by inadequate development of the agricultural economy. For example, in 1984, one state farm in Tajikistan had a population of 20,000 people, of whom 9,000 were capable of working – but only 650 work-places were available (Polykov, 1989, p. 32). Traditionalism influences the high birthrate: young people are expected to marry once they come of age; pregnancies are not to be inter-rupted; families are encouraged to have many children, and so on. But the high birthrate is not the sole reason for the pressing social problems that Central Asian society faces today; the economy also seems to be directly connected with the outbreak of conflicts. First of all, economic development has been dis-proportional. Under Soviet rule, Central Asia became a big producer of cotton in order to make the country independent of imports from abroad. Cotton soon became a monopoly crop which determined the entire economic policy of the region. As a result, the number of people now living below the poverty line amounts to 60% of the population in Tajikistan, 46% in Uzbekistan and 40% in Kirghizia and Turkmenistan (*Moscow News*, no. 19, 1990).

Moreover, the territories of all the Soviet cotton–growing republics are to a considerable extent poisoned by chemical weed and pest-killers. The water resources are exhausted, and the Aral Sea has nearly dried up, producing an ecological cata-strophe extending far beyond the region.

Table 2: Distribution of Nationalities in the Central Asian Republics (according to 1979 census, in thousands)

	Uzbekistan	Kazakhstan	Tajikistan	Turkmenistan	Kirghizia
Uzbeks	10,569	263	873	234	426
Kazakhs	620	5,286	9,6	80	27
Tajiks	595	-	2,237	-	23
Turkmen	92	-	14	1,892	-
Kirghiz	142	-	48	-	1,687

Source: *Brook*, 1986.

As *Pravda* wrote on 3 May 1990: 'departments have been extorting raw materials and continue to do it now'. In Uzbekistan, the major cotton-growing republic, only 10% of the raw cotton is processed at local enterprises, and 75% of the population do not have an opportunity to make use of the natural gas extracted there, as it is sold to France and Germany. The Central Asian republics have the highest death rate for children in the whole country, and infant mortality in Turkmenistan is twice the USSR average. The situation is worse only in the Philippines, Nigeria, Angola and Chad. In 1988, 53 children aged less than one year of age died per thousand in Turkmenia – corresponding figures for the USA and Japan are 10 and 5. These are a few examples which demonstrate the way the monopoly crop has developed into a principal source of social misfortune for the region.

The mechanization of agriculture has made redundant a great number of agricultural workers. This has also led to a considerable growth of small-scale commodity production, involving a great number of people. In its turn, such small–scale commodity production has paved the way for conservative movements and greater traditionalism. This may explain why, during the mass disturbances in Fergana, Dushanbe and Andizhan, some groups fought against the Soviet authorities under the slogans of Islam.

At the present stage of historical development in the Central Asian region, Islam as a form of social consciousness cannot serve as a supranational ideology; nor is there any serious role for this religion in inter-ethnic affairs. The trend of social development has now entered a phase of formation of nations who search for their own place in the world community. That is why internal conflicts today tend to assume a national rather than a religious character. Certain minor Islamic forces in their struggle for power are trying to kindle flames of conflict and foment hatred between ethnic groups. Also according to local sources in Uzbekistan, a new underground 'Islamic Party', which calls for a federation of Islamic Central Asian republics independent of Moscow, is spreading rapidly through the region. The Western press reports that 'rumours are rampant of arms from Afghanistan being collected in the Fergana basin' (*The Independent*, 6 June 1990). Small, fundamentalist Islamic groupings, as yet without much influence on public opinion, have also sought to form a union of all Turkic-speaking people in

Central Asia. They also call for the establishment of Islamic order in social life. However, such calls ignore the interests of some millions of non-Islamic people in the region, thereby provoking further inter-ethnic conflicts.

In February 1990, a demonstration occurred in Dushanbe against the migration of Armenian refugees to Tajikistan. This deteriorated rapidly into mass disturbances, causing heavy casualties and an attempt to seize power. According to official reports, this attempt was led by a group of high–ranking officials who used the support of 'Islamic fighters' (*Pravda*, 10 May 1990). On the other hand, we should not overestimate the influence of Islam on socio-political processes in the region, or ignore secular tendencies. The changing attitude of the state to religion in the USSR today, including Islam, can play a positive role in preventing social conflicts. In response to the action of the state aimed at guaranteeing real freedom of religion, spiritual leaders of the Central Asian region have become actively engaged in stabilizing relations between different ethnic groups. The Chairman of the Religious Board of Moslems of Soviet Central Asia and Kazakhstan has appealed repeatedly to the ethnic communities to put an end to their fratricidal clashes. Other Moslem leaders did the same during the ethnic unrest in Dushanbe and Osh. They usually base their appeals on the *suras* of the Koran, which ban violence against any human being. At present the mufti of Central Asia appears every week on TV with a sermon.

With *perestroika*, the state has shown a greater understanding of religion, and this has contributed to expanded contacts between administrative authorities and religious institutions. Coordination of measures between the two promotes the relaxation of inter-ethnic tension based on religious differences. The state is helping the Moslems of Central Asia to develop normal international relations with the Islamic world and with regional Islamic organizations. In 1990 many Moslems from the republics of Soviet Asia made pilgrimages to Saudi Arabia. In accordance with special decrees of Soviet President, M. Gorbachev, and the President of Uzbekistan, I. Karimov, all necessary assistance has been provided to pilgrims – special airliners to Saudi Arabia, free medical services and so on.

Cooperation between Christian and Moslem leaders also plays a positive role in the social life of the Asian republics. As an example of joint efforts aimed at consolidating the two main confessional groups in Uzbekistan we may note that the leader of the Christian church campaigned on behalf of the chairman of the Religious Board of Moslems of Soviet Central Asia when he was nominated as a candidate for the Soviet parliament. Having recourse to Islamic religious leaders to solve inter-ethnic problems is a new phenomenon in the social and political life of this region.

An important feature of Central Asia's conflicts is the coincidence of social stratification with national divisions. The local population in the rural regions is mainly employed in small private business; whereas large-scale industrial production in the republics of Soviet Central Asia is based on a labour force brought in from outside – an immigrant population. Large industrial enterprises requiring highly qualified labour tend to recruit people from the European part of the USSR, mainly ethnic Russians. As a result of complex social problems, the local population is very jealous of outsiders, who are granted priority in housing. Workers from outside the region arrive at a time when there is already overpopulation and a housing shortage – whereas in some regions of the Russian Federation many villages are deserted. This provokes a negative attitude on the part of traditional nationalists towards policies of the central authorities.

Inter-ethnic confrontation is exacerbated by the social stratification at work not only in the various branches of the economy but also in the towns and the countryside. In Uzbekistan during June 1989, clashes between Uzbeks and Meskhetian Turks occurred in Fergana and Kokand, involving knives and small arms. Many people were wounded and killed, and hostages were taken. Nor was the damage limited to Meskhet houses: administrative buildings belonging to the local authorities were set on fire and destroyed. Serious refugee problem emerged as a result of this conflict.

It is true that the Meskhetians occupied a more stable economic position than the local population, and enjoyed a higher standard of living. This can be explained by the fact that the Meskhetians tend to be more enterprising than the local population, and, in the areas where they concentrate, have often managed to monopolize small trade and the distribution of consumer goods. Meskhetian families are also not as large as Uzbek families. The local population blames these disparities on the Meskhetians as a group. Now, searching for the guilty among one's neighbours when there is a socio-economic crisis is nothing new. In the 1970s Shiite Moslems in Southern Lebanon came out against the presence of the Palestinian refugees, holding that they were to blame for all the misfortunes of the Shiite community. But the Central Asian conflicts have many causes. In Fergana, at the beginning of *perestroika*, the Meskhetians launched a campaign for their return to the motherland in Georgia, from where they had been violently deported. Some observers believe that the leaders of this movement resorted to force and ethnic provocations in order to attract the government's attention to the necessity of solving their problem as soon as possible.

Recent events in the southern republics of the USSR testify to the fact that ethnic problems appear as a result not only of a clash of interests between different communities within separate republics, but also of relationships at a higher level, in particular among and between republics and the central government. Some clashes have been territorial, such as those arising from the claims of some groups in Tajikistan to the Uzbek cities of Samarkand and Bukhara, or the border conflicts between Kazakhstan and Uzbekistan, or disputes over water resources among the various republics. These conflicts may be exacerbated by ecological problems. The massive project proposed to divert Siberian rivers to save the Aral Sea was widely criticized by Russian ecologists and writers and has now been dropped. But in Central Asia this development is seen as evidence of Russian unwillingness to help the Central Asian republics in tackling the serious problems facing them.[2]

Over the years a great potential for inter-ethnic confrontation has accumulated in Soviet Central Asia. In this connection two important questions may be raised: Which new or old conflicts could become violent, and how can this be prevented?

First of all, separatist movements, if widely promoted, may induce the threat of new inter-ethnic conflicts in Central Asia. The situation elsewhere in the USSR shows that separatism is always accompanied by the aggravation of nationalistic passions and encouragement of extremist demands.

During the national-territorial demarcation of the 1920s, the Central Asian region was carved up in such a way that conflicting territorial claims among different ethnic groups now prove a dangerous source of inter-ethnic tension. In the light of the demographic upsurge in Central Asia – which seems unlikely to subside even in the first decade of the next millennium –

there exists a real prospect of worsening inter—ethnic conflicts in such densely populated regions as the Fergana valley.

Inter-ethnic conflict in one region may have serious consequences for other regions as well. For example, social tensions in the Crimean area of the Krasnodar territory in Russia became aggravated as a result of the mass immigration of Meskhetians in the wake of ethnic clashes in Fergana. More than 10,000 refugees came there on their own initiative, but only 400 of them could find jobs. At the same time, local crime increased by 29%. This set the stage for possible inter-ethnic conflicts between locals and Meskhetians refugees. Indeed, in recent years the problem of refugees has become a serious potential source of inter-ethnic conflicts throughout the Soviet Union.

How, then, can new conflicts be prevented? Let us consider the viewpoint of two experts on Central Asian problems – analyst T. Pulatov, and Executive Secretary of Turkmenia's magazine *Siasi Sokhbetdesh*, M. Salamatov. Pulatov believes that tension can be relaxed through the market economy when land is no longer the property of the 'partocracy', an object of bargaining or a gift to those of a specific clan or nationality. M. Salamatov also expresses confidence in the ability of the market economy to help Central Asia weather the crisis. As he wrote in *Moscow News* (No. 26, 1990): 'A market system for our republic is not only a legitimate imperative, but a way to restore historic justice'.

NOTES

1. For instance, Australia's T. Bessemeres warned in his *Socialist Population Politics: The Political Implications of Demographic Trends in the USSR and Eastern Europe*, over ten years ago, that the nationalities problem would become increasingly important in future, not least due to demographic changes, and particularly in Soviet Central Asia (Bessemeres, 1980).

2. The prominent US specialist on Soviet water problems, Professor Phillip Miklin of West Michigan University, believes that the Soviet Government may be forced to return to this project in the 1990s 'not only for water, but also for political and social reasons' (in *Pravda Vostoka*, 28 March 1990).

REFERENCES

Bessemeres, J., 1980. *Socialist Population Politics: The Political Implications of Demographic Trends in the USSR and Eastern Europe*, New York: M. E. Sharpe.

Polykov, S. P., 1989. *Traditionalism in Contemporary Central Asian Society*, Moscow.

10

Inter-Ethnic Conflicts in Central Asia: Social and Religious Perspectives

Talib Saidbaev

1. INTRODUCTION

In recent years, especially during 1989 and 1990, inter-ethnic conflicts have engulfed the Soviet republics of Central Asia. Ferghana, Kokand, Kuvasaj and Namangan in Uzbekistan; Isfara and Dushanbe in Tajikistan; Urgen and Frunze (now Bishkek) in Kirghizia; Ashkabad, Nebitdaghand and Krasnovodsk in Turkmenistan – these are but a few of the 'hotbeds' of the region. Conflicts have taken place between the indigenous peoples of the region professing Islam (Uzbeks, Kirghiz, and Tajiks) and between the indigenous populations and representatives of other nationalities: Meskhetians Turks, Muslim peoples of the North Caucasus and Russian-speaking Christians. Although each of these conflicts has its own peculiarities they have much in common.

In all cases, the conflicts have involved mostly young people no older than thirty years, including teenagers. Nearly all the conflicts have had a mass character: in Kokand, Dushanbe and Frunze between four and six thousand people, in Ferghana more than ten thousand; in Osh *oblast* 20,000. According to official juridical authorities, 385 people were prosecuted in Ferghana; 290 in Dushanbe; and 54 and 94 in Andijan and Namangan respectively. Inquiries are continuing everywhere.

The methods used and the aims of those who initiated the conflicts were generally the same. In each case there was mass destruction and arson. Institutions, private homes, shops and means of transport were destroyed or looted. Participants acted with medieval cruelty and barbarity. In Namangan, for example, five soldiers were torn to pieces by a furious crowd of young Uzbeks, then doused with petrol and set on fire. According to the authorities, during the conflicts more than 400 people of different nationalities were killed and more than 800 went missing, including many children. Several thousand civilians, soldiers and militiamen were wounded.

Nationalistic and anti-Russian feelings were typical in all the conflicts, as was made clear by many slogans and demands: 'We strangle Meskhetian Turks, and Lenin's degenerate Russians!', 'Russians must answer for everything!', 'Aliens! Get out of Tajikistan!', 'Tajikistan is for Tajik speakers!', 'Uzbekistan for Uzbeks!', 'Meskhetian Turks must get out of Uzbekistan!'[1]

But the recent conflicts in Central Asia were not only confrontations between different nationalities: there were many cases of disobedience directed against the authorities and many demands for the resignation of leading statesmen, including republic notables. Almost everywhere Party premises were besieged and the local authorities were pelted with stones, beaten up and bombarded with Molotov cocktails. There were many attempts at vengeance against Party and soviet workers.

2. THE ROLE OF ISLAM

Inter-ethnic conflicts in Central Asia may be analyzed from various positions, but we are primarily interested in the complex and controversial role of Islam. The Party's political slogan of 1988, which claimed that for the Central Asian peoples Islam had become 'a living monument and vestige of the past', and that 'habit had become a stable ideological form for the unification of the people, the majority of whom are atheists', was refuted. The events of 1989-1990 have also posed many new questions. Without answers to them we cannot explain the upheavals or foresee the significance of the religious factor in the future political life of the region. A close look at the facts reveals that these inter-ethnic conflicts had a social and economic origin:

mass unemployment; lack of land and water resources; the financial difficulties faced by many Central Asian peoples; lack of trust in the authorities, and deep disappointment in the outcome of *perestroika*, which had awakened hopes of all-round improvement in life.

But what do the participants in these events see as a solution or alternative to the existing regime? How do they see the future of their region? They appear to see a brighter future, the revitalization of their hopes and a solution for present-day problems in *Islam* and its socio-political principles and ideals. Thousands of people were streaming down the streets and into the squares carrying green Islamic banners and shouting slogans: 'Long live Islam, the Muslim religion, Ayatollah Khomeini!' Appeals were launched: 'Wake up, Muslims! Rise up!' Thousands of people saw the proclamation of an Islamic republic and the creation of a Muslim state as their ultimate aim.

But how can one explain the complete absorption of Islamic values into the public consciousness, and the fact that most of the indigenous population, to all appearances, now considers religion a major force, capable of introducing a new energy into economic, political and spiritual life? And why are the majority of demonstrators young people who see Islam as a solution?

According to statements by various officials, including K. Makhkamov, First Secretary of the Central Committee of the Communist Party of Tajikistan and President of the Tajik Supreme Soviet, representatives of religious circles made already-strained ethnic relations more acute and played a significant part in the violent events. For instance, the plan for a pogrom in Dushanbe from 12 to 14 February 1990 had been discussed ten days before action began in one of the mosques. There were proposals to hand over government power to the clergy; and the young willingly followed the mullahs who urged them to go against the authorities and led them to storm the Party and state buildings.

Peoples of both Islamic and Christian background were involved in the conflicts, but the most bloody and cruel confrontations occurred among fellow Muslims: Uzbeks against Meskhetian Turks; Kirghiz against Uzbeks. How could this happen, when according to the Koran all Muslims are brothers? Was it accidental that the day before the events in Dushanbe marks appeared on the gates of certain houses? Some were marked with the Islamic half-moon, others with a cross. In Namangan the Christian church was attacked. What exactly was the role of religion in the confrontations between the Muslims and the Russian-speaking Christians? Is it true, as many ethnographers argue, that the attitude of Muslims to Europeans, whether believers or not, is largely determined by the fact that Europeans are not circumcised and eat pork? The true reasons are not as simple as they may seem – after all, the Koran speaks of the 'people of the Book' – the Jews and Christians – with respect, distinguishing them from followers of other religions. Hence, there must be other, more serious, reasons. We must closely analyze the historical past of the Central Asian peoples and the role of Islam in their personal and public lives.

3. HISTORICAL BACKGROUND

'A nation of believers' is a phrase used to characterize the religious life of feudal Europe. The same words can be used to describe the Central Asian population in the early 20th century. The region entered the present century and encountered the October Revolution while still in the feudal, medieval stage of development. It then by-passed a lengthy stage that elsewhere had included the creation and development of capitalist relations and the formation of bourgeois nations, paving the way for internationalization and secularization of social and private life and the shaping of democratic ways of solving social problems. The thirteen-century long history of Islam in the region is overwhelmingly feudal. The initial dissemination of Islam in Central Asia dates back to the late 7th and early 8th centuries, with the occupation of the region by the Arab Caliphate and the emergence of feudal relations. Islam continued to spread throughout the region up to the late 19th century, consolidating feudalism in the steppe regions. The success of Islamisation in Central Asia was prompted by one essential fact: the dogmas and demands of the new religion did not force the local population to give up ideas already rooted in their ethnic life. Islam was able to assimilate local customs and beliefs, interpret them in a new way and even strengthen them.

Of course, feudal society was characterized by a low level of productive forces and limited, stagnant relations among people

and with nature. The overwhelming majority of the population
lived in the countryside, working in agriculture and fully
dependent on the whims of nature. The lives of many generations would pass in one and the same village community,
within the same limited sphere of interests, duties and roles.
Community life was based on unqualified observation of the
written and unwritten laws regulating human relations. Each
generation simply repeated the material and spiritual life of
the previous generation, and any attempt to introduce something
new or unusual was disapproved of and indeed strongly
denounced.

Islam was a force that served to integrate society, securing
its stability and acting as a symbolic expression of social
solidarity. Production, distribution and consumption of spiritual
requirements; the whole process of moulding the personality and
adapting it to reality – these were completely subject to religion.
Islam regulated relations among people, the individual and
society. Centuries of Islam shaped a definite historical type of
individual perceiving the world only in the light of religious
ideas and unreceptive to new things unless sanctioned by Islam.

The peculiar ethnic histories of the Central Asian peoples of
Tajik, Turkmen and Uzbek nationality were formed (in the 16th,
14th-15th and 13th centuries respectively) at the expense of
tribes, once these peoples became Muslims. Likewise a Kirghiz
nationality evolved from the consolidation of Islam during the
late 18th century. Islam promoted an ethnic identity for groups
of tribes, which in turn formed a nationality. Important in that
process was a common cultural life – similar language, customs
and traditions; but without a common religion the emergence of
nationalities would have been out of the question. Hence, Islam
affected ethnic genesis, and professing Islam became a dominant
value for all Central Asian peoples.

Moreover, from the 15th century up to the mid-19th century
Central Asia found itself practically divorced from the outside,
non-Moslem world, and retreated into itself. This isolation
became another reason for a hostile attitude to everything non-
Moslem. There was a general suspicion of novelties in everyday
and public life and of everything that was unusual or extraordinary. Thus Islam became a pivot of the Central Asian peoples'
perception of reality. Islam stifled innovative social activity
among the masses and fostered patience and obedience, teaching

the people to consider earthly life a 'temporary deception' and to concentrate instead on an eternal after-life. On the other hand, Islam also contained something important which gave people hope and justified their earthly life, however full of misery and misfortune. The strongly developed egalitarian ideas in Islam could give to the destitute a feeling of moral satisfaction and inner superiority over those whom they served and on whom they depended. According to the Koran, Allah possesses qualities which personify for believers a possibility to punish those who deprive them of normal life, who misappropriate their goods and so on: 'He, Vigilant, Giver of Security, Settler of Accounts, Compassionate, Just, Strict in Punishment, Increasing the Means of Subsistence, Humiliating the Arrogant...'

Very popular among the people were legends – *khadises* – told in the name of the Prophet Mohammed. They denounced bribery, usury and stinginess, while encouraging generosity and attention to the poor, the destitute, children and those who by their actions do not offend others: 'Nobody shall rise over others: profit or non-profit of people is determined by their piety'; 'Allah cannot favour people where the weak do not get their share from the strong'; 'The keys to Paradise belong to those who love the poor and the unfortunate'; 'People who misappropriate the property of others will get to hell'; 'The arrogant will meet the anger of Allah in the other world', and so on.

Europeans had long been united by the common name of Christians. When the dissemination of Islam began in Central Asia, its population belonged to a wide variety of religions – Buddhism, Zoroastrianism, Manicheanism, Judaism, Christianity and various pagan religions – and Central Asia was to remain multi-religious for several centuries. During the 8th-13th centuries Nestorian Christianity was widespread among a number of tribes, as evidenced by the three Nestorian episcopates within the area. In the 11th century there was a Manichaean community in Samarkand. Throughout Central Asia in the 10th and the 11th centuries there were communities of Zoroastrians, and of idolaters and pagan cultists. In the 10th century there was a large Jewish community in Samarkand. Gradually *khanifite* (Sunni) Islam emerged as the single religion common to all the Central Asian nationalities. And then, from the 15th century, Central Asia severed its connections with the Christian world.

Thereafter, for several centuries the Central Asian peoples were 'stewing in their own juice'. Various feudal states emerged, waging endless internal wars for land, water and the right to subjugate other people. These wars, as everywhere in the Middle Ages, were fought under religious slogans: it was usual to call the enemy 'pagans who had broken with Islam' or, at least, 'Shiites', i.e., followers of another branch of Islam. Isolation from the outside world, coupled with the absolute domination of Islam in everyday life, sharply limited the world outlook of the Central Asian peoples. It fostered a groundless belief in the superiority of their own culture and mode of life, and an extremely hostile attitude to everything non-Moslem which did not correspond to their centuries-old prejudices.

4. EAST MEETS WEST

Then, in the mid-19th century, Central Asia was conquered by Tsarist Russia, a country with a much higher level of socio-economic and political development. At that time capitalist relations were solidly rooted in Russia and were developing rapidly. But the link to Russia did not lead to the removal of entrenched prejudices against the bearers of the Christian, Western culture. Instead, it deepened and intensified these prejudices, as well as giving a concrete focus for traditionally negative attitudes towards non-Moslems. The reason was not only that the invaders (who were not only Russians by origin) belonged to another religion and another civilization, with a foreign language, an unusual appearance and alien norms of life and traditions. There were other, more profound reasons.

To begin with, Central Asia's encounter with the Christian world began with massive bombardments, the storming of towns and fortresses, desperate street-battles, the liquidation of settlements and the killing of thousands of town-dwellers. The war was unequal – the advantage, naturally, lay with the Tsarist army, which was well-organized and well-armed, on a par with European armies. Nor was war the only thing to leave bitter traces in the historical memory of the Central Asian peoples. Tsarist Russia had invaded Central Asia with one definite aim: to turn it into a source of rare and expensive cotton for industry.

Hence arose a lopsided orientation of regional agriculture towards cotton production. Almost half of the industrial enterprises built by Russians over half a century were engaged exclusively in providing cotton for export. The rest served local needs which could not be met by the metropolis. The number of workers of local origin did not exceed 20,000, and among them only one in every seven was a skilled labourer. Europeans formed a kind of aristocracy, and Central Asia experienced practically none of the great achievements of capitalist industrial production or the related revolutionary and secularizing changes in social life. Central Asia also bypassed another phenomenon directly related to capitalism – the creation of bourgeois nations with their development of social rather than ethnic relationships.

There were, however, some major changes. Turkestan, after its occupation by Russians, saw the creation of over 300 settlements and villages inhabited by peasants from the central regions of Russia. Hundreds and thousands of local peasants were ousted from their centuries-old holdings. Many small villages were destroyed. Russian peasants, encouraged by official colonial policy, rapidly began enriching themselves. In 1917, a Russian who had settled in Turkestan had on average 15 times more land than a local inhabitant. Wealth was often accumulated at the expense of labour hired from the local population. Even before the Russian invasion the region had had a corrupt local administration. People were deprived of all economic and political rights, subject to arbitrary rule and to violence, humiliations and insults. The new authorities left the old administration intact, but created their own bureaucratic apparatus with superior powers. This new apparatus organized elections for the local administration, approved their results and had the right to dismiss any official without explanation. The Russian administration in Central Asia was staffed by an exclusive, self-contained and self-satisfied caste, which considered itself as the sole and proper master of the region, before whom the people had to shudder, render homage and pay tribute.

The economic and political inequality reflected the scornful attitude of the Tsarist administration towards local religious feelings and cultural development. In 1868 one of the most revered Koran manuscripts in the Moslem world was taken from

Samarkand to St. Petersburg: according to legend, it had belonged to the Khalif Osman. Christian Orthodox missionaries preached in the steppe regions denouncing the 'falsity of Islam' and extolling the 'truth of Christianity'. Mosques could not be opened, nor could mosques or Islamic schools function, without permission. Besides, a teacher in such a school had to know the Russian language – an unrealistic condition. Indeed, schools and mosques functioned illegally, in secret.

The activities of Moslem organizations were also curtailed. Lands belonging to mosques and Islamic schools were limited, and new laws prohibited further expansion of the property of Islamic religious bodies. Naturally, the Central Asian peoples sought in Islam protection from alien phenomena. Here is a message sent by the governor-general of the region to the Minister of War in 1908:

> *We should not forget that we have introduced to the Central Asian people a host of negative aspects of European culture: pubs, restaurants, opium dens, brothels, etc. have gained a foothold, not only in towns, but in all big settlements. The local youth have rushed to these enticements of spiritual and corporate debauch, to the terror and misery of the old people, glorifying in unheard-of violations of the Koran and the centuries-old traditions of the East of decency and good manners. Among the local youth there have appeared robbers, murderers, obvious debauchees and hooligans ...[and] respect for the elders and authorities is disappearing. If such decline in morals continues, it will be difficult to imagine what will become of the next generation of indigenes. Today's old people, mullahs, kaziis [judges] and elders, looking with regret at such a decline in morals, blame the Russians for everything, and, probably, in their heart of hearts they have felt more than once a secret urge to overthrow the yoke of the 'infidels'. This aspect of local life should be also taken into consideration as it is fraught with risks of the outbreak of serious popular discontent with far-reaching consequences, because the people are sure of the rightness of their cause.*

Thus, the local population perceived the change in traditions – which in fact is inevitable in the transition of any society to a new state – as being a result of their annexation by Tsarist Russia, and extended their hostility to all Russians and Europeans. It is no surprise, then, that popular resistance in Central Asia took the form of *gazavat* – a holy war. And the religious motive was strong even in cases when those killed, robbed or immolated were not Europeans, but local officials and the rich.

5. BEGINNINGS OF THE SOVIET ERA

It was natural to expect that the Soviet power would seek to put an end to the negative attitude of official Russia towards Central Asia, and to overcome the mistrust Moslems felt towards Europeans. The Bolsheviks' programme, the first document of the Soviet state, prepared and signed by V.I. Lenin, formulated the task of removing former economic and political inequalities. The address of the Soviet of the RSFSR People's Commissars 'To all working Moslems of Russia and the East', passed two weeks after the triumph of the October Revolution, pledged to respect their freedom, the inviolability of their beliefs and customs, the right to cultural establishments and to freely construct a national life.

However, things were to take a different turn. As a result of the civil war unleashed immediately after the Revolution, Central Asia found itself cut off from central Russia. Activities of the Soviet authorities remained heavily dominated by Europeans, infected by a colonialist spirit and frankly chauvinistic sentiments.

Climatic disasters also played a major role in what followed. The summer of 1917 was dry, which strongly affected food deliveries, as local agriculture was oriented towards cotton and not foodstuffs. Bread, arriving from Russia only sporadically, was distributed mainly among the European population. Moreover, the winter of 1917-18 proved to be very rigorous. The new Soviet administration carried out mass requisitions and confiscation drives among the indigenous population of town and countryside. Everywhere, local people were dying of hunger. Corpses were scattered all over – in the streets, at railway stations, on the roads. In some areas, the hungry population reportedly started eating the bodies of those who had starved to death. According to official data, human losses from cold, hunger and disease varied from 25% to 50% in Central Asia.

Initially the local population were granted no part in the administration of public affairs. The European communists treated Moslems as their subjects, and showed their scorn and open distrust by claiming that 'all Moslems are profiteers'.[2] As a result, a *basmach* movement took shape. Until recently, this movement has been dismissed as banditism, a form of class struggle against the Soviet power. However, modern historians now see the primary cause of its emergence and growth in the excesses perpetrated against the people's national feelings and religious beliefs. This movement, having started in late 1917, and continuing up to 1934 in some regions of Central Asia, was of a religious nature, and generally took the form of *gazavat* – holy war. Although life in the region, including religious life, gradually returned to normal in the mid-1920s, and mosques, Islamic institutions, schools and courts resumed their activities, it seems that present-day anti-Russian, anti-European sentiments are rooted in those first days of the October Revolution, a result of the gross mistakes made by Soviet power in policy towards Islam, its priesthood and organizations.[3]

When analyzing the relationship between Soviet/Communist power and Islam, one must note that for only seven years (1922-29) out of the 70-year history of the USSR was religious life in Central Asia allowed to proceed according to the laws and declarations proclaimed by the Soviet authorities themselves. During these few years the authorities permitted the establishment of mosques in sufficient number for the needs of the populace. Parents enjoyed an opportunity to teach their children the fundamentals of religion. But then, from the late 1920s, most mosques were closed down; many were destroyed; religious schools and institutions terminated their activities; mullahs were arrested, exiled or executed. Nor did local Moslems find much consolation in the fact that their fellow-believers in other regions found themselves in an identical situation.

Until recently, there were only 300 officially permitted mosques in the all of the Soviet Union. This represented about 1% of the pre-Revolution number, despite rapid growth in the Moslem population. For dozens of millions of Moslems, there was only one Islamic secondary school, with strictly limited entrance. The people also had no access to religious literature, while many anti-religious books were published, putting Islam and believers in a false light and distorting the genuine feelings of the people towards religion. The atheist publications urged 'an uncompromising and consistent ideological struggle against religion', and wanted to remove children from believers' families into boarding schools and Young Pioneer camps, so that they 'could stay outside the influence of their believer relatives'.[4]

The actions of the authorities and ideological workers towards Moslems and mosques were based on false postulates which ran counter to a truly scientific view of religion. Any open observation of Islamic rites or festivities was fraught with negative consequences, especially for Communists, Komsomols and intellectuals. Efforts were made to introduce new 'non-religious and Soviet' rites and traditions which, in essence and form, were simply imported European ones. Many local folk rites and customs were prohibited or abandoned as religiously tainted. For a long time many prominent pre-Revolutionary writers were consigned to oblivion – because of the religious motifs in their works. In some cases, places of pilgrimage were destroyed as well as books in Arabic. Of course, such heavy-handed measures failed to remove Islam from the life of the Central Asian peoples. Instead, Islam withdrew into people's inner life. Mosques and Islamic ministers continued to exist, although illegally. Religious rites were observed on a mass basis, and festivities were held as before; but the lack of opportunity to worship openly, and the propaganda offensive against Islam and believers – all this aggravated a feeling of national grievance. Once again Islam turned against Moscow, the Centre, as the initiator of its perse-cution – and, hence, against Russians and Europeans as a whole.

6. THE SITUATION OF YOUTH

Especially among the young people, who demonstrated in the streets and squares of Central Asian towns, national resentment served as a background for large-scale manifestations under religious banners, often levelled at the representatives of other nationalities. Why?

Many young people never ask what kind of socialism has been built in their country; never give a thought to whether this is a developed or a feudal socialism. It is difficult for them to identify the in-depth reasons for such indisputable facts as the following: up to one fifth of the indigenous Central Asian peoples have remained rural and the proportion has been increasing. In Tajikistan, urban residents now constitute less than one third of the whole population of the republic. This decreasing share of the urban population represents an unprecedented case in a world perspective. Moreover, this is a region where in many places each person engaged in agriculture has less than a hectare of irrigated land. The average village resident has less than one third of a hectare with completely exhausted water resources. Today's youth fails to comprehend still another thing: why, at the numerous enterprises in Kirghizia, Turkmenistan and Tajikistan, three quarters (in Uzbekistan, over half) of the workers and specialists are Europeans, occupying key posts and receiving good pay. They hardly know that before the October Revolution the Russians were responsible for less than a quarter of the industry of the region.

Today, after some 70 years of Soviet power, the Central Asian peoples lag very much behind the developed nations. They are still at the pre-industrial stage. Officially – thanks to the creation of union republics, and not to any internal economic or social development – they are considered 'developed nations'. However, there is much in their lives, not least the level of social development, that shows their pre-industrial position. And yet, as I say, many young people do not give a second thought to such problems. They judge the society in which they live by the surrounding reality – their own life, the life of their family and the atmosphere around them. The young have no past: they have nothing to compare with; they are just young. They have only the present and the future; but they are not doing well.

According to official data, almost 1.5 million young people are unemployed in Uzbekistan, the largest of the Central Asian republics. Among those engaged in domestic work and subsidiary farming, the young make up 51%. Average wages of a young person in Uzbekistan comprise half or, at best, two thirds of the wages of his or her peers in the European parts of the Soviet Union. Moreover, 87% of young families live below the poverty line defined in the republic; and 65% of the urban young do not have their own dwelling. In other Central Asian republics, young people are in the same position, if not worse.

7. THE PRICE OF SUCCESS

Today the indigenous population in the Central Asian republics is paying dearly for the activities of the administrative command system in Moscow and the local capitals, which has turned the territories of these republics into enormous cotton fields. In pursuit of their own advancement, which depend on crop records, responsible officials have mercilessly applied the strongest chemicals. These have now contaminated the land, nature and human organisms. For instance, in the Turkmenian countryside today, one hectare of land has 100 times more chemicals than in Japan, and 20 times more than the average for the Union. The level of pesticides in the milk of Turkmenian nursing mothers exceeds that in the milk of Vietnamese women in the war period when the jungles were polluted by defoliants. In some regions of the republic 75% of adults and over 90% of the children are ill with anaemia and vitamin deficiency, and are suffering from malnutrition and gastro-intestinal illnesses. In Tajikistan, 70% of the women and 67% of the children are said to be affected.

As before the October Revolution, people continue to live in wattle and daub houses with earthen floors. For years they do not see meat, or even fruits from their own plots of land, as they must sell them at the market to buy other necessities. They drink poor water. Indeed, a film from the Middle Ages could easily be made on location. Half the houses of the native population lack sewage facilities, running water and a heating system, and many houses have no gas line. Half the village families have no radio sets, washing machines or sewing machines. Every third family has no refrigerator, despite the hot climate. The results of such an existence are quite obvious. There is a decrease in the average height and chest volume of the young people of Central Asian origin. The share of malformed infants and handicapped children is growing, as well as the number of child suicides. Village school teachers note that children are not receptive to subjects requiring abstract thinking – physics, chemistry, astronomy. Today, experts are talking about 'depopulation' – about the degeneration of a people as an independent biological species, often using the word 'genocide'.

8.   YOUTH IN CRISIS

Thus, Central Asian youths begin their independent lives in unemployment, or with low wages and poor living conditions, getting no relief or credits from the state. Young people and young families are put in an embarrassing position of dependence on the social status of their parents. This in turn generates disappointment in social values, and some of the youth resort to illegal ways of getting the means of subsistence. All this weighs heavily on the young people. Critical appraisal of their socio-economic position, and constant comparisons with the lives led by their peers of other nationalities and from other republics, make them wonder: Who is to blame? How to find a way out?

Many factors prevent the young people from finding a place in society and escaping from their predicament. The young people have no relation to production – they do not produce material and intellectual values – hence the destructive nature of their actions. Remoteness from socio-economic and political life deprives youth of the chance to take part in decision-making. They are not used to protecting their interests within a particular organization on the basis of communal socio-economic activities, and have no idea about the intrinsic connections between the various strata of society. They stand apart from social processes, cannot find their own place in them, and do not realize that those processes bear a direct relation to them. It does not occur to them – and this is a vestige of Central Asia's feudal past – that they should seek a place in the sun for themselves, give up their bad habits, find other guidelines and values and shape themselves to live and work in different surroundings. They are not ready to live another life, different from that of their parents and previous generations. Their families have prepared and continue to prepare them to repeat the experience of their ancestors, to be like them, to act in the same socio-economic conditions.

But life has changed. Today it places quite different demands on the new generation, taking them out from their centuries-old niches, destroying their paradigms. The young must learn how to live differently, to choose another course in life. Young people have lost faith: in a solution to their problems, and in the local administration – its ability to solve their problems; its honesty and decency; its concern with human destinies. That is why youth who live in poverty and unemployment start negating the existing regime and its values. Incidentally, their thinking is quite critical of the values of the older generation – workers and collective farmers. Young people are refusing to agree with them in everything, and do not copy their patterns of behaviour.

The young generation feels that life is proceeding in strange and enigmatic ways, and they fail to grasp just where they are at variance with society. One thing is clear: they feel their uselessness; that there is no place for them in the surrounding reality, and that they will never be able to settle their problems. Young people see no way out: life is driving them into a corner. In such a situation they lose faith in everything previously thought important in life – in all the values acquired through socialization, family and school upbringing. Simultaneously, they lose contact with their families – they no longer fit in and they are a burden amongst peers who have somehow found their place in life. They are also alienated from the Komsomol, which never gave them anything and never bothered to protect their interests.

All this testifies to a deep crisis in the Central Asian republics and among their youth. The young find themselves in a deadlock, caused by the inability of society to solve the problems of its rising generation, and by the obvious gap between their own ambitions and the demands of modern industrial society. But why do they turn to Islam for a way out, and see a solution in its social teachings? Why is their discontent directed against representatives of other peoples and beliefs, and why does it show such cruel and destructive attitudes to other peoples? We should seek the answer in the peculiar socialisation of youth, and in the major role still played by Islam in the life of the peoples of Central Asia.

9.   EXPLAINING ETHNIC CONFLICT

Against a background of underdeveloped social ties and imperfect political structures, ethnic features come to the fore. Central Asian peoples live on centuries-old territories, chiefly in a mononational rural environment whose stagnant mode of life preserves the cultural and ethnic traditions and mentality formed under the strong impact of Islam. As in the past, everything connected with Islam continues to dominate the life of the family and the religion-oriented rural and urban communities. The Central Asian village does not recognize an individual, family or group mode of life as having two independent and parallel components – religious and secular. In the observation of religious rites, norms and festivals no serious change has taken place. Rites continue to unite the people. Through rituals they establish their nationality and their group and family solidarity, and demonstrate devotion to the customs of their ancestors. Islam is an indispensable aspect of social life, a passport into that life. Anyone who fails to observe its rites and traditions can become an outsider, opposed by his neighbours and fellow villagers.

No wonder, then, that the religious experience of the older generations is reproduced in the thinking and behaviourial stereotypes of the younger generation. The religious interpretation attracts youth by its simplicity, not demanding from them a complex analysis of reality or a strenuous quest for solutions to social problems, or any precise division of public life into the 'good' and the 'bad'. Young people cannot but be attracted by the social doctrine of Islam, with its egalitarian ideas which explain injustice, misuse of power and disregard for the interests of the people by deviation from religion. Additionally, we must note the common human tendency to idealize the past, especially in contrast to present-day difficulties.

All this should help us realize why the young Central Asian demonstrators agitated for replacing the existing state structure with a system based on religious principles. Nevertheless, the question remains: Why did the riots take the form of *inter-ethnic* conflicts, both between co-religionists and between representatives of different religions? To this there is no simple answer. I believe that the conflicts have become inter-ethnic for one basic reason: the indigenous youth has turned its anger against those who have jobs, high wages and decent material and living conditions, i.e., against those who are doing better in life. They fail to understand that these things are not acquired through one's national origin, but perceiving the prosperity of others as a personal insult. That is why in inter-ethnic conflicts the victims were both Europeans and fellow Moslems – indeed, the number of the latter far exceeded the number of the former.[5]

It would be wrong to derive the inter-ethnic character of the conflicts from the attitude of Islam to followers of other religions. Islamic doctrine contains points which can be interpreted in contrasting ways. Of greater importance, I feel, is the historical memory of the events of the remote and close past. Among them we have noted the traumatic events of the hunger of the post-revolutionary years, the destruction of mosques and the clergy and contempt for the dignity and culture of the Central Asian peoples. Still fresh are memories of recent years when the people had to conceal their faith, when everything related to Islam was proclaimed harmful and hostile.

On the other hand, we should not forget that Islam, like any other religion, cannot be totally unbiased. Moslems cannot remain neutral towards the followers of other religions and cultures: they necessarily consider their religion the true one and their mode of life the only correct one. This conviction, based to some extent on Islamic doctrine, has gained a firm foothold in Central Asia as a result of centuries of existence in a mono-religious and mono-cultural environment.

Despite the importance of religion, the fact that among the victims of the conflicts were co-believers, Moslems from other regions, testifies to the primacy of the social over the religious – economic interests prevail over religious ones in the national movement. When land and water resources or employment issues were raised, religious unity was rapidly overshadowed by material interests. The reason seems to lie in the prevalence of ethnicity in the present-day development of the Central Asian peoples, in the unfinished process of nation formation. In Central Asia, differences in language, traditions and customs have come to the fore, disuniting rather than unifying the people. Thus, in Central Asian towns it is not unusual for representatives of different nationalities to have their own clergy, even their own mosque – and thus lead an isolated religious life. This does not necessarily mean misunderstanding, or a disregard for religious unity. But the undeveloped national mentality, conditioned by the low level of social development, prevents the people from transcending the limitations of ethnicity, or from making Islam a force capable of preventing inter-ethnic conflicts.

10. THE FUTURE

What next? Will there be other inter-ethnic conflicts in Central Asia; and, if so, what will be the role of Islam? These are far from rhetorical questions. The basic social problems remain unsolved, and will hardly be solved in the near future. The transition to market relations recently initiated in the country will aggravate the position of the Central Asian peoples to an even greater degree: non-profitable enterprises staffed with local workers will be closed and unemployment will rise, not least because of the growing number of school leavers. Hundreds of thousands of new jobs need to be created for future school-leavers in Central Asia – but this is an unrealistic demand. Large-scale unemployment will parallel an acute shortage of skilled labour in industry, construction and transport – a shortage caused by the low level of training of the indigenous population, coupled with a massive emigration of the Russian-speaking population in the wake of inter-ethnic conflicts. Populist measures by republican governments can scarcely suffice to reduce the acuteness of outstanding social problems.

Perestroika has radically changed the religious situation in the region. Over the past few years the number of officially functioning mosques alone has increased five-fold, and in everyday life things are returning to the pre-Revolutionary situation, when each rural and urban community had its own mosque. More and more new Islamic educational establishments are being opened, and many religious books are being published. Also the mass media have launched a widespread religious campaign. The national intelligentsia, as if taking revenge for past insults, have strongly promoted this process. The role of Islam in all walks of social and private life is rapidly growing. Demands are being launched to put into life the postulates of Islamic law. Parties are created which see their major goal in restoration of religion and the creation of an Islam-oriented society. Moslem organisations enjoy the open support of top Party and state officials. Today, Islam can be discussed only in superlatives – few will dare to consider it critically from a colder, scientific point of view.

And yet, inter-ethnic conflicts have failed to be properly assessed. The genuine causes have not been identified, nor has the development of conflict been closely explored. Where can this lead? I would be so bold as to say that the painful inter-ethnic conflicts of the recent past constitute only the beginning, not the end, of massive social collisions awaiting Central Asia in the near future. And in these conflicts a major role will belong to Islam.

NOTES

1. Some indications of crowd violence: In the markets in Frunze (Bishkek), Uzbek tradesmen were beaten and banished; all Uzbek students had to leave Frunze because of possible aggression. In Osh 1500 Kirghiz were evicted by their Uzbek landlords. In Dushanbe a Russian boy was torn to pieces by a crowd and a Russian woman was thrown over a bridge, while a seven-month pregnant Tajik woman was raped because she was wearing a European dress (she hung herself at home), and other people wearing European clothes were beaten.

2. Chauvinist-minded Europeans perpetrated a great many actions aimed at undermining the honour and dignity of the people, and effecting a forceful change in their mode of life and religion, including destruction of cultural monuments. Where Soviet power triumphed, mosques and Islamic educational establishments were closed down, *shariat* courts were liquidated and the property of religious organizations was nationalized. Many Islamic ministers and judges were arrested. In one town, Soviet authorities burnt the Koran in public; in another they turned the main mosque into a barracks, where Muslim soldiers then indulged in vices; in a third they promised Moslems at a public meeting to 'free' them from Allah. Some mosques were turned into cattle-sheds. All this was accompanied by open plundering, burning of Moslem houses and acts of violence.

3. Such things leave deep imprints in the historical memory: not in the form of generalized, quantifiable facts, but rather in the form of conclusions drawn about 'us' and 'them'. Moreover, the 70-year history of the relations of the Communist Party and Soviet power with all religions and religious organisations (Islam and Moslem organisations included), far from encouraging the people to forget the injustices of the first years of the October Revolution, has given fresh grounds for bitter remembrance.

4. Even those published in the first three years of *perestroika*, i.e., in 1985-88, were still claiming that Islam 'for centuries impeded the cultural development of Moslem peoples', 'prohibited love of freedom' and made Muslims incapable of 'perceiving a fresh idea'. Propagandists declared that the 'moral and social precepts of Islam could give nothing positive to the man of the 20th century'; that its 'ideology is incompatible with progress'; that it 'does not recognize the friendship of peoples'; 'propagates contempt for other believers', and has been 'a source of national and religious strife'.

5. This, for instance, happened in Ferghana, where the Meskhetian Turks - who are Moslems - were victimized. Likewise in New Uzen, Ashkabad and Nebitag members of Caucasian nationalities - also fellow believers - were attacked.

11

Communism and National Self-Determination in Central Asia

Tair Tairov

1. INTRODUCTION

In Soviet writing there has been a widespread legend that Soviet power has managed to abolish inequality among nations and provide self-determination for many nationalities who allegedly lacked a separate identity before the Revolution of 1917. Recent developments in the Soviet empire have, however, involved a widespread search for the sources of national consciousness and a tremendous rise in nationalism.

According to recent Soviet estimates, there are currently between 20 and 30 disputes in progress over borders and territories among union republics, autonomous republics and autonomous regions within the Soviet Union. Most of these disputes stem from the demarcation policy of the Soviet authorities in the early 1920s, when the Union of Soviet Socialist Republics was created and the status of union republic was granted to minorities formerly living under Russian colonial rule; but the source of conflict is not solely the territorial issue. Apart from the obvious political sources of conflict, economic and social dependence play an important role, as well as the misery of everyday life for the bulk of the population in today's republics, especially in Central Asia.

Ironically, what Lenin wrote about imperialism being the highest stage of capitalist robbery of colonial nations was to prove applicable to the reality of Soviet Communist power, especially in Central Asia. The political philosophy and economic practices of the Bolsheviks, as applied to the populations of the former Russian colonies in Asia, were truly imperialistic. In the West it is often said that Russia was never a colonial empire like France or Great Britain. This, however, is quite contrary to historical truth. Even Lenin admitted many times that Russia was the greatest colonial power on the Eurasian continent. Yet Soviet historians as well as official authorities hide the littleknown fact that in the second half of the 19th century the Russian Tsars pursued ruthless colonial wars against three Central Asian states – Kokand, Khiva and Bukhara.

Internal splits prevented these states from building a united front against the Russian colonial expeditions repeatedly sent to this area, then known as Turkestan. But despite the weakness of their armies and a lack of modern arms, the Uzbeks, Kirghiz and Turkomans, as well as other local populations, resisted well-armed Russian colonial troops for decades. Reports from the colonial wars in Turkestan gradually reached Europe through British diplomats and military experts involved in wars with Afghanistan at the borders of Bukhara and Samarkand. It is an acknowledged historical fact that Russian troops under General Skobelev carried out genocidal policies among the local population, levelling many villages and killing thousands of people who resisted Russian expansion. During the Soviet period, however, official historians came to describe the colonial wars in Turkestan as a process of a 'voluntary unification' of the Central Asian population with Great Russia.

The population of Turkestan never accepted Russian colonial dominance. National liberation movements resulted in many upheavals and revolts: suffice it here to mention mass resistance in 1898 and again in 1916. In any case, by 1917 the Russian colonial empire was on the brink of disintegration. The colonies in Turkestan were demanding political freedom, equality with the Russian population and the elimination of national and racial discrimination. Social conditions in Tashkent bore a strong resemblance to South African apartheid: non-Russians were not permitted to enter the areas where Russians lived, to sit on benches with them or to use the same public transport. The Russian empire was not only racist and repressive but also imposed a colonial culture on non-Russians. It created privileged groups among local merchants, landowners and religious leaders, on whose support Moscow could then rely. But with the beginning of World War I the liberation struggle in Turkestan nevertheless acquired new dimensions. One theory holds that troops sent to Tashkent in 1917 by the Prime Minister of the Russian Provisional Government, Kerensky, to suppress the local liberation movement left him without sufficient support in Petersburg, and that this helped the Bolsheviks to overthrow him and declare the victory of the Great October Revolution.

2. REVOLUTION – AND THEN WHAT?

Russian social democrats led by Lenin promised freedom for the former Russian colonies in Central Asia. Under these circumstances new national leaders managed to launch the first political parties, such as the party of *jadids* in Tashkent or the Young Bukharans who joined the Social Democrats in their military struggle against the colonial administration and the Tsarist military contingents in Turkestan.

But what ensued after the Revolution was not the promised freedom and self-determination. The old Russian colonial policy was replaced by a Bolshevik colonial policy under the rhetoric of Communist brotherhood. If it had not been for the Russian Revolution, the war to liberate Turkestan from the Russian yoke could have been continued. It was due to Lenin's national slogans and the Bolsheviks' iron-fisted policy that the Russian colonial empire was preserved and even strengthened through Communist policies of exploitation and political isolation of local nationalities in Central Asia.

Today, the roots of conflict in Soviet Central Asia lie in the colonial policies of the old Russian empire during the 20th century – territorial expansionism and annexation of new lands – policies also pursued in the Soviet period.

A policy of terror against the civilian population and destruction of historical and cultural monuments was used in the conquest of Bukhara in 1920. This event is still fresh in the memory of the Central Asian peoples. Seventeen years before Guernica – when the Nazis employed surprise air raids to destroy that Basque town in order to terrify the local population and break the republican government – Lenin's government was the first to use air forces in massive attacks against a civilian population, wreaking incalculable damage on the ancient city of Bukhara.

Officially Bukhara was a protectorate of Russia. But it enjoyed a relatively independent foreign policy, and had its own fiscal system, army and foreign trade. On the other hand, the Bukhara Emirate was far from democratic: it practiced ruthless repression of any political dissent. By 1920 the Red Army had decided to occupy vast areas of Bukhara. Giving 'international' help in the class struggle of the Young Bukharan party against the Emirate was the pretext for the Red Army to storm the gates of the old town. In close consultation with Lenin, the Commander-in-chief of the Red Army in Turkestan, Mikhail Frunze, decided to use airplanes to attack the town. In the course of one week in August 1920 a dozen planes dropped hundreds of bombs on the horrified population and the historical monuments of Bukhara. Even Ghenghis Khan had not dared to destroy the legendary architecture of Bukhara. But Frunze did not hesitate to level hundreds of mosques, palaces and schools in order to establish control.

There are many more pages in the annals of 20th century Central Asian history to illustrate the violence widely used against the local population. Here we may mention two examples: the collapse of Kokand Autonomy in 1918, and the struggle against the Basmachi movement – a Central Asian type of armed struggle against Soviet power. In fact the Basmachi movement continued to exist until the early 1930s, with many groups of armed resisters against Soviet power active in the mountains and deserts of Central Asia.

The Russian and Soviet annexation of new lands in Central Asia and the military crackdown on national separatist and autonomous movements were accompanied by the classical policy of divide and rule. Nevertheless, the October Revolution gave a chance to some national groups to establish their statehood for the first time. The Revolution did give Turkomans, Kirghiz and others the chance to form their own territories. But the borders between the newly-ordained republics were drawn up artificially, and so areas with a dominant Uzbek population fell under the Kirghiz and Kazakh Republic, while Kazakh and Tajik areas fell under the Uzbek Republic. This confusion about borders has led to turmoil in relations between republics, and is exploited by extremist nationalist forces in the various Central Asian republics today.

But the main issue between the Central Asian republics and the central government remains economic and socio-political. Flagrant examples of the imperial nature of centre-periphery relations can be found in the history of economic, national and social policy in Uzbekistan. Today this historical background represents the greatest source of conflict in and between the republics of Central Asia.

3. MONOCULTURE AND ENVIRONMENTAL DISASTER

In the Soviet period Central Asia became a supplier of raw materials. From the very start, a special policy was elaborated to provide the Centre with essential materials and agricultural products from Central Asia. Cotton monoculture was developed. As early as February 1918 a special decree was adopted 'on the confiscation of reserves of cotton' in Turkestan, imposing the death penalty on those who refused to obey. That was followed in 1920 with a new decree issued by Lenin which militarized institutions and enterprises involved in cotton production and irrigation. The production of cotton was declared a monopoly of the state. Administrative orders and military enforcement became the main instruments in managing cotton production in Central Asia.

By the mid-1920s the formation of new Central Asian republics was accomplished. Each of them had obligations concerning the amount of cotton to be supplied. With plans for industrialization and military build-up in the 1930s it was necessary to increase the production of cotton, so Moscow started extensive cultivation of new land. In order to justify cotton monoculture in the Central Asian republics, and especially in Uzbekistan, a new political slogan was invented – 'cotton independence'. More than 100 products of various types – food, cloth, oil, etc. – are made from cotton, including several kinds of explosives. In order not to be dependent on imports, the central government declared the necessity of providing the cotton entirely at home, mainly in Central Asia. Ever since the 1930s, and right up to the present, the official propaganda with all its ideological machinery has continuously preached the advantages of cotton independence.

Cotton monoculture proved to be an environmental and socio-political tragedy for Central Asia. For more than 30 years, aircrafts used defoliants to prepare the cottonfields for the picking machines. Without defoliants, the machines could not collect cotton, which had to be free of leaves. These were the same kinds of defoliants that were used by the US Army during the war in Vietnam. Besides defoliants, a pesticide called butafos has been widely used to boost productivity.

Contaminating substances are still being used in Central Asia to increase production. People in opposition movements in Uzbekistan came to realize that under the pretext of cotton production Moscow had in fact been waging decades of chemical warfare. Among the results were casualties because of health deterioration, and the contamination of underground waters – the main source of drinking water for the local people.

Prices for cotton are established arbitrarily from Moscow. Until recently, for one ton of raw cotton, collective farmers received from the state between 200 and 300 roubles, depending on the quality. For the peasants, this was the only source of income. Those who picked cotton by hand were paid 10 kopeks for 1 kilo; until recently the monthly income of the farmer or his wife or his sister was 30-40 roubles. These people were often the only ones who could earn money for families with five or more children. Recently Moscow has increased the payment to three roubles for one kilo of cotton fibre, while on the world market the equivalent sum is between five and 20 dollars. Child labour is also widely used in Uzbekistan. Despite efforts to ban it, in distant rural areas pupils from seven years old are involved in cotton picking, either helping their parents or on their own.

For centuries the agricultural lands of Central Asia were considered very rich and fertile. Nowadays, however, the lands and waters are contaminated. Traditionally, rivers and wells have been the main source of potable water in Uzbekistan and the rural areas still lack centralized water supplies. But according to the latest government studies there is today not a single river in the republic which can provide safe drinking water (Tskanderov, 1990, p.11).

Child mortality in Uzbekistan is twice as high as the average elsewhere in the Soviet Union. Whereas child mortality in the Soviet Union in 1989 was 22 per thousand, in some areas of Uzbekistan it was 52. In agricultural areas where children and teenagers are involved in cotton production 86% of all children examined are unwell, while 18% suffer from three or more chronic diseases, and 15% lag behind in their normal physical development.

Cotton monoculture has led to an ecological catastrophe of global dimensions – the drying up of the Aral Sea. As far back as 1971 the Soviet government elaborated a plan according to which all the Aral Sea was to be used for irrigating cotton. As a result of overuse of land and water, the Aral Sea has practically ceased to exist. The water level has dropped 15 metres in comparison with 1961. The total surface area of the Sea has shrunk 60%, and 54% of the total volume of water has disappeared. Salination continues to ruin fertile lands, contaminating water and soil alike.

Politically, Uzbekistan was transformed into part of the administrative-command system. Moscow's party-political and administrative institutions were reproduced and extended in Uzbekistan. The goal of political self-determination, proclaimed after the early years of the 1917 Revolution, was gradually abandoned. In addition, the social and economic well-being of the population was sacrificed for the sake of monoculture and the uncontrolled export of such strategically significant resources as gold, uranium and gas.

Today, 80% of a population of almost 20 million are living in the rural areas, half of them with a standard of living below the poverty line. Eightyfive per cent of cultivated land continues to be used solely for cotton.

The government has cut back slightly on cotton production; but it has not given up the notorious theory of cotton independence. Gold and uranium mines as well as other strategically important extraction industries continue to be the absolute monopoly of Moscow. There is no official information about how much gold is actually excavated in the Bukhara region, but figures between 70 and 110 tons of gold per annum are mentioned. Even with 50 tonnes of gold per year Uzbekistan could provide itself with enough currency, not counting other goods – silk, cotton and natural gas – for its internal needs.

4. WAVES OF CHANGE, OR REPRESSION?

Recent political and economic reforms in the USSR have opened
up new chances for the people of Central Asia. The struggle for
national dignity and self-esteem has acquired new forms. But
unlike the Baltic republics or the Transcaucasus, Uzbekistan
cannot be viewed as a region undergoing rapid change. Some 70
years of communist rule have resulted in a very strong and
reliable local Communist elite, loyal to the central administrative system in Moscow. There are still powerful Communist
party leaders who belong to the traditional Stalinist type of
politician.   They are relatively young, but are firm proponents
of Stalinist methods of leadership. Under the direction of this
kind of party official, elections to the Supreme Soviet of Uzbekistan were recently held, with I. Karimov being elected President.
The practice of individuals holding more than one office has been
introduced practically everywhere. The result is the continuing
subordination of the soviets to the Communist Party.

The 22nd Party Congress of Uzbekistan issued a unanimous
condemnation of the recent democratic transformations in the
western part of the USSR, declaring itself the successor of the
Stalin/Brezhnev type of CPSU in the ideological sphere. The
Congress resolved that the Communist Party of Uzbekistan has
the right to choose the way of development of the republic if
'destructive forces' (as party members call the democratic forces)
should prevail at the Centre. Uzbek communist leaders oppose
the new independent members of the Moscow and Leningrad
City Councils, and the increasingly independent Russian Federation led by Boris Yeltsin. They oppose democracy and de-ideolo-
gization of coercive state bodies – army, militia, courts and KGB
– speaking up in favour of 'democratic centralism' and the unity
of the party instead.

The activities of the party leadership are not widely welcomed by the population, however. Party power rests upon
paramilitary troops, the militia, the KGB and the zeal of the
Procurator's Office and the courts, all of which are still being
used as punitive instruments by the party apparatus. The
republican party leadership manipulates the sentiments of the
local population who want to see Uzbekistan independent; but
nowadays the balance of political forces is such that independent
Uzbekistan could well become a Stalinist type of state based on
the dictatorship of the local party leaders.

Violation of human rights has remained the order of the day. Members of democratic organizations are repeatedly persecuted – fired from their jobs, arrested or terrorized by the press. Gatherings are not allowed in the republic, to say nothing of public meetings and demonstrations. No official recognition has been granted to *Birlik*, the major democratic organization in Uzbekistan. This movement enjoys broad support among the entire population, but people are still afraid of the totalitarian regime which has been in existence for decades.

Together with a stagnating old-style party bureaucratic apparatus, Uzbekistan is subject to the added strain of territorial claims from other republics, as indeed are neighbouring republics. It is estimated that there are 28 areas in dispute between the various Central Asian republics (*Moscow News*, No. 11, 17 March 1991, p. 8). Conflicting territorial claims are used by local party leaders and mafias to fan nationalistic feelings and divert the attention of the population from their basic needs. This has resulted in many armed conflicts and clashes among local nationalities and between local nationalities and people of European origin, mainly Russians and Armenians.

The most tragic events took place during 1989 in the Fergana Valley: a massacre by the Kirghiz against the Uzbek population, causing the deaths of hundreds of women and children. In 1924, after the elimination of 'Turkestan', the city of Osh and its suburbs became part of the Uzbek SSR. Some 70% of the population were Uzbek; but in 1936, following a decree issued by Stalin, these lands were given to Kirghizia, turning it from an autonomous region into a union republic. Today the Osh region has two million inhabitants, 700,000 of them Uzbeks. The early 1970s saw the replacement of Uzbek leaders by Kirghiz ones. The rights of the Russian-speaking population were also infringed, and the authorities turned a blind eye to repeated skirmishes between Uzbek and Kirghiz youth.

The demand of the Kirghiz informal organization *Osh Aimagi* to distribute Uzbek-owned lands to Kirghiz was refused by villagers. However, the regional Party Committee headed by U. Siddikov openly welcomed the Osh Aimagi movement, and the Regional Soviet's Executive Committee decided to give sowing areas to the Kirghiz. The party authorities then came to Osh to conduct negotiations; but despite promises made by the party leaders, the issue exploded into open conflict. On 4 June, the city Executive Committee approved a meeting of the Uzbek population. During this meeting, however, the militia opened fire, causing 20 deaths and 100 wounded, all of them Uzbeks. On 5 June, Uzbeks were attacked by Kirghiz extremists who wore red ribbons on their foreheads. The slaughter resulted in over one thousand deaths in the town of Uzgen alone, and several thousand deaths throughout the region as a whole. The government of Uzbekistan demanded that Soviet President Gorbachev should give orders to deploy paramilitary troops but they came too late. Officers and soldiers were shocked by the atrocities – bodies of elderly men and children disfigured, women raped and killed, pogroms and arson.

The Kirghiz government did its best to cover up the crime. Indeed, it was the First Secretary of the Communist Party of Kirghizia, A. Masaliyev, the Prime Minister of the republic, Jamangulov, and other party leaders who were behind the policy of discrimination against the non-Kirghiz population. The Russian-speaking population fell victim as well, resulting in a mass exodus of Russian families from Kirghizia. These tragic events were not 'spontaneous' happenings. Preparations had been underway for a year. Foodstuffs and armaments were stored in caves, and MI-8 helicopters were used in the slaughter of civilians. A month before the events started, Uzgen sewing workshops were manufacturing those red ribbons on the instruction of the directors. Clearly, the operation had been planned. Nor was the tragic ethnic conflict in Osh and Uzgen a unique event. It was preceded by conflict between Uzbeks and Meskhetian Turks sent in exile from Georgia. In the Fergana Valley about 100 people were killed.

Finally, we should note that local authorities sometimes used the pretext of nationalistic riots in order to suppress democratic movements and manifestations. In Kokand, during the Fergana tragedy a meeting was held in front of the building of the city Party Committee. Those attending called for an improvement in the socio-economic situation, for measures to combat unemployment and the ecological crisis, and to ensure the security of the citizens of Kokand. The authorities responded by calling in troops to disperse the crowd. Soldiers were ordered to use guns against demonstrators, and as a result 26 people were killed and about 90 wounded. In 1989, similar bloodshed took place in the town of Parkent. Here the result was ten dead and 40 wounded.

Throughout the region, the mass media are under the strict control of the party apparatus. No independent political organization is officially recognized by the authorities or permitted to exercise its constitutional rights – neither the popular movement Birlik nor other new political parties and citizen movements in Uzbekistan.

And finally, let us stress that the peoples of Central Asia are not the only victims of totalitarian Soviet rule. Russians as well as other nations have suffered in their own way from the dictatorial rule of the one-party system. Real democratic reform is a precondition for raising standards of living in Central Asia, and for solving unemployment and the other tragic social, economic and ecological problems of the people.

FIGURE 5: CHINA

UNIVERSITY OF SYDNEY
Cartography

RUSSIA

HEILONGJIANG
Harbin

JILIN ●Changchun
Shenyang
LIAONING

NORTH KOREA
SOUTH KOREA

JAPAN

MONGOLIA
Ulan Bator

INNER MONGOLIA A.R.
Hohhot

BEIJING
TIANJIN
HEBEI Shijiazhuang
SHANXI Taiyuan
Yinchuan
NINGXIA-HUI A.R.

SHANDONG
Jinan

JIANGSU
Nanjing SHANGHAI
Hangzhou
ZHEJIANG

RUSSIA

GANSU
Xining
Lanzhou

QINGHAI

SHAANXI
Xian

HENAN
Zhengzhou

ANHUI
Hefei

HUBEI
Wuhan

JIANGXI
Nanchang

FUJIAN
Fuzhou Taipei
TAIWAN

SICHUAN
Chengdu

HUNAN
Changsha

GUIZHOU
Guiyang

GUANGDONG
Guangzhou

XINJIANG - UYGUR A.R.
Urumqi

Disputed Boundary

TIBET A.R.
Lhasa

YUNNAN
Kunming

GUANGXI-ZHUANG
Nanning

PAKISTAN

INDIA

NEPAL

BHUTAN
BANGLADESH

BURMA

LAOS VIETNAM

THAILAND

PHILIPPINES

A.R. | Autonomous Region
— | Province Boundary
● | Province Capital

0 — 1000 km

pK760śmb HS=800 25/9/91 B RoLoN Pattern ON Resolution STD SWAP B/W

12

The Brewing Ethnic Conflicts in China and Their Historical Background

Harald Bøckman

1. INTRODUCTION

The recent dramatic political changes in Eastern Europe and the Soviet Union have not only been centred around the disintegration of the socialist system. In several cases, the resurgence of nationalist movements and ethnic conflicts has played a crucial role. This has drawn attention to the fact that the Soviet Union inherited the geopolitical configuration of Czarist Russia.

There is also another former imperial power which conditioned the geopolitical configuration of a socialist successor, namely China. Recently, the outside world has focused mainly on the repression of the Chinese student movement, but reports about ethnic unrest in China are becoming more and more common. This paper will give a brief historical outline of ethnic relations in China and of Chinese Communist policies in this field. We also discuss possible scenarios for the future development of ethnic relations in China. This is indeed a vast topic, and the space allotted allows only a preliminary identification, delineation, and discussion of the main issues.

2. THE TRADITIONAL CHINESE WORLD ORDER

In the Confucian tradition, China's ethnic minorities and neighbouring peoples have been regarded as 'barbarians' of one kind
or another. Even in the earliest historical sources, there is a
lively concern about the various barbarian peoples who lived in
the regions around the core areas of Chinese culture of the times
(see e.g. Eberhard, 1942; and Pulleyblank, 1983). A strict distinction was made between those peoples who had been sufficiently
influenced by Confucian political ethics, and those who were not.
The more benevolent attitude towards the barbarians stressed
that the Empire would benefit if they would 'come and be transformed' (*lai hua*) by the superior Confucian culture. But on the
whole, the dominant notion was and has been *not to integrate*
the ethnic minorities and neighbouring peoples, but rather *to
control* them . This reflects a basic tenet in Confucian political
philosophy which stresses the importance of upholding the
separation between what was perceived as the civilized world
and the barbarian world, instead of being lax and inclusive in
this respect. Thus, control of the outlying regions and peoples
were intended just as much *a defense measure* as a strategy for
imperial conquest as we know it from the West and other
empires, like that of the Mongols.

The 'foreign relations' between the Empire and the people in
surrounding areas were perceived as an external expression of
the principles of social and political order that existed within
Chinese state and society. These relations were accordingly
regarded as non-egalitarian and hierarchically ordered, just like
Chinese society itself. Because of this, we cannot talk about
international relations or 'foreign policy' as such, but only of a
hierarchically ordered world with China as its centre (Fairbank,
1968a).

The states on the periphery of China were expected to send
regular tribute as a token of their submission to the Empire.
The tribute system was an elaborate system for regulating the
relations between the Empire and the various states and
peoples. This was always a bilateral relationship, and served
several functions. In the first place, it regulated the relationship
between the Empire and the state/people concerned. This relationship was normally expressed in terms of family relationships, where the Emperor always was the senior. In the second
place, it represented a certain control mechanism for the Empire.

Thirdly, it gave to the local ruler a certain legitimation for enhancing his power vis-a-vis local opponents and neighbouring polities. Fourthly, the tribute system also involved trade activity; this was especially valued by the tribute-bearing envoys, since the Empire bore all the expenses for the tribute mission itself. Furthermore, envoys would receive prestigious goods like silk in connection with the 'investiture' ceremony. Finally, they were entitled to trade for a number of days either in the capital or at the border. Trade thus became an integral part of the tribute system (Mancall, 1984, chs 2 and 3).

As Fairbank has pointed out (1968b, p. 3), the Empire was faced with the constant problem of making its ideological claim of being the one and ultimate centre of civil society correspond to actual practice. The basic problem was that the Sino-centric world was much larger than the region where Chinese culture was dominant. This was particularly the case with the Central Asian region, whose cultural features were in many ways fundamentally different from features of the Han socio-cultural organization. (Societies in this region might differ from the Chinese in characteristic like pastoral nomadism; tribal organization; using alphabetic script; professing Islam/Shamanism/Lamaism). The Chinese Empire was constantly faced with the military threat from sophisticated armies of mounted archers, and developed a number of strategies to neutralize them. These strategies aimed at keeping the barbarians in what has been freely translated as 'loose reigns' (*ji mi*), and included cultural and economic measures, strategic donations of brides (*he qin*), the system of appointing native chieftains (*tusi*), the policy of making the barbarians control barbarians (*yi yi zhi yi*), etc. (Yang, 1968, pp. 31-33). The strategic perspectives of the Chinese Empire thus extended far beyond the regions that the Empire normally controlled.

3. MINORITY POLICIES IN THE REPUBLICAN ERA

The downfall of the Qing dynasty in 1911 heralded a post-imperial era for China. The new government adopted a new national flag consisting of five horizontal bars in different colours. Each colour was to symbolize the five 'races' of China: the Hans, Manchus, Mongols, Tibetans, and the Tatars (a term for the various Turkic- speaking peoples). This division reflected the relative prominence of these ethnic groups during the Qing dynasty rather than any conscious theory of the ethnic composition of China.

In fact, Sun Yatsen (Sun Zhongshan), the founding father of the Republic, asserted that in China, the state and the nation (*guojia*) were one and the same. (He had admittedly good reasons for saying so, since the term for 'state' and 'nation' is the identical in Modern Chinese.) Because of the absolute prominence of the Hans, Sun was of the opinion that the Chinese state for practical purposes consisted of one nationality, and that the aim was to 'facilitate the dying out of all names of individual peoples inhabiting China,....and unite them in a single cultural and political whole' (Sun, 1953, p. 181). Later, under the influence of Comintern agents working with the Guomindang (Kuomintang) (GMD), the concepts of self-determination and autonomy for minorities were formulated as part of GMD policy, but they were never implemented in practice.

As Dreyer has pointed out, Guomindang concepts about the national question were at best traditionalist. The expressed aim was to promote an assimilationist (*tonghua*) policy towards the minorities (Dreyer, 1976, p. 40). However, this had only limited practical consequences for the minorities themselves, because the outlying regions in China remained warlord regions par excellence throughout the Republican period.

The pre-1949 policy of the Chinese Communist Party (CCP) concerning the minorities may – like the overall CCP political strategy for the liberation of China – be divided into a pre-1935 and post-1935 period. This coincides with the period before and after the ascent of Mao Zedong (Mao Tse-tung) as the supreme leader of the CCP and before and after The Long March.

In the pre-1935 period, the CCP followed closely the theoretical and political guidelines laid down by the SUKP and Comintern. As early as at the 2nd Congress of the CCP in 1922, the Manifesto of the Congress proposed that China proper (including Manchuria, the present Northeast), was to be a true democratic republic and that the three regions of Mongolia, Tibet, and Turkestan (present- day Xinjiang) were to be autonomous, forming democratic, self- governing regions. China, Mongolia, Tibet, and Turkestan would then unite on the basis of their own free will, thereby establishing a Chinese federal republic. (Brandt et al., 1952, p. 64).   This stance was reiterated throughout the 1920s.

The CCP established its first lasting 'soviet' base-area in Ruijin in Jiangxi province. In November 1931, it adopted a Draft Constitution of the First All-China Congress of Soviets and also passed a lengthy resolution on the national question in China – both modeled after the 1924 Soviet Constitution.

According to the proclamation of the Chinese People's Republic on 1 October 1949, China is *a unified, multi-national state*. In this formulation, there is no longer any mention of the idea of federalism or the right to secede. Accordingly, from 1935 and until 1949, a dramatic change of attitude concerning the national question must have taken place in the CCP. This attitude seems – along with the other strategic changes brought about by Mao's leadership – to have undergone a process of gradual sanification. Unfortunately, there is a dearth of documentation which can shed full light on this process.

The shift in CCP policy, formalized in the October proclamation of the People's Republic of China, may be explained in several ways, none of which are completely satisfying. In the first place, the Long March and the subsequent establishment of the Yan'an base area had given ample opportunity for the Chinese Communists to gain concrete experience with various minority peoples and become aware of the complexity of the minority situation. This experience was not always a particularly pleasant one (Dreyer, 1976, pp. 68-9).

Furthermore, the Communists were faced with a situation where there was a real danger that several of the minorities might ally with foreign powers in order to rid themselves of oppression from the Han Chinese. The Japanese had already established their puppet state in Manchukuo and were active in the eastern part of Inner Mongolia, were they enjoyed considerable backing. Among the Hui – Chinese-speaking Muslims – there was a strong pan- Islamic feeling at the time (Snow, 1968, pp. 306 ff.). In Xinjiang, the CCP had every reason to distrust the Soviet designs there. On the anniversary of the October revolution in 1944, an anti-Han riot broke out in the Ili valley in Xinjiang; subsequently, an East Turkestan Republic was established, only to be negotiated back into the Chinese fold by the end of 1948 (Clubb, 1971, pp. 365 ff.).

But the Yan'an period also provided a good opportunity for the CCP to get experience in how to handle the national question locally and regionally. In 1941, autonomous areas for Mongols and Huis were established in the liberated areas.

In the same year, a Nationalities Affairs Commission and a Nationalities Institute were established. In 1947, the first large-scale autonomous region, the Inner Mongolian Autonomous Region, was created.

4. MINORITY POLICIES DURING THE EARLY YEARS OF THE PEOPLE'S REPUBLIC

After national liberation in 1949, the Chinese Communists set about implementing a policy in the minority regions similar to the one they had implemented during the Yan'an period. Because of the precarious international situation of the People's Republic of China in the early 1950s, efforts to consolidate the minority areas – which were largely border regions – were given high priority (see e.g. Moseley, 1973). The only times the Communists met with significant armed resistance were in Tibet, among the Huis and the Kazakhs of Xinjiang.

The CCP strategy was to ally with the traditional leadership in minority regions, termed 'the patriotic upper strata'. At the same time, the CCP vowed that social and political changes could only come from within the minority societies themselves, and would not be imposed from outside.

In order to encourage this process of transformation, the CCP initiated several measures. In the first place, they started various types of relief work, introduced new technology, provided medical services, etc. Secondly, they started training large numbers of young people from the different minorities as cadres who would gradually take up positions as new leaders in their own regions. And thirdly, they launched large-scale studies of the social formations, the social history, and the languages of the various minority communities.

The purpose of these studies was twofold. One basic need was to determine the specific social formations of the various ethnic communities and how they differed from each other. Another need was to collect enough material to determine which ethnic group actually constituted a separate nationality and which groups could be said historically to belong to the same nationality. This was a rather sensitive issues: some groups who insisted on having the status of a distinct ethnic unit could be found to be a branch of an already existing group (for example, there were many groups with 'special cultural characteristics' that turned out to be ethnically Han Chinese), and others could be found to constitute a distinct ethnic group despite their own claims of affiliation with an already existing group.

This process was important for those involved because recognition as a distinct nationality would entitle the ethnic group to special rights and benefits. The most significant among these was the creation of a system of autonomous political entities. These entities were organized on three levels – as regions (*qu*), as prefectures (*zhou*), and as counties (*xian/qi*). The majority of them were established by 1958, but the process is still going on today in the form of local adjustments. As of today, there are 159 minority areas, divided between five autonomous regions, 30 autonomous prefectures and 124 autonomous counties. These regions account for about 64% of China's total territory; 78% of China's total minority population live in such autonomous areas.

5. THE LEFTIST YEARS

Looking back, 1957 must be regarded as a watershed in China's policy towards its minorities. Until then, the policies initiated in the Han areas and the minority areas had followed different courses, but from 1957 on, policies towards the minority areas generally became subordinated to the overall national political priorities. The late 1950s saw the beginning of the radical experiments of the People's Communes and the ensuing Great Leap Forward. The policy of allying with the upper strata in the minority areas came abruptly to an end, and was replaced by open class struggle. Whereas CCP propaganda until this time had mainly been directed against traditionalist Han Chinese attitudes towards the minorities, labelled 'Great Han chauvinism' (*dahan zhuyi*), the propaganda guns were now directed against ethnic resistance to the rapid transformation, which was branded 'local nationalism' (*difang minzu zhuyi*).

The reactions to this leftist wind in the minority areas were widespread, the best-known being the uprising in Lhasa in March 1959. But there was unrest in several other minority areas, the most conspicuous being the exodus of around 60,000 Kazakhs across the border to Soviet Russia in 1962. This was partly a response to the efforts of forced social transformation, and partly conditioned by the Sino-Soviet rift, (Moseley, 1966).

The early 1960s saw a retreat from the most radical experiments of the late 1950s. Efforts were made to patch up the
alliance with the upper strata among the minorities; but on the
whole, the process of social transformation in the minority areas
continued. With the widening Sino-Soviet rift, the border war
with India in 1962 and the preludes to the Vietnam War, the
minority areas became increasingly strategically sensitive areas
for the Chinese government.

The years of the Cultural Revolution led to renewed emphasis on class struggle and subsequent unrest in the minority
areas. In the drive against 'the four olds' – i.e. old customs,
habits, culture, and thinking – devastating losses were inflicted
upon the traditional culture of the minorities, especially in Tibet.
There were even those who proposed to abolish the system of
autonomous areas altogether. Renewed exodus of young Hans
from the urban areas did not, however, have a decisive impact
on the minority communities, since they were often settled in
specially designed camps or quarters. Minority rights were
curtailed, their economy brought further into line with that of
Han China, and the ethnic cohesiveness of their areas further
reduced. It is clear that these years also brought increased
tension within the minority groups themselves, and not only
between the Hans and the minorities. However, on the whole, as
Dreyer puts it, the difference between the radicals and the mod-
erates during the Cultural Revolution may be viewed as differences of opinion as to the timing of various measures, rather
than differing opinions as to end goals (Dreyer, 1976, p. 234).

6.   THE POST-CULTURAL REVOLUTION PERIOD

After the Cultural Revolution, the CCP changed its emphasis
from ideological struggle to economic work, initiating a restructuring of the economic and social relations, especially in the
countryside. As on earlier occasions after 1957, this turnaround
in national political priorities was also reflected in the minority
areas. The wave of 'reassessment' of almost all former policies,
as it was expressed by Hu Yaobang during his inspection trip to
Tibet in 1980 (*Beijing Review* no. 24, 1980, pp. 3-4, see also Hool,
1989, pp. 57ff), should to a certain extent be regarded as a
sincere effort to take a fresh look at the real political conditions,

but it was also used as a part of the political power-game after the Cultural Revolution.

There is no doubt that the policies initiated in the 1980s have given the minorities more room for articulating practices and policies specific to their own cultural traditions. Also, the new economic policies have created new opportunities for entrepreneurial minority people. For example, although reports in the West say that the Han Chinese have completely taken over local trading in Lhasa, in fact this is run mostly by Huis from Qinghai and Gansu.

However, recent economic reforms have also had the adverse effect of increased pressure on the minority areas. They have become 'boom areas' for entrepreneurial Hans, who flood into these areas, creating conditions reminiscent of 'the Wild West'. Even if there has also been a tremendous increase of prestige goods in many minority regions, the general feeling is one of having been victimized in an unequal race towards prosperity, since these minority regions in most cases are remote from the coastal boom areas. This is becoming an increasingly sensitive issue, because the manifest local riches – the abundant natural resources – are generally channelled out of the areas for processing. Moreover, complaints are frequently voiced about the increasing brain-drain from minority regions.

7. FORMS OF ETHNIC AWARENESS

An omnipresent cause for persisting ethnic awareness is the pressure caused by the large-scale immigration of Hans into traditional minority regions. This is a process that had been going on for a long period before 1949, but very unevenly. Whereas especially the former Manchurian homeland in the Northeast and the agricultural parts of Inner Mongolia had been receiving Han immigrants for several generations, immigration to the Xinjiang region primarily took the form of military-agricultural settlements (*tun tian*). Tibet had traditionally not experienced any Han immigration. Against this background, the Han presence in Tibet represents the most dramatic change, but on the other hand Tibet is the only significant minority region where the original population is still definitely in the majority.

Another important factor is the overall and long-term effects of the many-faceted process labelled modernization. Crucial to this process in terms of preconditions for a modern ethnic awareness is the introduction of general education and increased social and physical mobility. Modernization may of course also be viewed as tantamount to Hanification – as indeed it often has been interpreted by the minorities. This includes a whole range of processes from technological change to social and political transformations. Since these changes in the main have been initiated from outside, they have in many cases been perceived as outright efforts at Hanification.

Another important area is religious and cultural life. In some periods, minorities have experienced a strong pressure for secularization and even outright iconoclasm, when their religious centres have been looted and traditional 'backwards' cultural features have been banned. It is not surprising, then, that some of the most prominent features of renewed ethnic consciousness have taken the form of religious revival, especially among the followers of Islam, Tibetan Lamaism, and the Dai (Tai) Theravada Buddhists in the Southwest. This is the most conspicuous element of what we may call neo-traditionalist movements among many minorities today. Under certain conditions, this may evolve into alternative processes towards modernization also involving regional trans-border cooperation. The Dais in Xishuangbanna in the southernmost pocket of Yunnan are actively promoting the example of Thailand as a case where religious life and economic modernization have gone hand in hand.

Another factor likely to play an increasingly prominent role in the changing pattern of ethnic awareness is what we could call 'the contamination effect' of what goes on in similar surroundings in other parts of the world. The ethnic unrest in Soviet Central Asia is one obvious source of inspiration for the 'cousins' in Xinjiang, but the introduction of modern electronic media is also important. When Chinese television shows, for example, reports of the *Intifada* movement in Palestine in order to show the oppression of the Israelis, this may easily backfire for the Chinese authorities, in the sense that, for example, it may inspire Tibetans to try similar methods of resistance.

Finally, we should mention one feature of this whole process which is frequently overlooked. The 'cosmopolitan' Han culture has always been present throughout history. This has created a

tradition of material and cultural dependency as well as differing degrees of adaptation to and voluntary inclusion into the
Chinese World Order. In some periods, the minority peoples
moved away from the Hans, but they have also in periods
gravitated towards the Hans. This long-established pattern
has no parallel in any other major culture today, and this
'Chineseness' of the various minorities is undoubtedly still
very much a real fact. New York and Paris as centres of modern
living have not yet assumed any significance. It is still Shanghai
and Guangzhou, but increasingly Hongkong, which are seen as
the trend-setters.

For many, the bottom line of all the issues discussed above
concerns the crucial question: who has the final say in minority
issues – the Hans, or the various minorities? It is of course the
Hans, because of the simple fact that party- and state leadership
is dominated by Hans. But, as the Chinese saying goes,
xianguan buru xianguan – which admittedly loses somewhat in
translation: 'The county [higher] official cannot match the
[lower] official in charge'. There is considerable room for minority leaders to wield regional and local power. The reason for this
is as follows: under the imperial bureaucracy, the general rule
was that an official would never be posted to his native region.
Under the CCP, minority leaders, especially in the regions
adjacent to China proper, were for the first time allowed to
become officials within their native areas. Thus, today, we find
a strong and powerful stratum of minority officials with a vested
interest in continued CCP rule. In fact, many of the local and
regional minority leaders can be characterized as 'hard-liners' or
even 'maoists'. These labels may not have much ideological
substance, but they do illustrate the existence of an ethnically
based elite that is both strong and loyal. On the other hand,
recent developments in the Soviet Union vividly show that such
regional and local power-holders may shift allegiances when
their fortunes are challenged.

We will round off this discussion on ethnic sentiments with
a very brief overview of the situation in the major geographical
ethnic regions in China.

The only major ethnic group in the Northeast are the Koreans, who live adjacent to the Korean border in the Yanbian
region. They seem to have retained a large degree of ethnic
identity, and political developments on the Korean peninsula
will undoubtedly influence future developments among these
Koreans as well.

The Mongolian population in China is spread all over the Inner Mongolian Autonomous Region and also in Gansu, Qinghai, and Xinjiang. The looming headache of the Chinese authorities is the revival of Pan-Mongolism: future developments in the Mongolian People's Republic will undoubtedly be decisive in this respect. On the other hand, the Mongolian population in China is far from uniform. Whereas the nomad part of the population share many features with their kinsmen north of the border, the agricultural part of the population is much more acculturated to Han society.

In the vast northwestern region, mainly in what is now called Xinjiang ('the New Marches'), we find the largest concentration of Turkic-speaking people like the Uighurs, the Kazaks and the Kirgiz. This is also the main Islamic region of China, although there is no full overlap between Turkic-speaking groups and followers of Islam. There are Mongol-speaking Muslims as well, and above all the Chinese-speaking Huis, whose core region is in the Autonomous Region of Ningxia and Gansu Province, but who are also found in every province of China. The two main fears – as seen from Beijing – are the rise of pan-Turkic movements and the rise of Islamic movements. Turkic nationalism has resulted in attempts to establish independent states, like the 'Turkish-Islamic Republic of Eastern Turkestan' in Southern Xinjiang in 1933-34 (Forbes 1986, pp. 112 ff.); but on the whole, the region has traditionally been marked by conflicts between and among the various peoples there. The peoples adhering to Islam are mostly Sunni Muslims, and Islamic movements have not taken on a fundamentalist nature as we know it from the Middle East and Iran today. Historically speaking, it is actually the Chinese-speaking Huis who have been the most vigorous in staging ethnic-religious revolts against the 'infidel' Hans in modern times.

The situation in Tibet has been highly publicized. This is the region where the Chinese government has faced and undoubtedly will continue to face its biggest challenge. This is also the one region where calls for independence have been internationalized. Nowhere is the Han presence felt as massively as in the capital city of Lhasa – yet it is at the same time a place most resident Hans would be happy to leave if they were given better opportunities in the interior. The notion that there has been a strong pan-Tibetan urge for independence is, however, a popular Western assumption. Traditionally, both the Amdo and the Kam regions have resisted Lhasa dominance. Even if the resentment against Han Chinese oppression has given Tibetans from the various regions a new sense of common cause, it is unlikely that we will hear of widespread demands that go beyond real autonomy in the Kam and Amdo regions.

Finally, we have Southwestern China, where the complex ethnic pattern takes the form of a veritable Tower of Babel. However, there are only a few groups where the issues of ethnicity may result in major conflicts. The first one is the Muslim Huis, mentioned above. The second is the Dais (Tais), who live in two distinct areas in southern and southwestern Yunnan. There was formerly a strong irredentist movement in Thailand because of the mistaken assumption that Yunnan was the historical homeland of the Thais, but that seems unlikely to play any major role in the future.

8. FORMS OF HAN CHINESE RESPONSE

The main problem for the Chinese authorities would appear to be a sort of disbelief over the shortcomings of their own policy. They do not seem to understand that *they themselves have created the preconditions for modern nationalist and ethnic consciousness among the minorities*. The discrepancy between the theoretical framework and the practical results is experienced as very bewildering, most tellingly in the case of the Tibetans. Whereas the Lamaist state impeded the development of modern nationalist consciousness in Tibet prior to 1949 (Goldstein, 1989, p. 815ff), it has now become a major headache for the Chinese authorities.

Another factor likely to have a negative effect on Han/ minority relations is the general decline of social order in China. An unexpected by-product of the process of modernization has been the revival not only of traditional economic and social organization within Han communities, but also a revival of traditional Han prejudices against minorities. These popular assumptions depict non-Hans as backward, ignorant and dirty, although their cultural traditions and customs are at the same time the object of curiosity and fantasies. This form of folklore is also promoted actively for the sake of developing tourism. In some cases, this has also led to strong reactions from the minorities, even if they generally favour opening their areas for foreigners. Tourism is a field that will take on greater significance in the future – not only as a source of hard currency, but also as a channel of communication with the world outside China. The control of tourism in the minority regions is certain to become a tricky issue for the central authorities in the years ahead.

It then remains to discuss one feature of Han sentiments towards their own country that cannot be overemphasized. That is the paramount importance placed on 'the unity of the motherland' (*zuguode tongyi*) and the corresponding abhorrence of 'the splitting up of the motherland' (*zuguode fenlie*). The concept of unity, or rather 'unitarianism', runs deep in traditional Chinese political and philosophical thinking (Pye, 1985, pp. 64, 184). Because of this, what to an outsider may seem 'monolithic' in Chinese Communist theory and practice is not at all experienced as something alien that was imported to China with the ascent of CCP (Schram, 1985). China today may be characterized, to use a common saying, as a state where the regime 'has lost the hearts of the people but not yet the land/world of men' (*shi min xin er meiyou shi tianxia*). The collapse that was predicted in the wake of the Beijing massacres in the summer of 1989 did not occur, and the regime has been fairly successful in promoting 'unity and stability', even if it is fragile. The task of the times is to 'perfect the system', and not to seek fundamental changes. Within this conceptual straitjacket, we may come to see a surprisingly diversified and active policy towards the minorities of China. We may see active measures being taken to redress grievances from the minorities, we may see a diversification of measures according to differing conditions, an effort to 'perfect' the system of regional autonomy, and even moderate concessions towards real power-sharing, by including potentially troublesome elements into government bodies. For those who enter into active opposition, however, there will be no early warning or period of grace: '...we must fight resolutely and do everything we can to wipe out their splittist and sabotaging activities before they begin to spread' (Li, 1990).

9. A FEDERAL SOLUTION FOR CHINA

How, then, to envisage a development in China that neither lead
to fragmentation nor to a more authoritarian regime, a development that at the same time takes into account the legitimate
interests of the various ethnic groups? Everything depends on
the fate of the Central government. Prolonged power-struggle in
the Centre may leave it partly paralysed, with an ensuing
break-up of the country. If, on the other hand, gradual political
transformation can take place without excessive pain, the scene
may open up for what is possibly the sole viable solution to the
national question in China: namely, a federated China.

This solution will, however, not come easily. The very idea of
federalism is so alien to traditional Chinese political thought
that it is instantly equated with schemes for 'national division'
or 'national separation'. As of today, the concept of federalism
may, for tactical reasons, be applied to the Taiwan issue – but it
is not applied to any of the minority regions. The concept of the
unified, multinational state with an inalienable territory seems
as strong as ever in the minds not only of the rulers in
Zhongnanhai, but among the Chinese populace in general. A
federal solution for China would mean changing the main trend
of Chinese political thought and action in modern times. As
Lucian Pye has put it: 'The struggle of modern Chinese nationalism has been a Herculean effort to squeeze a civilization into the
framework of a nation-state' (Pye, 1985, p. 64).

However, the development of China itself is likely to force
the question of federal solutions onto the agenda. The reason for
this is the situation not only in the minority regions, but also
within the various regions of China proper (Schram, 1985;
Waldron, 1990). It may well prove impossible to rule such a huge
country in the same centralized way as before, once the country
reaches a certain level of modern development. Recent developments in the Soviet Union have shown how difficult it is to
restructure a relatively young but industrialized empire. This
chapter has, I hope, shown what a gargantuan task it will be to
initiate and carry through similar measures in the ancient and
industrializing empire which is China.

198   *Brewing Ethnic Conflicts in China*

REFERENCES:

Beijing Review, 1980. 'New Principles for Building up Tibet', no.24, pp. 3-4.

Brandt, C., B. Schwartz, and J.K. Fairbank, 1952. *A Documentary History of Chinese Communism*, Cambridge, MA.: Harvard University Press.

Clubb, O. Edmund, 1971. *China and Russia. The 'Great Game'*, New York: Columbia University Press.

Dreyer, June Teufel, 1976. *China's Forty Millions. Minority Nationalities and National Integration in the People's Republic of China*, Cambridge, MA: Harvard University Press.

Eberhard, Wolfram, 1942. *Kultur und Siedlung der Randvölker Chinas*, Leiden: J.E. Brill.

Fairbank, John K., ed., 1968a. *The Chinese World Order. China's Traditional Foreign Relations*, Cambridge, MA: Harvard University Press.

Fairbank, John K., 1968b. 'A Preliminary Framework', in Fairbank, John K., ed., 1968a, pp. 1-19.

Forbes, Andrew D.W., 1986. *Warlords and Muslims in Chinese Central Asia. A Political History of Republican Sinkiang 1911 – 1949*, Cambridge, MA: Cambridge University Press.

Goldstein, Melvyn C., 1989. *A History of Modern Tibet 1913-1951. The Demise of the Lamaist State*, Berkeley: University of California Press.

Hool, Cathrine, 1989. *Die chinesische Tibetpolitik unter besonderer Berücksichtigung der Jahre 1976-1988*, Bern: V. Peter Lang.

Li, Peng, 1990. 'Perform Our Work Well Among Nationalities and Strive for the Common Prosperity of All Nationalities'. Speech delivered at a national conference of directors of nationality affairs, 15 February 1990. BBC Monitoring Service, 23 February.

Mancall, Mark, 1984. *China at the Centre. 300 Years of Foreign Policy*, New York: The Free Press.

Moseley, George, 1966. *A Sino-Soviet Cultural Frontier: The Ili Kazakh Autonomous Chou*, Cambridge, MA: East Asia Research Centre, Harvard University.

Moseley, George, 1973. *The Consolidation of the South China Frontier*, Berkeley: University of California Press.

Pulleyblank, E.G., 1983. 'The Chinese and Their Neighbours in Prehistory and Early Historical Times', in Keightley, David N., ed.: *The Origins of Chinese Civilization*, pp. 411-66, Berkeley: University of California Press.

Pye, Lucian W., 1985. *Asian Power and Politics. The Cultural Dimensions of Authority*, Cambridge, MA: The Belknap Press of HUP.

Snow, Edgar, 1968, *Red Star Over China*, London: Victor Gollancz.

Schram, Stuart, 1985. 'Decentralization in a Unitary State: Theory and Practice 1940-1984', in Schram, Stuart, ed., *The Scope of State Power in China*, London: SOAS, University of London.

Sun Yatsen (Sun Zhongshan), 1953. *Memoirs of a Chinese Revolutionary*, Taibei: China Cultural Service.

Waldron, Arthur, 1990. 'Warlordism versus Federalism: The Revival of a Debate', *China Quarterly*, no. 121 (March 1990), pp. 116-28.

Yang Lien-sheng, 1968. 'Historical Notes on the Chinese World Order', in Fairbank, 1968a, pp. 20-33.

13

Linguistic Conflicts in Eastern Europe and Their Historical Parallels

Miroslav Hroch

1. INTRODUCTION

This chapter will analyze the relation between language and national identity conflicts in contemporary Eastern and South-eastern Europe, against the historical experience of nationalist movements in multi-national empires like the Habsburg monarchy and Czarist Russia during the 19th century. Analogies between current developments and the past can be justified only if we can view today's movements and conflicts in Eastern Europe as a kind of 'repeat performance' or fulfilment of a more or less successful Phase C or Phase B of their nationalist movements in the 19th century. By 'Phase C' is meant the third fundamental phase of nationalist movements: the rise of a mass national movement. This phase follows a successful Phase B – the period of patriotic agitation. During Phase B, language, or more correctly, the linguistic programme, has played an important role.

It is beyond question that the empires of the 19th century, like most contemporary states of this region, have a multi-ethnic character: on the territory of these states lived (and today live) several ethnic groups. Before the nationalist movement started, this multi-ethnicity was mainly an administrative problem: how to achieve a situation whereby different ethnic groups could communicate among themselves and with the state administration, without problems.

The situation changed with the onset of signals announcing 'national revival', a nationalist movement of the hitherto non-dominant ethnic group. How should we define 'nationalist movement'? Generally speaking, it was (and is also today) an attempt by the leaders of the non-dominant ethnic groups to obtain for their group all the attributes and rights characterizing the already existing nations:

• their own language and national culture;

• a complete social structure including ruling classes and intellectual elites;

• some degree of political self-government (autonomy).

In all instances, at the forefront of demands was the call for a national language – the linguistic programme.

2. THE LINGUISTIC PROGRAMME

To explain why language had priority in national movements involves a problem we cannot resolve without differentiating in terms of time, place, and – above all – content. What is usually called the 'linguistic programme' in nationalist movements of the 19th century and also in national conflicts of our days, in fact covers several aims which emerged only gradually. Earlier demands merged with those formulated later. The final linguistic programme was unthinkable without the previous formulation and realization of goals by the earlier movements.

From this perspective, I distinguish four strata of the national linguistic programme, in line with four stages of creating such a programme during the 19th century. Today, however, they are combined into one almost closed complex.

1) Interest in language as a subject of scientific research and of aesthetic value, an interest that mostly becomes a celebration of the language. This interest is linked not only to Enlightenment scholarship, but above all to the influence of the philosopher

J.G. Herder, who added to the celebration of the aesthetic, historical, and emotional values of a language a principled ethical and philosophical justification. In his view, language expresses a nation's way of thinking – indeed, almost the same as national thinking, a 'philosophy'. Without such a national thinking, expressed in literary language, the national character cannot emerge, nor can a nation emerge as a community. This model of thinking is still applied in some ethnic conflicts.

2) Language as an expression of national character cannot exist solely as a matter of celebration. It must exist as a written, literary language as well. This then gives rise to another stratum in the linguistic programme: efforts to create linguistic standards, cultivation of a new language, safeguarding its 'purity'. A non-written language cannot be used as an instrument of national identification. This stratum then involves three aims:

• self-identity of the language (different from other tongues);

• standardization and codification of the language;

• cultural intellectualization of the language (in literature, theatre, scientific activities).

Using the literary language tends to become the moral duty of all intellectuals from the ranks of the non-dominant ethnic group.

3) Normalized and codified written language can fulfil its role only if it is mastered by members of the given ethnic group (nationality). Thus, yet another goal enters the national programme: to have the new literary language taught in schools, and to have it made the language of instruction at all school levels. Different national movements have achieved very different results in these efforts during their Phase B and C of national movement, differences that are still relevant. Thus, for example, the Czech national movement achieved this goal during the second half of the 19th century, but not the Slovaks, who were thwarted by 'Magyarization' after the 1870s. The Finnish national movement has been more successful than the Estonian

one, which in turn has been more successful than the Lithuanian.

4) The highest, most challenging component of the linguistic programme is the demand that the written language of the non-dominant ethnic group be made equal to the language of the ruling nation – i.e. that it should become the language of administration, of the courts of justice and of trade in areas where the given non-dominant ethnic group is in the majority. This includes the demand that, in areas inhabited only or mainly by members of the non-dominant ethnic group, their literary language should become the ruling language, whereas the 'lingua franca' of the Empire (Russian in Russia, German in the Habsburg monarchy) should be used only in relations with the central authorities.

Historically, the older of these four components became integrated into the more recent ones during Phase B and Phase C. Thus it happened that admiration and celebration of the language remained within the linguistic programme and in the national consciousness of small nations, even in later periods when the nation was no longer threatened by assimilation and when it had won the right to introduce this language into administrative use. In other words: by the time when the written language of a small nation found a firm place in society, the mythological image of the national language was no longer confined to the actual role of every language: mediating social communication.

Language acquired an ideological mission, a purpose beside that of simple linguistic communication. It became the symbol of national identity and cultural independence, with a new, supra-linguistic and supra-communicative function. Such an adoring, overestimating attitude towards language can be found in the thinking of small nations in Eastern and South-Eastern Europe – even after successful movements managed to establish national states in the 20th century. The members of the former ruling nation still cannot understand this mentality; they have tended to regard language as merely a straightforward instrument of communication – as well as (though not always consciously) a symbol of their own privileged ruling position.

3. LANGUAGE AND NATIONALIST MOVEMENTS

How should we explain the role of the language in national movements? Generally we can say that the linguistic programme originally articulated new and separate interests – like the growing self- awareness of Czech craftsmen, and their resistance to the German-speaking elite and the state bureaucracy; or the freedom-seeking Estonian and Latvian small peasants in relation to their German landlords.

But how could language articulate various interests and conflicts which, in fact, had very little or nothing in common with language? The deeper reasons can be found in the process of social transformation from agrarian to industrial societies. Economic growth and innovation in the capitalist economy and its administration presuppose social mobility and communication. In turn, the need for mobility and communication compels a growing number of individuals, to become literate and capable of standardized presentation of messages. Thus language, together with culture, becomes for the individual the 'real entrance-card to full citizenship and human dignity', to use the words of E. Gellner.

However, this does not give a sufficient answer to why educated individuals from the non-dominant ethnic group, instead of turning to the standardized and routine use of the ruling state language, should choose instead a more complicated path for their involving mother tongue. One of the aims of the national movements and their linguistic programme has been to abolish bilingualism and to insist on the primary identity of the mother tongue and the written language. Only when such a language can be used by all educated persons is it possible to attain the status of a cultural entity that can bridge internal differences and conflicts within the national society. At the same time, the illusion of a 'conflictless' society gradually becomes an integral part of the national consciousness.

There is another important reasons for the over valuation of the linguistic programme of small nations. The patriotic agitators were the product of societies with an incomplete social composition, and they addressed their activities to the same societies. Whether these were primarily craftsmen or farmers, they were a group who during Phase B had no political experience or education. Such societies could hardly have become enthused by a politically articulated programme of civil rights. The linguistic programme, by contrast, was basic; it was familiar and understandable to them. They not only adopted it, but also passed it on to subsequent generations. That is why linguistic demands became for some decades the most suitable articulation of various interest conflicts in advanced societies – disputes in which conflicts of interest combine with the difference in language.

4. LESSONS FOR TODAY

How can a knowledge of the role of linguistic programmes in the multinational empires of the 19th century help us understand various national or ethnic conflicts in contemporary East and Southeast Europe? Current developments in this region should not be described as a new wave of 'nationalism', but as nationalist movements similar to those of the 19th century. Those movements have their own legitimacy, their cultural and social roots, try to repeat the stereotypes of national movements from the 19th century. Some of these movements have now arrived at Phase C (Estonians, Lithuanians, Slovaks), while others are still in Phase B (Ukrainians, Byelorussians etc.).

   We have all heard of the major role of linguistic differences in current political conflicts e.g., in the Soviet federation, and in Yugoslavia. However, is language really the main factor, the decisive reason for centrifugal efforts? Or is it only a superficial variable? What can we learn from the history of 19th century nationalist movements?

   Five fundamental lessons can be learned from the extraordinary role of the 'linguistic programme' in European nationalist movements:

1) During the 19th century, language began to serve as an instrument of agitation at a time when members of the non-dominant ethnic group had no political experience of a civic society and therefore could hardly formulate political argumentation. Today, after about half a century of Communist dictatorship, the situation is analogous. For similar reasons, then, language and the linguistic programme play a political role also at the present time.

2) During the Habsburg monarchy and in Czarist Russe, linguistic differences became an argument used by nationalist movements in opposition to the oppressive system. In Communist-ruled countries, the character of political oppression had changed, compared with the 19th century, but the Russian language remained the official language, the language of bureaucracy. To the members of a small nation or national minority, it is a symbol or even an instrument of political oppression.

3) An awareness of linguistic identity became central at a time when the old regime was disintegrating, with old ties disappearing as a result of political reforms or revolutions and as a consequence of the industrial revolution. The concept of linguistic identity brought together people from different social groups and later also from different political camps. Similarly, at a time when the planned economy and communist centralism are disintegrating, language suddenly and spontaneously takes over this integrating role.

4) The linguistic programme maintained its position at a time when the national identity was being formed. Even for those members of a small nation who held an administrative, economic or educational position, the language usually became something more than just a means of communication. Use of the mother tongue became a matter of honour, prestige, identity. When the Soviet system in the Baltic region or elsewhere pushed out the local language from most of administration and schools, this became a source of tension and dissatisfaction, although this was far from being a threat of Russification. Defense of the charismatic mother language has again become a matter of national identity and political prestige.

5) Another, motivation is to be found under the surface of events. After a certain stage in the nationalist movement comes a struggle for positions in the administration, army, courts of justice, etc. The local intelligentsia from families of the non-dominant ethnic group in the Habsburg monarchy or Czarist Russia found it very difficult to accept that imperial elites mostly filled from within their own ranks, and that many high officials in the province had been placed in positions by the Centre. They did not even have to know the language of the local

population. Very similar to this is the contemporary experience with officials from the Russian nomenklatura posted in the Baltic republics, or with Romanian bureaucrats in Hungarian and German areas of Transsylvania.

5. FURTHER CONSIDERATIONS

What further lessons can be drawn from these five parallels? One can argue against them by saying that the linguistic programme loses its justification as soon as the principles of equality of nations are realized. A state of equality based on individual human rights and determined by contemporary law and constitutions should – in theory – not give rise to conflicts. But this is true only in theory. Ethnic conflicts have become more prevalent than before: we can find them both in Phase B and in Phase C of the 'repeat performance' of nationalist movements.

Why has the linguistic conflict still such potentially explosive effects, even in situations where linguistic equality or rights are guaranteed by law? The main reason is that linguistic equalization, or language law, do not provide a guarantee of justice. Such equalization is in most cases not symmetrical: therefore, the equivalence of two theoretically equal languages does not exist.

Although more and more members of the non-dominant ethnic groups or small nations and ethnic minorities had to master the language of the ruling nation in the interest of their own professional success, members of the ruling nation were not forced to learn the language of a small nation, even when this formed the majority population in the given political or administrative territory. Most of them (e.g. Germans in Bohemia and Moravia or Upper Silesia) absolutely refused to learn this language. In their view, only their own language (i.e. the language of the ruling nation-state) was useful and important.

This asymmetry also has socio-linguistic implications: the language difference may come to serve as a social barrier. If we distinguish between the spoken and written (literary) language, then the written form becomes a kind of 'second language' that must be learned (as is the case with German, English, French, etc.). Analogous is the relation between the language of a small nation and the language of the ruling nation-state – with the latter being a language that must be learned. This means that children of the educated strata are at an advantage, since for them the language spoken at home is close to the written language, and the language of the ruling state-nation is routinely encountered. These children quickly learn at school to perform correctly in the state language. In contrast to this, children from families where parents have only a rudimentary education and where the mother tongue is different from the state language show inferior results. They have to surmount two barriers: between spoken and written language, and between mother tongue and alien state language. Naturally, they tend to achieve poorer results at school.

Members of a small nation and also of an ethnic (national) minority, especially members of the lower classes of these minorities, have therefore been disadvantaged by the unwillingness of the ruling nation to accept a real equality of the minority tongue and the state language. In such cases, formal laws guaranteeing 'language rights' to minorities or small nations cannot yield an acceptable solution.

This problem became even more complicated after World War I in cases where the former members of a ruling nation-state became a minority in new states ruled by the former 'small nation' – like the Czechs, Latvians, Lithuanians, Poles, or Romanians (in Transsylvania). When the German minority in Czechoslovakia or Poland, the Polish minority in Lithuania, the Hungarian minority in Romania, etc., refused to learn the language of the new nation-state, this unwillingness produced serious conflicts, ending in the political collapse in the late 1930s. In this context, we must not forget the dangerous role that was played by the 'mother-nations' (German, Magyar, etc.) of these new minorities.

This, probably, is the key parallel and the most important historical lesson for the outlying Soviet Republics – especially the Baltic republics. It also applies to Croatia. Just as the German minority refused to accept Czech or Polish as an alternative language of communication in Czechoslovakia or Poland after World War I, today many members of the Russian minority are refusing to learn the language of the local population. If in the 1920s and 1930s the unwillingness of the German minority led to an escalation of national tensions, preparing the way for political instability and foreign interventions, then surely the same tendency would threaten the further development of the free Republics, in the Baltic region and elsewhere.

The multi-national empires of Eastern Europe broke up after World War I so suddenly that there was little time to reach solutions to one set of challenges before another set of problems arose. An analogous situation could involve an accumulation of nation- building and minority challenges over a very short period of time. Ethnic differences could make the process of democratization very difficult, because ethnically un-integrated states could be faced with disruptive pressures from outside (the 'mother-nations') and from inside (new minorities).

6.   RECOMMENDATIONS

Finally, then, some historical experiences could indicate possible recommendations:

1) The linguistic difference must not become an articulation of conflicts of interest between two or more social groups; here, qualified explanation of the true character of such conflicts of interest in the mass media and school education would play an important role.

2) Proportional participation in administration of *all* ethnic groups living within the state-territory could diminish conflicts of interests.

3) Such participation needs to be made conditional on a symmetrical, bilingual mutuality: the majority learns the language of the minority to the extent that it can at least understand it, and likewise, the minority does not refuse to learn the language of the majority.

14

The Ethnic Conflict In Bulgaria: History and Current Problems

Borislav Tafradjiski, Detelin Radoeva and Douhomir Minev

1. INTRODUCTION

Bulgarian society is made up of a variety of ethnic entities. The country's crossroads situation in the Balkans and the dramatic historical destiny of its population have resulted in the formation of many layers of diverse ethno-cultural models and traditions, as well as in varying interpretations of the relationship between the agents of these differing cultural models. The modes of interaction between the various ethnic groups have themselves their own specific histories. Important here are the ideological models that interpret the essence of the coexisting groups and prescribe relationships between them, especially in the context of the formation of the Bulgarian nation.

Already the Bulgarian National Revival Period (18th-19th century) was dominated by the widespread belief that Orthodox Christianity determined the 'Bulgarian' ethnic and national identity, while the 'Turkish element' was identified with the Islamic faith. A normal phenomenon in the conditions of the struggle for state independence, which was also a struggle for affirmation of a Bulgarian national identity, this ethno-religious differentiation was not re-interpreted in the post-

National Revival period. The Third Bulgarian national state (19th and 20th century) failed to yield a new idea of Bulgarian ethnic and national identity.

Here, we shall only note that historians generally hold that the incomplete process of national consolidation in modern Bulgarian history paved the way for the subsequent evolution of ethnic processes and the accumulation of distrust between Bulgarians, Turkish-speaking Christians, Bulgarian-speaking Moslems and Turkish-speaking Moslems (Genchev, 1990).

2. HISTORICAL PERSPECTIVE

Ethnic differentiation based on both language and religion became ideologized during the Bulgarian National Revival. This resulted in several large-scale migrations towards Turkey and towards Bulgaria in the late 1800s.

With the Russo-Turkish war of 1877-1878 and the signing of the Berlin Treaty (1 July 1878), which granted independence to part of the territories occupied by ethnic Bulgarians, came largescale, spontaneous migrations in both directions: thousands of refugees from the Bulgarian territories which remained under Ottoman domination (like Macedonia and Western Thrace) rushed towards the Principality of Bulgaria and towards the autonomous region of Eastern Rumelia; at the same time, about 730,000 Turks migrated to Turkey.

Dimitrov has maintained that despite this 'shift of layers', in 1883 in North-East Bulgaria, Moslem Turks (without any clear-cut Turkish identity) accounted for 51% of the population, Greeks and Armenians – 1%, while Bulgarians numbered less than 48% (Dimitrov, 1990, p. 117). These facts meant serious problems for the policy of the Third Bulgarian State. But even then – irrespective of the historians' opinion that these regions had been populated by Christians as early as the 17th century and that the domination of Moslems should be regarded mostly as a result of assimilation – in the long run, official policy did not reconsider the established criteria of ethnic identification, but encouraged the migration of Turks from Bulgaria. This laid the foundations of a state-regulated migration policy, an almost century-long process of periodic migrations which, besides being self-reproducing on the basis of the transboundary networks of kinship ties, has kindled the ethnic differentiation of Bulgarians and Bulgarian Turks in Bulgaria. This migration flow ever since Bulgaria's liberation from Ottoman domination till the present day can be regarded as a major factor in the periodic aggravation of ethnic contradictions in the country.

Official data on migration are available from 1903, and from the Balkan Wars and immediately afterwards. At the end of these wars (1913) the peace treaty concluded between Bulgaria and Turkey included a special clause which for the first time dealt with the question of the 'ethnic minorities' in both countries, as well as a number of conditions regarding policy towards them, migration included.

1913 and 1919 saw large-scale immigration of Bulgarian refugees, mainly from Aegean Thrace. This process intensified with the signing of the Neuilly Treaty in 1919, under which (under pressure from the Entente) Bulgaria lost both its outlet to the Aegean and about 11,000 sq.km of its territory.

It is worth noting that in 1912, immediately before the Balkan Wars, the government of the Popular Party in Bulgaria (under Prime Minister Ivan Geshov) introduced some nuances in national policy towards Bulgarian Moslems. It encouraged the spontaneous formation of a Bulgarian national identity among Moslems, to be accompanied by a voluntary replacement of Turkish by Bulgarian names.

In 1913, however, in connection with the Balkan Wars, the next Bulgarian government under V. Radoslavov reverted to the conservative policy towards this population. The authorities put an end to the voluntary change of names and forced already Bulgarianized Moslems to restore their Turkish names.

Migration towards Turkey intensified especially after 1919: after World War I it was stimulated by both the Bulgarian and the Turkish state authorities. Kemal Ataturk's government, which came to power in 1919, pursued a policy of attracting all fellow-citizens to the 'Motherland'. In the 1920s and 1930s Turkey launched an official propaganda campaign for the migration of Bulgarian Moslems, resulting in an increased flow from Bulgaria to Turkey.

At the same time, especially after 1922, Turkey began a purposeful campaign to implant Turkish national consciousness among the Bulgarian Moslems of Bulgaria. Turkish organiz-

ations were set up among this population, as was a Union
of Turkish Teachers. Turkish textbooks were used in schools,
etc. The Bulgarian authorities let these processes continue
unimpeded. After 1932, however, Turkey revised its migration
policy and restricted the admittance of refugees.

Between 1919 and 1932, the problems pertaining to migration and minorities were almost invariably in focus in inter-
state relations in the Balkans. The many inter-governmental
negotiations, treaties and agreements are indicative of the
varying tensions linked with these questions. One aim was to
ensure the rights of the Moslem minority in Bulgaria and the
Bulgarian one in Turkey as guaranteed by the Neuilly and
Lausanne Treaties, respectively. Similar provisos are found
in the Mollov-Kafandaris agreement signed between Bulgaria
and Greece on 29 March 1928 for the settlement of migration
problems.

In practice, the two countries implemented these agreements
differently. While Turkish refugees in Bulgaria were able first
to sell their property and then leave the country, the property
of Bulgarian refugees (mainly in Turkey and partly in Greece)
had to remain there and they received no compensation.

In the second half of the 1930s, Bulgarian authorities once
again set about promoting the process of Bulgarianization of
Moslems in the country. They promoted the activities of
voluntary organizations (e.g. the Rodina cultural and charity
organization in the Rhodope mountains) which popularized the
Bulgarian origin of Bulgarian Moslems and worked for the
restoration of Bulgarian names and customs among this population. The process of voluntary adoption of Bulgarian names
again gained momentum; according to some sources, by the early
1940s a sizeable portion of the population already had Bulgarian
names (Zerov, 1990).

During World War II cases of migration were rare. Then,
after 9 September 1944, the official (Communist) authorities
radically changed their attitude towards ethnic Turks and
Bulgarian Moslems. This was prompted not by a new idea of
national unity, but by a re-interpretation of the ideological
model inherited from the National Revival in terms of the 'class
approach' and internationalism.

The Moslem and Turkish-language inhabitants of Bulgaria
were officially proclaimed to be ethnic minorities. Their ethno-
cultural differentiation, on the basis on the Turkish language,

was promoted. The new power launched a campaign of restoring Turkish names to Bulgarian Moslems. According to some sources, registers with their Bulgarian names were destroyed. Employees of pro-Bulgarian ethno-political organizations were persecuted for their loyalty to the 'former regime'. (Zerov, 1990)

These changes stirred discontent among the pro-Bulgarian minded part of this population and boosted the self-confidence of the pro-Turkish segment. Thus, in the 1947 census, a sizeable portion of the Rhodopean Moslems, although considering themselves Bulgarians, stated that they were Turks.

The new government proclaimed a new approach to minorities in Bulgaria. A number of Communist Party and government decisions between 1948 and 1951 outlined and implemented special measures for:

• the accelerated social and economic development of regions with Turkish population;

• giving priority to young people of Turkish origin in high school and university admission;

• setting up special funds for the cultural development of Turkish-populated regions, etc.

The Turkish language began to be taught in primary schools in areas with predominantly Turkish population, and Turkish secondary and high schools were founded in the bigger towns of these regions. Teachers from Azerbaidjan were invited, at the expense of the state. An inspectorate of Turkish schools was set up under the Ministry of Education. Two newspapers and one magazine in Turkish began publication. In regions with Turkish population the radio stations transmitted in Turkish, and the national radio also had some broadcasts in this language. Turkish drama theatres were founded in Kolarovgrad (Shoumen), Haskovo, and Rousse. Various Turkish amateur art ensembles gave performances in all-Turkish regions.

Registration of Turkish ethnic affiliation was made easier in a number of ways. For instance, every citizen who certified with the help of two witnesses that he professed the Islamic faith and spoke Turkish, could be registered as a Turk after filing a written application with the local council. As a result, about 130,000 Tartars, Gipsies and Bulgarian Moslems were registered as Turks. These provisions were cancelled in 1955, however.

The first major migration wave after 1944 occurred in 1950-1951, when about 150,000 Bulgarian Turks left for Turkey. Among them were many Gipsies and Tartars who had registered as Turks – this was later used by the Turkish authorities as a pretext for terminating the migration.

In 1958, the Bulgarian authorities introduced corrections to their policy as regards ethnic Turks. They continued to adhere to the official concept that the Turks were an ethnic minority, but their ethno-cultural differentiation was restricted. The 1958 Plenum of the Central Committee of the Bulgarian Communist Party took a decision to reduce Turkish-language education. Turkish began to be studied mainly as an optional subject, the circulation of Turkish newspapers and magazines decreased, as did radio-broadcasts in Turkish. Special emphasis was laid on halting Turkish-language education among Gipsies, Tartars and Bulgarian-speaking Moslems. Instructions were given that children of mixed marriages were to be registered as Bulgarians.

These inconsistent changes, made within a little over one decade, intensified the already existing mistrust, especially among Bulgarian Moslems, towards the ethnic policy of the state. Witnesses testify that in 1964, there was a riot of Bulgarian Moslems in South-West Bulgaria against one of the many changes of names (from Turkish into Bulgarian) forcibly carried out in 1962. The government then discontinued the Bulgarianization campaign and restored their Turkish names.

Another 120,000 people migrated to Turkey between 1968 and 1978, while two or three times that figure were willing to leave. This migration took place within the framework of a 1968 bilateral agreement concerning divided families where family members had migrated to Turkey prior to 1952. After the expiry of the agreement term in 1978, the two countries agreed to stop discussing the refugee issue in their further relations.

As a whole, the 1960s saw the launching of a differentiated policy towards Bulgarians believed to be of Turkish ethnic origin. The Bulgarianization policy in that period was oriented mainly towards Bulgarian Moslems. Forcible adoption of Bulgarian names was undertaken, but only in some regions, sporadically, and in the nature of an experiment.

After 1970 came an intensification of the work (mainly ideological and political) for 'national identification and patriotic education of Bulgarians professing the Moslem faith'. By the late

1970s nearly all had Bulgarian names, due to administrative pressure. Amateur Turkish cultural organizations and centres were abolished, as were Turkish schools. Newspapers and magazines intended for ethnic Turks were now published in the Bulgarian language only.

Bulgarian Turks were encouraged to adopt Bulgarian names, which they then did gradually and mainly voluntarily. By 1984-1985, however, this had become a large-scale campaign carried out through forcible command-and-administrative methods: all Turkish-Arabic names were replaced by Bulgarian ones.

Already in April-May of 1985, Bulgarian Turks organized underground resistance against this forcible assimilation and for the restoration of their cultural rights. The authorities responded with repression and attempts at moral discrediting of ethnic Turks through propaganda and involvement of the local Bulgarian population.

As a whole, the years 1985-1989 were a period of 'cold war' in ethnic relations. Ethno-national ideas and values gained ground among the Bulgarian Turks, and the movement for restoring their ethno-cultural rights grew in scope. It intensified further alongside the overall crisis of Bulgarian society, and in the spring of 1988 took the form of open protest. On the other hand, ethnic Bulgarians developed a syndrome of chauvinism.

With the global crisis and the politicization of some sections of Bulgarian society in 1988-1989, and with the formation of oppositional social and political organizations and movements (some spontaneously backed by ethnic Turks), the ethnic conflict got out of control.

In April 1989 the Politburo of the Central Committee of the Bulgarian Communist Party adopted a decision 'for the further consolidation of the Bulgarian socialist nation'. This contained special instructions for ideological and political work among Bulgarian Turks and for accelerated development of the regions with such populations.

In May 1989 a powerful protest wave spread in regions with a homogeneous Bulgarian Turkish population: hunger strikes, protest rallies, sit-down strikes, demonstrations, etc., which were often discontinued after clashes with the authorities. The demands launched were mainly for the restoration of Turkish names and former religious and cultural rights. Parallel with this, protests were aimed against Bulgaria's political system, as personified by the Zhivkov regime. Some time later, Ahmed Dogan, the leader of the Rights and Freedoms Movement, explained thus the essence of the Movement:

> For us, the basic problem lies not so much in the name, though it occupies an important place in the value system. Social security is the first major problem. When the state cannot guarantee equal participation in public life, in the choice of a profession, in the study of a language, then this section of the population is restricted in its possibilities of public performance. (Dogan, 1990)

Meanwhile, many ethnic Turks prepared to leave for Turkey, taking advantage of the amendments and supplements made to the Law of Foreign Passports in May 1989. Regions with such populations faced great difficulties in industry and agriculture, trade, supply, services and health care. There was an acute shortage of manpower. Some enterprises were on the brink of closure; crops were left unharvested. The Bulgarian population from the affected regions, as well as people from all over the country (students, soldiers, workers and pensioners) rushed to help, working non-stop up to 15 hours a day, six days a week, with no summer holidays.

Data from sociological studies carried out at that time show that the migration was accompanied by profiteering, pillaging and fraud. The victims were the Bulgarian Turks who were preparing to leave for Turkey and were in a hurry to settle their property problems. (Cf. Petkov & Fotev, 1990)

Then, on 22 August 1989, Turkey unexpectedly closed its borders to Bulgarian citizens, who were coming in droves, and introduced a visa regime.

All in all, in May-August 1989 about 330,000 people left Bulgaria for Turkey, of whom 105,000 had returned by 21 January 1990. According to the Turkish newspaper *Milljyet*, 421,000 Bulgarian citizens arrived in Turkey, and 120,000 had returned to Bulgaria by 20 March 1990.

As a result of changes in the ruling Party and the Bulgarian government after 10 November 1989, on 29 December 1990 Bulgaria's State Council and government adopted a decision which denounced the errors and violations committed during the so-called 'restoration process' (1984-1989). It stressed the need for a radical change in policy on the national question. This decision provided for restoration of the Turkish names of all those who so wished and of the religious and cultural rights of Bulgarian Turks.

On 31 December, only two days after the government's decision was proclaimed, a wave of protests swept the regions with mixed population: Bulgarians staged rallies and strikes, cars with protesting people set out for the capital, a live chain surrounded the Parliament. They protested against the authoritarian way in which this decision had been adopted (without any public opinion poll) and against its national-nihilistic nature. They voiced fears for their own security and that of the country. On their part, Bulgarian Turks held counter-rallies in support of the decision and demanded more extensive rights.

Though democratic, the further steps taken by the political forces did not help ease tensions. Representatives of the government met with demonstrators in Sofia and in the countryside. It became clear that the conflict was assuming nationwide proportions. A Public Council for National Conciliation convened; and between 8 and 12 January this Council held round-table talks with representatives of all parties concerned. It proved possible to reach consensus, and three days later the Parliament adopted a Declaration on the National Question.

A Parliamentary commission on the national question was set up which, assisted by the non-parliamentary opposition Coalition of Democratic Forces and representatives of ethno-political movements, drafted a new Law on the names of Bulgarian citizens. Adopted by the Parliament on 5 May 1990, it aims at restoring the names of all those who so wish.

Generally speaking, after April 1990, the main emphasis of the ethnic conflict shifted to demands linked with housing, labour, legal and other social problems that arose on the return of ethnic Turks from Turkey, and that were related to the unwillingness of Bulgarians in the respective regions to have them back.

Most initiatives that the authorities took for curtailing the conflict after 29 December 1990 were based on the idea of seeking dialogue and consensus. However, in the context of the rapid political changes and polarization in the country they remained ineffective, blocked by the two ethnic groups' distrust of the state, and by the local authorities' distrust of the political elite. A sociological study in December 1989 on the attitude of local Party functionaries towards the ethnic policy 1984-1989 showed that many of them had a dual attitude: on the one hand, they believed that this policy was inconsistent, lacked a clear-cut strategic goal, and was characterized by unfounded decisions and many tactical mistakes (Petkov & Fotev, p. 226). On the other hand, they upheld the view that 'what has already been won should not be given up' (ibid., p. 223).

3.   INTERPRETING THE CRISIS

Discussions on the background and reasons for the ethnic crisis in Bulgaria, launched in the mass media and in the scholarly community, have outlined two kinds of interpretations – which have little in common at present.

The *first* interpretation, which is widely held, maintains that the ethnic crisis is linked mainly to definite *historical* and *geopolitical* realities, These include the differences between the two ethnic groups in terms of demographic and residential structure, and of the employment structure depending on their family and kinship models, as well as religious differences. All these historical differences, geopolitical circumstances, social peculiarities and cultural features are considered as natural background factors in the crisis. Moreover, they are not believed in themselves to reflect the specific features of the now disintegrating socio-political system of the past 45 years. In this context, the reasons for the ethnic conflict that erupted in 1989 are sought mainly in the 'mistakes' made by the camarilla of the former head of state, T. Zhivkov, rather than in the deeper contradictions rooted in the so-called 'existing socialism'.

This approach underrates the importance of concrete historical and social phenomena in the appearance of social and cultural differences between the ethnic groups and in their juxtaposition. Furthermore, it generally regards the existing differences as stable characteristics of the ethnic groups themselves (language, religion, origin, educational and employment models, etc.) – rather than as a differentiating set of characteristics which define these groups as related to one another, and each of them as related to the state and the civic society (Lijphart, 1990).

The *second* type of views emphasizes the *social nature* of the differentiation of the ethnic groups. This approach proceeds from the idea of the inherent link between totalitarianism and ethnic confrontation. One argument cited in favour of this is the assumption that the totalitarian state and political system is not an outsider as regards public life. Instead, it is seen as generating its own inertia in society by force of such basic characteristics as the state's total penetration into civic society (Zhelev, 1982), the penetration of politics into the economy (Kornai, 1985); or, 'its ability for a permanent limitation of the possibilities for autonomous activity in any sphere of social activity' (Rupnik, 1990, pp. 290-1).

Viewed in this context, the contradictory and conflicting nature of ethnic relations relates above all to questions of power. It is assumed that the forms of class domination and social control under totalitarianism, through the specific mechanisms and tools of control, influence and modify the differentiating peculiarities of the ethnic groups, and contribute to the accumulation of tension between and within these groups, suppressing any autonomous instance of cultural originality and social initiative. Totalitarian bodies and mechanisms of management and social control block many of these possibilities for spontaneous regulation of ethnic contradictions – or rather, they leave space for autonomous regulation only in an alternative form.

Generally speaking, the degree to which the preconditions and reasons for the crisis in ethnic relations are sought in the context of socio-political and socio-class realities under socialism, also indicates the distance between the above two interpretations. This differentiation does not apply only to researchers and politicians in Bulgaria, or only to those from former socialist countries. During international sessions of experts held in Bulgaria recently, this differentiation was also manifest among scholars and politicians from Western Europe, the USA and Canada, who assessed the country's ethnic crisis from the position of 'outside observers'.

Proponents of the idea of 'realities' should not simply be dismissed. It is an indisputable fact, for instance, that there were mass migrations of ethnic Turks even before the establishment of the socialist system in Bulgaria. On the other hand, there are proofs that in most cases migrations of ethnic Turks have coincided in time with mass migration of ethnic Bulgarians. According to official data, at present about three million Bulgarians live outside Bulgaria. Under socialism, there was no mass migration of Bulgarians, because all citizens were denied the right to migration. Temporarily and purely as an exception, however, this right was granted to ethnic Turks at a time when the social tensions in the country had to be remedied.

We cannot deny the existence of a number of historical conditions for the ethnic problem, which leave open the question of whether and to what extent the Turks and the Bulgarians in Bulgaria are diaspora communities, or have native status in the territorial homeland. The Bulgarians are a nationality formed by the merger of the tribes of the local Thracians, Slavs and the Turks – protoBulgarians from Central Asia. These orgins favoured the later adoption of a sizeable part of the Turkish conquerors' ethnic culture. On the other hand, during the five-century-long Ottoman domination of Bulgarian lands, the original population was subjected to systematic assimilation by its conquerors, which turned religious characteristics into criteria of ethnic division. This created a situation of non-defined ethnic differentiation which complicates relationships even today.

The geographical situation of Bulgaria and Turkey, sharing a state border, is another 'reality' which conditions the long-existing ethnic problem. Following World War II, the two countries came to join opposite military alliances – the North Atlantic Treaty Organization and the Warsaw Treaty. The military-political confrontation, a constant source of tension between the two countries, was also transferred to relations between the two ethnic communities in Bulgaria. During periods of inter-state political confrontation, tensions were reflected in everyday relations between Bulgarians and ethnic Turks. Geographical proximity made real the intentions to migrate, as well as facilitating the dissemination of Turkish propaganda among ethnic Turks in Bulgaria.

Some proponents of the idea of the 'natural' character of the differences between the two ethnic groups underline the role of religious differences. Specifically, they refer to a particular aggressiveness seen as typical of Islam, which is easy to revive and kindle, especially given the existing possibilities for propaganda among the relatively compact groups of ethnic Turks in Bulgaria. This view is often backed up by reference to the fate of Cyprus.

Obviously, the ethnic division in Bulgaria has deep historical roots which go beyond the concrete historical scope of socialism. However, to overrate them in explaining the crisis is useless, as well as potentially dangerous. It can make the country's future ethnic policy ineffective or even lead it into an impasse. The same holds true if we overemphasize the 'situational' factor. As a whole, the explanative paradigm of 'realities' obscures the presumption that the ethnic crisis is hardly likely to be indirectly controlled by changing the specific social conditions which determine it. Much more effective would be political approaches that relied mainly on a direct and special regulation of ethnic relationships. Given the overall aggravation of Bulgaria's socio-political situation and the growing social tension during its transition to democracy and market economy, such an approach poses grave dangers as the ethnic crisis has become a national issue.

The *second* approach to interpreting the ethnic crisis is based on the general principle which Wallerstein (1974) formulated thus: '... initially small differences, which grow in the process of social interaction, consolidate and can be defined as "traditional"'. From this point of departure, the reasons for the ethnic crisis are sought, whereas the 'traditionality' itself – the so-called 'realities' – are regarded in a specific way. It is tempting to use traditionality as an explanation of events, but as Wallerstein points out: '... the traditional has always been an aspect of the establishment of the present and never of the past.' (p. 98.)

Given such a premise, particular significance attaches to the differentiating processes which increase differences between the two ethnic groups in the spheres of labour, forms of labour organization, the way of formation and size of incomes, degree of preserving ties with agricultural work and rural lifestyle, degree of preserving family-kinship ties and family models, and so on.

On the other hand, the differentiating processes are often linked with the total crisis of the previous social system and with the specific ways in which this crisis manifested itself in the individual spheres of social life.

Proponents of this view place the emphasis on several aspects of the social crisis, without arranging these aspects into a cause-and-effect chain. Often these aspects include basic characteristics of the totalitarian regime, although formulations may differ. But no matter whether speaking of power-managerial reasons, political systems or of the so-called leading role of the Communist Party, researchers underline the super-centralization and super-organization characteristic of the totalitarian regime. The goal was to gain complete domination over all objective (institutionalized) and subjective (personified) power resources on the part of the Party-and-state nomenclature, which had permeated the legislative, executive, economic and cultural-semiotic means of power. (Stavrev, 1990)

The economic crisis is generally associated with totalitarian power. This is so because, on the one hand, such power inevitably dooms the economy to growth by extension, confining economic development to quantitative expansion and a simple increase of the invested resources. The exclusion of other types of economic development is seen as a key economic factor in maintaining the former power system.

On the other hand, economic life under this power system was triggered mainly by the administrative commands of the ruling centre. But even in the early 1970s it was growing obvious that the effectiveness of these commands was on the wane. Even the simple quantitative expansion in the economy was becoming complicated – due to the increase in production-economic ties, which the centre tried to focus within itself, even when this had become practically impossible. Thus, by 'expanding' the production-economic system, the centre itself generated the cause of its diminishing control over this system. Ironically enough, striving to retain power leads to losing it.

An essential question in studying this aspect of the social crisis concerns the growing tension in the relationship between the national centre and the various administrative-territorial (local) management centres. This is sometimes interpreted also as a growing tension within the structures of the ruling party.

Researchers often focus on the social aspects of the crisis. In practice, this covers a vast range of different manifestations of the crisis and their consequences. It is worth noting the view held by some sociologists that it is impossible to orient the super-centralized, super-organized and extensive production-economic sphere to the needs of the population. The continuous growth in resources invested in this system of 'production for production's sake' inevitably restricts the possibilities of meeting people's demands, and exerts pressure on the population. This development can also be interpreted as a weakening link and even a rupture between the economic and the social sphere. One of the basic ties in society – that between labour and consumption – becomes dissociated. Not only is the development of the social sphere delayed, but violations of and deviations from its normal functioning also increase. This applies to housing construction, education and health care – to mention only some examples.

The appearance of parallel structures in the economy and of malformations in the labour and economic behaviour of the population is a predictable and important consequence of these processes. The 'second and third' economy – or, from another point of view, the so-called self-welfarization – acquire prominence. More and more of the population's standard of living is formed outside official structures and mechanisms, and remains beyond the centre's control and influence.

The data we have so far are insufficient to assess the scope of this phenomenon, but there is reason to believe it involves the real income of nearly half the population of Bulgaria. Especially within agriculture, conditions are quite favourable for its manifestation. As is well known, the 'swindling' of finished products and raw materials became so widespread that special measures had to be taken. No less current was the 'swindling' of labour, equipment and so on, from public farms to the privately owned ones. According to some experts, about one-third of products got 'distributed' in this way. Some simple calculations yield results in line with the above estimates. Finally, we should bear in mind that the imminent global crisis of society manifests itself in a specific way on the local level. The limitation and gradual disintegration of the municipal economy as a foundation of local management gradually deprived it of real power, confining it to lower-level activities linked mainly to re-distribution of resources and immediate control of the population.

4.   THE SOCIAL DEVELOPMENT OF BULGARIA'S ETHNIC
     COMMUNITIES

The relation between the various aspects of the global crisis in society and the changes in ethnic relationships in Bulgaria could be summarized as follows:

The pressure brought to bear on the population affected in different ways every ethnic group, which in turn responded to it in its own manner. These differences are particularly clear when considered in the light of the discrimination of local communities.

Over the past few decades in Bulgaria, most settlements with mixed population have become ethnically 'clearer', with increasing territorial differentiation and concentration of the population into ethnically homogeneous groups. These processes have been stronger in the countryside than in towns. Ethnic differences have also taken shape according to the type of settlement: most ethnic Turks have remained in the villages, while Bulgarians have tended to move to towns. The Bulgarians who have remained in the villages are mostly pensioners, while among ethnic Turks there is a more even age-distribution.

The two groups have reacted differently to industrialization, with Bulgarians joining the industrial sphere to a greater extent than ethnic Turks. The ethnic Turks have developed a model of employment quite different from that of the Bulgarians: it includes specific spheres of employment such as construction, trade and services, light industry, health care – all of which are spheres of economic stagnation.

Among ethnic Turks we may also note a high relative share of unskilled manual labour, mostly under poor working conditions. They also preserved links with agricultural work and combined industrial and agricultural labour, etc. The two groups have also developed different educational structures and specificities.

The main effects of the social differentiation characteristic of the disintegration of the local community have favoured the different development of ethnic groups within society.

Firstly, Bulgarian families have become much more torn apart: coexistence between several (at least three) generations has been hard to maintain. Moreover, the young Bulgarian family frequently finds itself in an urban environment, and has more or less adopted an urban way of life. The situation of the Turkish ethnic population is quite the contrary. There the disintegration of the three-generation family has been less pronounced; the tie with the land and farm labour has been preserved; their environment has remained largely rural.

Secondly, the two ethnic groups have different income sources (and therefore different incomes), as well as different living conditions.

These two consequences (which in turn give rise to others) are also key points in a comparatively long process of disintegration of the local community. Differences in income sources can be seen from the fact that ethnic Turks have depended on earnings (in cash and in kind) from the privately owned farm, from the state sector of agriculture, and only marginally from salaries from industry. For the Bulgarian population, the share of the various sources in the gross income has been quite different. If, for instance, an average of 60 or even 70% (in the last few years) of the overall income of a Turkish family has been generated from work in state and personal farms, for a Bulgarian family this figure has not exceeded 35-40%.

The extended family, which preserved its tie with the land and was engaged in farm labour even if some of its members began work in industrial enterprises, remained closely linked with agriculture. This difference turned into an advantage in the 1970s and the early 1980s, in connection with the sizeable expenses for food in the overall family budget in Bulgaria, and in terms of stimulating the production of certain kinds of farm products and the promotion of private farms and self-subsistence. Combining industrial and agricultural employment was also advantageous, due to the increasing disorganization within the economy on the municipal levels which allowed for transferring labour from the industrial sector to agriculture while preserving the incomes obtained from state enterprises. This can be illustrated by the increase in overtime work and the simultaneous increase in unused working time (lost working days). Both our and other studies carried out in Bulgaria show that such a situation satisfied both industrial workers and managers: it allowed the former to engage intensively in other income activities besides their employment in state enterprises, and the latter to compensate for some consequences of the overall disorganization of production.

Moreover, income differentiation at the municipal level (due to the growing incomes of ethnic Turkish families) was influenced by the possibilities of misappropriating state property, especially in farming. It is not accidental that reports on and measures against 'wasteful practices' have occupied a prominent place in various official documents on agriculture of late. Special measures were adopted to combat these malpractices, which were considerable. Studies have indicated that they were much bigger than official data show. If we consider not only the direct appropriation of output, but also the shift of working efforts, the use of machinery, materials, fuels, etc., we can assume that about 20-25% of the 'public' sector in farming was in practice private.

The above specificities of the social development of the ethnic Turkish community can help to explain the sizeable gap in incomes – which are well-known, published in information sources and controlled by the state authorities – and savings, which do not correspond to the incomes of this group.

This also leads to another, more important conclusion. Over a long period of time, Bulgaria's ethnic Turks have lived and acted within a system of production relations greatly differing from that of the bulk of the Bulgarian population. The two groups have developed along different 'social coordinates'. An invisible wall has separated them far more effectively than any material barriers. This 'wall' is the most important characteristic and consequence of the disintegration of the local community under the pressure of the totalitarian state. Additionally, we should note that the characteristic reactions to this pressure have differed. The Bulgarian population proved more susceptible and vulnerable to it, and therefore gradually became an amorphous aggregate of people. By contrast, the ethnic Turks built an isolated community and worked for its growing consolidation and isolation from the surrounding social milieu. Covered by a specific network of social relationships and developing within a definite social specificity, the Turkish population can be regarded as not belonging to the fellowship or community. It was isolated as a social milieu, as a network of relations. To all intents and purposes, this population inhabited community territory, but it became increasingly consolidated, isolated, closed within itself – and inevitably moved towards a point of uncontrollable spontaneous action. These were the changes we had in mind when speaking of the disintegration of the local community.

Particularly important in these processes were the already mentioned factors: specific spheres of employment; sustained links with farm labour and the rural way of life; the preserved and increased role of family-kinship ties among ethnic Turks. From a social point of view, the Turkish ethnic group 'left' the community, the social milieu of a local community characterized by definite social relationships. In fact, the high authorities acted to consolidate and intensify private life and private business among one section of the population which, moreover, had ethno-religious specificities. In this way, ethno-religious differences became coupled with other differences; in the long run this has led to the appearance of an isolated social sphere.

The better preservation of the traditional family and the importance of kinship ties among ethnic Turks have played a particular role in this respect. In such families, elder members have the final say, and the family is a major means of handing down traditional values, especially religious ones, to the younger generations. The religious faith of this population has by no means weakened over the years. Therefore it grew increasingly sensitive to any pressures on religion and to violations of its religious feelings. Deprived of the possibility to express its demands in a normal and legal way, this community accumulated explosive attitudes which peaked in connection with the name-change policy. The coordinated actions, the quick spread of common attitudes and the adherence to share ideas confirm that this group was already well-consolidated. Faced with a problem which they had themselves created, the higher authorities only triggered off the avalanche of events with their decision to change the names of ethnic Turks. Worth noting here are another two factors. The first is the commuting migration of ethnic Turks. Its social equivalent is the preserved family of many generations, the preserved link to the land and the appearance of a specific group. The latter did not adopt the urban workers' culture and way of life and therefore did not turn into a group of 'real workers'; at the same time, however, it did not remain a group of 'real peasants' confined to rural life, traditions and culture.

Due to the marginal situation of the 'worker-peasant' group, their behaviour is difficult to observe and control. They can transmit strong impulses among different groups and communities, and are prone to extreme actions and inadequate reactions.

On the other hand, the appearance and expansion of this group, bridging two socio-cultural realities, also contributed to the consolidation of the traditional family and its values, instead of changing and eroding it. When the local community disintegrated socio-culturally, this group was left with one possibility – to resort to the family sphere, culture and traditional values and to find a spiritual refuge there. This is not a specific feature of one region only – in all probability the same processes have taken place elsewhere under similar conditions. They have also been observed in quite different circumstances. The US scholar R. Nisbet, for instance, has described a similar situation in the USA, pointing out that no local community can be sought in a mass society (see Nisbet, 1969). Bulgarian developments under a totalitarian regime are not identical, but there are similarities. In Bulgaria the disintegration of local communities has not turned the 'national flag into a tribal totem'. But it has led to the appearance of other symbols, to the consolidated consciousness of another ethno-national affiliation. If we paraphrase Nisbet, the need to belong to some community was transformed for ethnic Turks into a religious fervour for the symbols of another national affiliation. Given all this, the ethnic crisis in Bulgaria seems a logical manifestation of the hidden, but deeprooted social crisis. Parallel with that, the events of 1989 proved to be a loud beginning to the end of the totalitarian age.

5. NEW PROBLEMS IN SEEKING A WAY OUT

Bulgarian society has now embarked on the road towards neutralizing a dangerous and destructive ethnic crisis, which by the early 1990s had become a national crisis. Yet we cannot maintain that concrete and effective decisions guaranteeing any quick way out have been found and implemented.

The radical changes now underway in society quite often aggravate existing ethnic problems and conversely the latter quite often hamper the implementation of changes.

A typical example is the outburst of discontent and the additional deterioration of relations between the two communities which followed the essentially democratic decision to restore the names of ethnic Turks. On this occasion, Bulgarians, mainly from regions with a mixed ethnic composition, marched against the capital. This forced the authorities to waver in their policy of abolishing a human rights violation.

Many examples can be quoted of difficulties which the ethnic crisis has created for the democratization of society and the solution of Bulgaria's economic problems. Economic reforms can hardly be implemented without national consensus – this is one of the gravest problems facing today's disunited Bulgarian society. The ethnic crisis comes on top of many other things dividing the people, and this impedes the achievement of a much-needed consensus. It also gives rise to various fears concerning the implementation of privatization and land reform. For instance, many believe that private ownership of land might favour demands for autonomous regions.

There are also fears in connection with the forthcoming elections of local management bodies. The Parliament itself has found it difficult to determine the composition of the provisional commissions which are to replace the existing mayors until elections of local bodies of power are held. The Bulgarian population in regions with a high relative share of ethnic Turks is quite sensitive on this question and would hardly accept an ethnic Turk as mayor. In this way, what was meant as another step on the road to democracy – elections to new local bodies of power – may become an occasion for new ethnic conflicts.

Naturally, political organizations must take into account their electorate's views, not only as regards the ethnic question. The Union of Democratic Forces was on the brink of being isolated, though for a short time, when it supported the decision for restoration of names. The pressure 'from the bottom up' concerns more than the attitude and behaviour of the political forces as regards the ethnic question. It also affects other aspects of their activity. One case in point is the discussion in Parliament on the term of military service. This was a question of major importance in the process of dismantling the totalitarian structures, and depoliticizing the army. In the end, however, it was decided that the army could not be weakened excessively.

The importance of the ethnic crisis in terms of democratization became most obvious during the elections to a Grand National Assembly (Parliament) – the first democratic elections in 45 years. Many explain the electoral victory of the Bulgarian Socialist (former Communist) Party by the re-orientation of the Union of Democratic Forces – to the Movement for Rights and Freedoms. The issue is more complex than that, but it is quite possible that the ethnic split between those of the electorate who did not vote for the Bulgarian Socialist Party has also played a major role.

REFERENCES

Dimitrov, Strashimir, 1990. 'Expert opinion on the sociological research "Mass Emigration Psychosis (June–July 1989)"', in Kr. Petkov and G. Fotev.

Dogan, Ahmed, 1990. 'The national question', interview in *Pogled*, 26 March.

Genchev, Nicolai, 1990. 'Issue on the national question in Bulgaria', paper presented at a session of Glasnost and Democracy Club, 27 March.

Kornai, Janos, 1985. *Economie de la pénurie*. Paris: Economica.

Nisbet, Robert, 1969. *The Quest for Community*. New York: Oxford University Press.

Petkov, Kr. and G. Fotev, eds., 1990. *Ethnical Conflict in Bulgaria – 1989*. Sofia: Sociological Archives, Institute of Sociology.

Rupnik, James, 1990. *L'autre Europe. Crise et fin du communisme*. Paris: Odile Jacob.

Stavrev, Svetoslav, 1990. 'Power premises for the Third National Catastrophe', *Trud*, no. 172, 31 August.

Wallerstein, Immanuel, 1974. *The Modern World-System*, vol.I, *Capitalist Agriculture and the Origins of European World-Economy in the Sixteenth Century*. New York: Academic Press.

Zerov, Assen, 1990. 'I want no revenge from anyone', *Pogled*, no. 4, 6 January.

Zhelev, Zhelyo, 1982. *Fascism*, Sofia.

15

National Identity in Post-Communist Hungary[1]

György Csepeli

1. HISTORICAL, SOCIOLOGICAL AND SOCIAL-PSYCHOLOGICAL CONSIDERATIONS

1.1. Re-acquisition of history

The late Soviet dictator, Josef Vissarionovich Stalin, used to assert that 'history belongs to God'. This is a truism favoured by dictators of all kinds throughout history, but it is definitely not true. It implies that the masters of the present can rule and dictate everything – including the past and consequently the future. In the case of Stalin, this implication has failed. There are many alternative interpretations of the recent abrupt changes in Eastern Europe ('silent revolution', 'velvet revolution', 'transition from state socialism to capitalism', etc.). In relation to the issue of nationality we would like to offer an interpretation indicating that, as a result of the changes, historical continuity has been re-established in Eastern Europe. At last, the people of this historical wasteland have got back their history.

The re-acquisition of historical continuity leads to many benefits, but there are also immense costs. The past four decades of state socialism meant an almost Münchhausian effort to dismiss the discontent within a historical heritage full of intergroup conflict, hatred, aggression and prejudice. The illusion of socialist society was that it could rid Eastern Europe of ethnic hostilities through an ambitious modernization programme to be

231

implemented on the foundation of a Stalinist a-historical *tabula rasa*. Social justice, equality, manifold development of human resources, and international understanding were offered. Lacking the adequate means to realize these ambitious positive ends, however, the socialist dream became transformed into a totalitarian nightmare of negative modernization (Hankiss et al. 1984).

Many actors and observers of the current Eastern European scene now think that everything is to be started anew, as if the recent decades (1945-1989) were to be excused from history. From their point of view, the region is merely an arena of reborn national conflicts where forces advocating the nation as supreme value and those disparaging it are to be clearly distinguished.

Progress in national development centred around the establishment of an independent nation-state, and progress in social development centred around the establishment of political democracy; a class structure based on equality of conditions, and a market economy – these seem once again contradictory. This contradiction has in fact been the characteristic feature of the historical heritage so recently reconquered.

Arguably, however, the past four decades also belong to history. As controversial as these decades have been, they have had a formative impact on the societies of Eastern Europe. In most of the countries concerned, generations have grown up without having been exposed to overt national and social demagogy. The socialist proletarianization process completely demolished the remnants of the former semi-feudal, semi-capitalist ways of proletarianization. The social structure of Eastern Europe prior to state socialism, with its vast inequality and injustice, had been fertile soil for nationalism, anti-semitism and hatred against every kind of minority.

The virus of intergroup conflict might be the same, but the circle of possible recipients is much narrower today. Paradoxically, although socialism was unable to achieve the aims of the promised egalitarian post-bourgeois society in Eastern Europe, it was successful in eradicating the traces of the feudal past, while simultaneously and unintentionally promoting a process of embourgeoisement (Szelenyi, 1988), which in the long run proved to be the decisive undermining factor in the final collapse of the socialist experiment. The 'prodigal son' of socialism – embodied in the *second economy*, limited spheres of market activity, consumption, autonomy of private life, and citizen's self-help movements – killed 'the father', embodied in a planned, redistributive economy, with its one-party rule and total control over society (Szelenyi, 1988).

The various Eastern European countries exhibit striking differences in respect to levels of embourgeoisement. The higher a country was on the scale of socialist embourgeoisement vs. socialist proletarianization, the more marked was the tendency to make the transition to post-Communism in a peaceful and non-violent way. The goal was to overtake countries in the West which had long sine begun on the path to positive modernization through the structures of a market economy, parliamentary democracy, and a class society centred around a strong middle class.

1.2. National sentiment

There are many analyses of the nature of national sentiment. Few of these discussions deny the fact that groups who define themselves and others in terms of national category are products of relatively recent historical developments (Szücs, 1988).

The word 'nation' is definitely not new, but its meaning in the sense of an assembly of people as a limited category of self-identification was unknown before the French Revolution of 1789. We may regard this date as a symbol of the transition from traditional social organizations into modernity. During this period, the modern values of liberty, property , equality and the establishment of institutions aimed at realizing them (such as parliamentary democracy, market and class society) invalidated previous categories of self-identification as legitimizing the new social order. In this new order, economic and political actors, linked by contradictory interests, came to perceive each other outside of their traditional collective identities. The only reliable base for formation of a new social collective identity was class. The contradictory nature of this identity formation, however, created a huge obstacle that precluded the formation of a legitimized order requiring a more cohesive collective identity. Today, traditional identities in terms of religion, region, city, estate, profession, etc. have been partially or totally abolished and their psychological force drained. The 'national' category can consequently be viewed as an attempt to fill the growing legitimization vacuum. This category has remained the sole one which can serve as a 'common denominator' for all social groups, providing a sense of collectivity and a basis for political and social consensus.

In the everyday manifestation of national sentiment it is easy to recognize the implicit assumption that the nation is a 'natural grouping', in line with the general characteristic of everyday knowledge based on what is 'natural'. We tend to take the world around us for granted, as a natural 'given'. But in the case of national attitude this assumption should be investigated with greater precision. Closer historical and sociological investigation may demonstrate that the assumption of the nation as a 'natural' group is a learned set which has developed as a result of indoctrination and socialization. What we have to identify first is the role of underlying national ideologies in the formation of the 'natural' attitude toward nation.

1.3. National ideology

Ideologies of the nation can be categorized by the extent to which they rely upon arguments stressing the biological and organic roots of the national existence.The arguments concerned are by no means simply fabrications, or products of 'false consciousness'. Not surprisingly, they come from the ethnocentric heritage of the national attachment which involves emphasis on descent, the mother tongue, and the cultural values and norms that differentiate the in-group from the out-group. In the framework of feudal society, the myth of the ethnic origin of the nation was a monopoly of the ruling estate which sometimes shared, sometimes did not share, the ethnic stock of the ruled social strata. Ethnicity could not have played a major role in the formation of social identity because other categories were also emphasized – religion, status, region, and vocation.

As a result of political democratization (which was the function of a broader modernization process) these categories lost their legal and psychological efficacy. This is how ethnicity came to the fore. This development was facilitated by ethnicity's close link with language and culture. As the classical languages of Greek and Latin lost their central role in maintaining political, legal and cultural institutions, each individual European country had to seek a language of its own for the concomitant literary tradition. The language concerned naturally had to be perfected in each case, but it was already spoken and widely used as a vernacular. In most cases this vernacular was far from being the only one in an area, so alternative tongues had to be suppressed.

On the basis of the development outlined above, we may differentiate a twofold typology of national ideology. There were countries in Europe (mostly west of the Rhine) where the category of the nation, defining every member of a given society, emerged as a consequence of prior economic,social, cultural and political developments. Unity defined in terms of the nation followed facts established by firm administrative, legal, and cultural institutions. A nation of this type can be characterized as one having its own *state*. In such cases, there has been less need for an emerging ideology to justify the ethnocentric heritage. The nation could afford to legitimize existing power relationships in terms of modern political ideology stressing the values of property, liberty and equality.

In the other type of national development (usually east of the Rhine), national unity was formulated as a wish that lacked adequate economic, social, political and cultural foundations. Here the notion of the nation came before the establishment of the relevant national institutions; the emerging national ideology had to refer more actively to such elements of the ethnocentric heritage as descent, cultural values and norms. Moreover, there was a total or partial lack of relevant autonomous national institutions (e.g. a capital city, a sovereign, a legal system, internationally recognized borders, currency, customs, army, police, postal service, an academy of sciences, educational institutions, etc.).

This type of national ideology became dominated by an overwhelming concern with fictions and symbols. The imagined realm of the 'nation' was created by the language of historical writing, literature, anthropology, by paintings and sculptures. This type of national ideology was centred around the idea of the nation defined in terms of *culture,* in contrast with the previous type centred around the idea of the nation defined in terms of *state.*

Cultural nationalism, however, cannot be viewed solely as a means of romantic or poetic expression of nationhood. With its concern for the values of economic and social development, it also served as a powerful modernization force, motivating members of the nation to realize the dream of the full-fledged national state.

There is, however, a third type of nation and ideology which is of a purely political and legal nature. No ethnocentric heritage plays a role in nation-formation in this case, because its only basis is a written *constitution*, with national membership defined solely in terms of citizenship irrespective of ethnicity, religion or cultural self-identification.

These three ideal-type versions of national ideologies are rooted in various historical trajectories of national development and cannot be seen as mutually exclusive entities. Rather they are mixed, and aspects of each can be found in all. Individual national ideologies differ to the extent that they tend to follow one of these three ideal types.

1.4.　The stock of knowledge of national identity

National identity as a modern means of self-identification can be analysed as a set of affective and cognitive components (Smith, 1986). The formation of the psychological set is a result of national socialization along the lines of the ruling pattern of national ideology. The basis for this set is the *spontaneous national identity*, where faith in the existence of the nation makes possible the identification of self and others in terms of perceived nationality.

The assumption of the natural and self-evident nature of the nation is also inseparable from this spontaneous national identity. By the latter we mean pride and preference along the lines of one's nationality; assumed similarity in terms of the national in-group and assumed dissimilarity in terms of the national out-group follow concomitantly. The psychological importance of the spontaneous national identity is linked to its behavioural potential, elicited by situational variables of national context. National symbols and rituals tend to elicit spontaneous behavioral responses in terms of one's own nationality. Encounters with foreigners and permanent or temporary stays abroad also provoke salient national identification.

The ability to categorize – to name or classify – dimensions of the world as 'national' is the result of the operation of the spontaneous national identity. This would be impossible without themes determined and defined by the national ideology and considered as belonging to the 'essence' of the nation. The scope of *thematizations* can embrace a broad spectrum from such realms as geography, anthropology, psychology, morals, aesthetics, culture, politics, economy and history. These themes, when defined in terms of national ideology, make possible the construction of the world in terms of national ideology, facilitating the narrative communication of facts and values connected with national existence.

While thematizations serving the formation of the national experience will vary greatly as a function of the type of national ideology, a process of *typification* occurs in every case. National prototypes and stereotypes result. These cognitive products make visible the world of the nation for those who identify themselves with their national group. Additionally, these cognitive products often act beyond the realm of mere perception. Once acquired, they not only mirror but in fact create the national environment. Typifications lead not only to judgements of description but also to the definition of what is 'typical' and what is not in terms of national character. Typifications usually imply judgements as to what is 'normal' and what is 'deviant'.

Probability judgements are motivated by hopes and fears related to the nation's perceived options in the past, present and the future. They organize the time experiences completing the creation of the national scenery with the nation's typified space (homeland), time (history) and its agency (compatriots).

The *values* cultivated by the national ideology will determine in every field of national existence what is to be approved and what is to be disapproved. In acquiring these values, members of the national community develop national attitudes which orient their judgement and action in the fields of economy, politics, culture or everyday life – whenever life-issues of national existence appear as relevant.

This review of the components of the national consciousness that operate as a stock of knowledge for members of the national community cannot be complete without mentioning the structures of cognition that serve as a means of interpretation and explanation for the affairs of the nation's geography, sociology, psychology, morals, culture, politics and history. *Evaluation, dichotomization, attribution, compensation* and *comparison* are the main means of understanding available to those who are interested in being conscious participants in the life of the nation. The operation of these cognitive structures demands considerable *knowledge of facts.* Factual information, however, often becomes of secondary importance, since in most cases the aim is not to acquire a correct and precise appraisal but instead to form a cognitively balanced national belief system free from dissonance and strain. Justification, defence, biased views of the nation's role in international affairs. Blind and rigid self-perception are the results.

There are, however, also instances where the outcome is just the opposite. Sensitivity to contradictions, openness of judgement concerning national existence, tolerance and readiness to be familiar with the other side's opinion and a kind of 'international empathy' can be the consequences of organizing cognitive structures in a manner which can tolerate a certain degree of cognitive dissonance. The contents and structure of national identity vary widely as a function of the type of the national ideology. Furthermore, they show a remarkable distribution among the various social groups within society. Social-economic status, as measured by educational level, occupation and level of social mobility, seems to be the most important variable behind the presence of the more simple or the more sophisticated contents and structure of national identity.

2. 'GEMEINSCHAFT' AND 'GESELLSCHAFT' PARADIGMS OF NATIONAL IDENTITY

2.1. The experience of being Hungarian
In Hungary, investigations of national identity have been conducted within the framework of public opinion research since 1969. The emergence of such research was a result of the 1968 reform initiative aiming at introducing modern socio-technological means of social administration and establishing some forms of market economy. Subsequent surveys on national identity dealt with facets of spontaneous national identity such as ethnocentrism, sentiments and feelings, national autostereotypes, national heterostereotypes, knowledge of Hungarian national minorities in Czechoslovakia, Austria, Yugoslavia, Romania, and the Soviet Union, and reception of relevant messages transmitted by the media. National and selected samples of the adult or the young population were exposed to questionnaires administered by trained interviewers. The results of this research, however, have scarcely been published to date. Access to the results remained limited to high ranking-party and state officials – who were not really interested in reading scholarly reports on Hungarian national identity.

These investigations demonstrated that nationalistic feelings of Hungarians are pronounced (Csepeli, 1989). Large numbers of Hungarians accept affirmative statements(82 to 94%) and reject negative statements(87 to 93%) about their country and its people. Most respondents show considerable pride in being Hungarian. On the other hand, national pride in Hungary proved much weaker than for instance in the USA or in Ireland, although stronger than in the Netherlands. Youth were generally in agreement with adult response patterns, but they tended to consider national sentiment as somewhat less relevant. The majority of a sample of Hungarian high school students displayed ethnocentrism by accepting positive stereotypes and rejecting negative ones about their country, whereas a completely different pattern of acceptance/rejection of the same stereotyped statements was displayed in relation to other countries such as Slovakia, Romania, Poland, etc. Younger Hungarians were less optimistic than older Hungarians about their national existence, but both groups also had high numbers of pessimists and non-respondents. Better-educated Budapest citizens were among the most pessimistic respondents. Older people, villagers and less-educated respondents gave more positive and less ambivalent national trait responses than did younger, urban and more highly-educated respondents.

The causes for Hungarian successes and failures were also studied. Successes were attributed by a national sample to strong allies and national solidarity. Failures, however, were attributed to enemy superiority, endurance and strong allies – thus allowing the in-group to shirk responsibility for the perceived tragedies and avoid cognitive dissonance. Better-educated, interested and urbanized respondents were less likely to choose such options, however, preferring moral or psychological explanations for Hungary's defeats. There was also a general tendency to view Hungary as an actor that had played a passive role in the past. Hungarians compensate cognitively for their country's size by accepting the proposition 'Our country is small, but it has great achievements and great men'. Similarly phrased positive statements about the Netherlands (also a small country) were, however, rejected. The cognitive scheme of 'small country-great achievements' consequently serves as a means of compensation, much as the mass media have taught Hungarians to do in judging their own nation's fame, worth, and achievements.

The surveys have indicated continuing and increasing interest in Hungarian minorities in Yugoslavia, Austria, Czechoslovakia, the USSR and especially in Romania, where Hungarians live in great numbers. Concern for those perceived as discriminated against because of their Hungarian nationality had mainly to do with presentation of one's own national identity.

These results strongly support the conclusion that despite campaigns of 'socialist patriotism' and 'internationalism', which had formed part of efforts to de-nationalize the citizens of Hungary, national identity has managed to survive, becoming a political factor as the crisis of the state socialist system increased. Hungarians were outraged to hear of the plans of Romanian dictator Ceauşescu to tear down between six thousand and eight thousand villages, including a great number of old settlements inhabited by ethnic Hungarians in Transylvania, who number about two million. Public opinion responded with anger at reports that Hungarian schools had been closed, towns of historical importance deprived of their Hungarian names, and cemeteries and statues destroyed in order to erase any vestige of Hungarian identity in Transylvania.

A large anti-Romanian demonstration was held in the summer of 1988; it was unofficial but the regime clearly had not the power to stop it. In spring 1990, free elections were held, the first since 1947. A major factor behind the victory of the conservative Hungarian Democratic Forum was the bloody massacre in Tirgu-Mures (Marosvasarhely) across the border. The victims were local citizens belonging to the Hungarian minority in Transylvania. Andras Suto, resident of Transylvania and one of the greatest living Hungarian authors, was severely injured and half blinded.

The transition from state socialism to post-Communism in Hungary, however, has not been able to remedy the wounded national identity. The new government has not managed to improve the position of Hungarian minorities in neighbouring countries; indeed, it is difficult to resist the conclusion that its rhetoric is meant solely for home consumption. On the other hand, the increase in unresolved tasks (privatization, marketization, Western economic orientation, investments in infrastructure and human development, etc.) and the emergence of domestic problems (perceived incompetence of the government, unemployment, inflation, pollution, low life expectancy, mass poverty, political apathy, ignorance and arrogance of the new political elite, etc.) have diminished the importance of issues stemming from national ideology ('Who is Hungarian, who is not?', 'Is the prime minister of the Republic of Hungary responsible for the fate of Hungarian minorities abroad or not?', 'Hungarian participation in alliance with Nazi Germany in World War II against Soviet Union, United States and United Kingdom can be justified or not?'). Under state socialism, Hungarian society – or at least part of it (young, educated, skilled, entrepreneuring men and women) – had been taught the lessons of pragmatism and survival; they seem not to forget it despite the increased anti-Communist and nationalistic efforts of the ruling coalition (Hankiss, 1990). Newspapers and mass media efforts focusing exclusively on issues of national ideology failed to arouse interest and support. Local elections held in the autumn of 1991 resulted in an overwhelming victory for the liberal opposition. It is tempting to assert that Hungarian society is in fact more liberal and less ethnocentric than its present government.

2.2. Intellectuals and national identity

Previous research on national identity has shown that the level of education and the level of social mobility are the principal explanatory variables of the nature and kind of national attachment. Knowledge of facts of history, economy, culture, geography and the ability to interpret this factual information in the context of national ideology may be confined to a minority of the population – the elites, intellectuals, professionals, politicians and opinion leaders. Indeed, intellectuals have always performed a key role in the development of national ideology. In Hungary, as in most Eastern and Central European countries including Germany, *men of letters* (literary authors, clergy, 'prophets') were instrumental in elaborating and distributing the content of the national ideology centred around norms, values, and standards of culture, morals and psychology. In countries where state and nation coincided, it was the duty of professionals to elaborate the message of national ideology in terms of politics, legal rights and economic tasks.

Among Hungarian intellectuals, then, to what degree do various patterns of national identity ('Gemeinschaft' pattern of cultural nationalism, 'Gesellschaft' pattern of state nationalism) exist and prevail? Two surveys were conducted in 1983 and 1989. Samples of university graduates (n=600 in 1983, n= 671 in 1989) were selected, taking into account the variables of age, religious background and social mobility. The impact of religious background and social mobility on the nature of national identity has been demonstrated. The second survey also showed a remarkable shift toward more pronounced and polarized response patterns among respondents. Various questions were used to test the presence of different underlying ideological paradigms in spontaneous national identity.[2]

2.3. Measures of spontaneous national identity

Many respondents justified their sense of being Hungarian by reference to the national category as a means of their self-definition or the formation of their citizenship. Other respondents justified their national self-ascription by mentioning the circumstances of their birth – birthplace, parents' nationality, mother tongue. The same type of difference was revealed when respondents described the criteria for being 'Hungarian'. Some respondents held the view that anyone should be considered Hungarian who refers to him/herself as Hungarian, while others associated this categorization primarily with mother tongue or descent.

There were questions related to national and European identities. Some respondents considered their loyalty to the nation more important than the adoption of an European identity, which they felt was vague and distant. Among other respondents, the dominant pattern found was adherence to a European identity; these respondents had difficulties in accepting national loyalty as their basic and continuing means of identity. In some cases, national pride acted as a balanced national sentiment free of dissonance; in other cases, the sense of national pride, of being Hungarian, was mixed with shame, resulting in ambivalence. Some respondents compensated cognitively for Hungary's economic, social and historical weaknesses by resorting to comparisons presenting Hungary as a 'great power' in chess, hunting, philately , gastronomy or other such areas. Others simply chose the strategy of not responding to this question. While some respondents asserted that if they could choose, they would remain Hungarian, others expressed neutrality or indifference on this score.

Different subjective probabilities were found with respect to a question on how Hungarian minorities abroad would or would not be assimilated into Romanians, Slovaks, Serbs, Ukrainians or Austrian Germans. The rated likelihood of assimilation is conceived as a measure of strength of national attitude, with a strong and devoted national attitude contradicting the perceived assimilation of Hungarians into other national group. One group of respondents was pessimistic about the ultimate fate of Hungarian minorities abroad, believing that their fellow nationals would finally be devoured by the respective national out-groups. Other respondents considered such complete assimilation of Hungarian minorities impossible: they predicted their national and cultural survival, irrespective of the country where the Hungarian minorities live. Respondents were also asked to estimate the Hungarian population world-wide. While many respondents gave accurate figures, a clear distinction among underestimaters and overestimaters was to be observed.

Finally, attitudes toward the Hungarian national coat of arms were investigated, as such national symbols are important in the formation of national consciousness. In 1989, as a part of the transition process, Hungarian public opinion strongly supported changing the unpopular Soviet-tailored coat of arms (which was imposed by the state-socialist system) into one of the traditional coats of arms. There were two basic options: one was a version representing the republican and revolutionary tradition of the country (coat of arms with red and silver stripes and the cross of Lorraine); the other one – with the Holy Crown of Saint Stephen, first king of Hungary – representing conservative tradition linked with the Kingdom of Hungary. Not surprisingly, the parliament, dominated by the coalition of Hungarian Democratic Forum, smallholders and Christian Democrats, opted for the version with the Holy Crown.

2.4. Measures of ideological national identity

Structures and contents of ideological national consciousness were also investigated. The questionnaire contained 60 key-words representing six thematizations (politics, culture, economy, psychology-morals, society, history) – thematizations important in any construction of a national consciousness. Respondents had to decide how meaningful were the words embedded in national context. They had to decide if such expressions as 'Hungarian face', 'Hungarian fate' or 'Hungarian blood' have any meaning and relevance from their national point of view. The list of words most frequently chosen as meaningful and relevant in the semantic space of 'Hungarian' shows dominance of terms concerning politics and culture. Words like *independence, constitution, state* and *liberty* were among the most preferred political words, while *science, literature, art,* and *school* formed the most preferred words of culture. The list of most preferred words was topped however by the word *intellectuals,* which may be considered a reflection of professional achievement and self-ascription of the respondents. On the other hand, this result also shows the survival of the traditional ideological importance of the notion of 'intellectuals' in Hungarian ideological identity. The list of least preferred words is also not without interest. *Homeland, peasant, past, soil, mentality, fate, present* are to be found on the list. There were semantically 'empty' words such as *superiority, form, blood, face, hero, mission, value.* These words seem to belong to the past national ideology full of romanticism and ethnocentrism. *Socialism, cooperative, trade union, steel* also failed to elicit responses – which can be interpreted as result of the twilight of the state-socialist ideology. Six years earlier, in 1983, these words had elicited far more meaning in the context of national ideology. Primary component analysis of the responses revealed three characteristic patterns. The *first primary component* (HARD) consisted of words belonging to *economics, politics* and *society.* Words from *psychology, morals* and *culture* were found in the *second primary component* (SOFT). The *third primary component* consisted of words of the *orthodox ethnocentric national ideology* (ORTH).

Attitudes toward living and dead persons were investigated as measures of ideological national ideology, since such reference persons are generally seen as major orientation points in the formation of national ideological frameworks of thought. Names of well known persons (literary authors, historians, journalists, essayists, politicians) representing characteristic ways of the Hungarian political tradition (democratic, socialist, populist, national socialist, communist) were included in the list. Persons representing ideological extremes (Communism and National Socialism) were avoided, however. Three distinct patterns emerged, reproducing a long-standing tradition of thought about the nature of Hungarian nation: 'Populist Intellectuals', 'Urban Intellectuals' and 'National Democratic Intellectuals'.

Respondents were also asked to compare Hungary with other European countries in realms of economy, political culture, arts, history and everyday habits. Two major patterns of comparison emerged: one composed of countries of the late Austro-Hungarian Monarchy, the other consisting of smaller Western European countries.

Analysis of probability judgements on the future economic and cultural success of Hungary showed three basic types: cultural optimism, economic optimism and economic-cultural pessimism were the major primary components of the national future image.

When different versions of the definition of national sovereignty (maximalist, optimal, minimalist) were presented to the respondents, the majority chose the optimal one. The idea of limited sovereignty was accepted by only 7% of the respondents in 1989. The same definition had been accepted by 26% of the respondents in 1983.

Romania and Czechoslovakia were perceived as countries in conflict with Hungary. In the case of Romania, the most frequently mentioned source of conflict was discrimination against the Hungarian minority. In the case of Czechoslovakia, the perceived source of conflict was the plan to build a huge and costly hydro-electric dam and power station over the Danube in one of the most picturesque areas of the Hungarian landscape. Both are neighbouring countries and belonged at that time to the same military alliance, the Warsaw Pact. By contrast, no country belonging to NATO was perceived as a source of possible national conflict from the Hungarian point of view.

Investigation of the narrative schemes of national historical consciousness showed an overwhelming presence of scenarios of defeat and a striking absence of scenarios of victory. The majority of respondents considered the Treaty of Trianon[3] following World War I to have been the deepest historical trauma of Hungarian history. In 1989, 78% of the respondents shared this opinion, as against only 64% in 1983. (Earlier studies had not contained this question because the issue of the Trianon Treaty was one of the few taboos of the Communist public communication.)

Respondents held a negative evaluation of Hungary's role in World War II. As a result of Hungary's participation in World War II, hundreds of thousands of Hungarian Jews were deported to Nazi concentration camps or murdered in Hungary. According to the majority view the German Nazi government and the occupying German Army were to blame for the genocide. The minority view held that responsibility for the mass murder of Hungary's Jewish citizens lay with the Hungarian government and the Hungarian gendarme.

Analysis of attributions of historical, political and economic successes and failures reveals different patterns of perceived causes of national success and failure. In the case of national success, mainly moral and psychological national virtue are attributed (internal and unstable causes), but in the case of ill fate, the causes are seen as misfortune and unfavourable geopolitical circumstances, and external national isolation (external stable causes).

2.5. National ideological profiles

On the basis of measures of spontaneous and ideological national identity, a cluster analysis has been carried out, revealing five clusters. Two clusters (A and E) showed consistent national identity patterns differing from each other, while the remaining three (B,C,D) proved inconsistent and lacked marked characteristics of national identity. Because the sample was not representative, the ideological trends represented by the clusters must be considered more important than the numbers showing the actual distribution of individual clusters among respondents.

'Gesellschaft' Pattern of National Consciousness (Cluster A)
This cluster can be characterized by a national identity related to the framework of the nation-state. This framework is free of spontaneous and affective characteristics of natural national involvement. The nation is presented as a democratic political community; and Hungarian national history emerges here as a sequence of serious failures, culminating in the state-socialist period. Attributing national failures to stable external causes (Soviet occupation, lack of Western support) and stable internal causes seems to be crucial. These include economic underdevelopment and backwardness of social structure.

Optimistic National Consciousness (Cluster B)
On the basis of spontaneous and natural national identification, some positive probability-judgements as to the Hungarian

national future can be found. Such cultural factors as language, literature, historical writing, the arts, and education seem to play an important role in the formation of this pattern of national identity, which sees Hungary as a leading country in the Central European region. Attraction to a *third road* is pronounced. This is conceived of as a middle way between socialism and capitalism. This ideological preference is, however, free of dogmatism, as indicated by respondents' choice of anti-populist reference persons.

Emotional National Consciousness (Cluster C)
This cluster reflects the operation of the elements of spontaneous and natural national identity focusing on the psychological consequences of national self-ascription. This is a naive version of national identity, since it does not include acceptance of the importance of political and legal bonds in national affiliation. The depth of affective components correlates with an absence of complexity of cognitive components of the national attitude. The structure of cognitive components is inconsistent; however, inconsistencies of national belief system are not revealed by the respondents.

Low Profile National Consciousness (Cluster D)
Characteristic traits of spontaneous and ideological national identity are lacking from this pattern. The nation is broadly conceived as a social psychological community united by cultural tradition, which facilitates communication among people who consider themselves members of that community.

'Gemeinschaft' Pattern of National Identity (Cluster E)
This pattern of national affiliation is balanced by the mutual presence of elements of spontaneous national identity and themes, attitudes, beliefs and values of cultural national identity (ethnic purity and distinctiveness, folklore, cultural tradition, literature, the arts, language, national character, democracy of Hungarians defined by cultural prescription, etc.) When confronted with the vision of national decay, respondents here consider positive alternatives of concentrated moral and psychological action as a means of defence.

2.6. Some conclusions from the cluster analysis

What are the basic sociological variables explaining these clusters? *Age* was a significant indicator. Younger respondents were more likely to belong to clusters where national identity was seen as a result of legal and political involvement in the national group. Older respondents tended to belong to clusters where the traditional, cultural formulation of national identity was dominant.

Religious background and *social mobility* proved to be major explanatory variables of national identity among Hungarian intellectuals. We have no data, however, on religious affiliation, as attempts to measure directly the religious affiliation of respondents failed to elicit sincere answers. Religious background was instead measured by the religious affiliation assigned by the respondent to his/her four grandparents. A Jewish background was found to increase the likelihood of the 'Gesellschaft' type of national identity. Respondents with a Jewish background were also more prone to belong to cluster C, which stresses emotional and self-ascriptive components of national affiliation. Respondents with a Christian background tended not to favour a 'Gesellschaft' type of national identity. Protestants seemed to share a 'Gemeinschaft' type of national identity; some of them were attracted to the naive versions of national identity. Catholicism was found to increase the tendency to belong to Cluster D (low profile national consciousness).

Effects of social mobility are less pronounced. The 'Gesellschaft' type of national identity occurs less frequently among intellectuals with parents from a non-intellectual background (first-generation intellectuals). Emotional national identification is more frequent among members of this category of intellectuals. Enacting the role of the intellectual in Hungary would of course be impossible without assuming patterns of ideological national identity, and second- or third-generation intellectuals are more likely to assume one of these patterns.

Investigation of the joint effects of religious background and social mobility on national identity shows that the spontaneous and natural experience of being Hungarian is embedded in various ideological frameworks which can be traced back to different socio-cultural traditions. The 'Gesellschaft' type of national identity is from the outset part of a Jewish socialization background irrespective of the level of social mobility. This type remains part of a political tradition transmitted through generations. National identity among intellectuals with Christian backgrounds can be characterized at the outset as emotionally loaded. This type of identification is gradually replaced by a 'Gemeinschaft' type of national identity which is more frequent among intellectuals of the second and third generation than among intellectuals from families of workers, peasants, or self-employed small owners.

The category of national self-ascription can be considered as a conglomerate of all persons who identify themselves with a given category. Nevertheless, psychological homogeneity does not erase traces of the past cultural bonds. 'Gesellschaft' and 'Gemeinschaft' types of national ideology can be seen as competing paradigms of national identification. On the basis of a pluralistic and democratic political and ideological discourse, this competition would lead to a peaceful coexistence of alternative programmes of national modernization. In the absence of conditions favouring open and uninhibited public discourse on issues of nationality, however, there is the danger that competition between alternative paradigms of national identity may result in stigmatization, scapegoating, exclusion, intolerance and mutual prejudice between adherents of the individual paradigms. Such a development could unleash a vicious circle of misunderstanding between Hungary and its neighbours who are facing the same problems in defining their own national identity.

Finally, then, in light of current ideological and political events in Hungary – and throughout Eastern Europe – there does not, unfortunately, seem to be much hope of avoiding malignant developments of competition within and among the individual countries, unless mutual understanding, cooperation, exchange of goods, services, information and people can come to replace the dangerous heritage of destructive conflict.

NOTES

1. This is a revised version of a paper presented at the conference 'National and Political Identity in Post-Stalinist Societies' organized by Forum for Soviet and Eastern Europe Studies held in Oslo, 6-7 December 1990, at the Norwegian Institute of International Affairs.

2. The two studies on the national identity of intellectuals were carried out in the Mass Communication Centre supported by the Institute of History of the Hungarian Academy of Science, the Institute of Hungarian Studies of the Hungarian Academy of Science and the Institute of Sociology of the University of Eotvos Lorand in Budapest. The second project in 1989 was carried out in collaboration with Tibor Zavecz, research fellow at the Mass Communication Centre, which had been renamed the Hungarian Public Opinion Research Institute.

3. According to the terms of the 1920 Treaty of Trianon, signed by Hungary and the Allies (excluding the USA and USSR), Hungary's territory was reduced by one-third and the country lost its access to the sea.

REFERENCES

Csepeli, Gy., 1989. *Structures and Contents of Hungarian National Identity. Results of Political Socialization and Cultivation*, Frankfurt/New York: Peter Lang.

Hankiss, E., et al., 1984. 'Modernization of Value Systems: Indicators of Change in Cross-Cultural Comparisons', in Melischek. G., K. Rosengren, J. Stappers, eds, *Cultural Indicators: An International Symposium*, pp.461-72, Wien: Akademie der Wissenschaften.

Hankiss, E., 1990. 'In Search of a Paradigm', *Daedalus*, Winter, pp.183-214.

Smith, A., 1986. *The Ethnic Origins of Nations*, London: Blackwell.

Szelényi, I., 1988. *Socialist Entrepreneurs. Embourgeoisement in Rural Hungary*, Madison, WI: The University of Wisconsin Press.

Szűcs J., 1988. 'The Historical Regions of Europe', in John Keane, ed., *Civic Society and the State*, pp.291-332, London: Verso Press.

16

Cognitive Adequacy of Sociological Theories in Explaining Ethnic Antagonism in Yugoslavia

Sergej Flere

1. INTRODUCTION

Yugoslavs have often boasted of their uniqueness in liberating themselves during World War II 'without foreign intervention', and have boasted even more of constructing a unique system of 'socialist self-management' within which historically rooted ethnic antagonisms have been resolved. This institutional system paid considerable attention to ethnic (national) parity and equivalence in representation and economic assistance to the less developed regions.[1] Equality of representation of ethnic groups contributed much to the profuse and complex institutional system. It was officially held that such an institutional arrangement represented a strong barrier against centrifugal and conflictual tendencies among the various ethnic groups in Yugoslavia.

After the death of President Tito in 1980, however, ethnic antagonism has been growing in Yugoslavia, taking on numerous forms – institutionally political, and direct face-to-face disputes among inhabitants and groups. At times, clashes have become violent and have included demonstrations, sit-down demonstrations, marches, riots, 'media warfare', 'severing of relations between republics', football fan clashes, and the rise of ethnically-determined inter-personal distance. As for the political aspects of the matter, the very integrity of the Yugoslav

polity is in question. This chapter seeks to explore the verita-
bility and plausibility of various contemporary sociological
theories, bypassing those which are evidently inapplicable. The
models contained in these theories will be contrasted with
Yugoslav reality, offering a possibility of analysis. After
conducting such a procedure with four theories, we will attempt
an explanation of our own.

2.   EXPLOITATION AS A SOURCE OF ETHNIC TENSION

Various paths within Marxist explanations lend themselves to
considerations of ethnic tension and antagonism. Basically, the
Marxist view holds that – behind ethnic tension and antagonism
– we always find an infrastructure of exploitation, which
assumes ethnic dimensions, among others. According to this
view, ethnic relations are directly and fully reducible to class
relations, exploitation and class rule. In the simplest case, this
means that the exploiters and the exploited are also ethnically
distinct groups, so that exploitation takes on ethnical colours.

This way of thinking may be operationalized by means of
dominant-class use of a reserve labour army composed of a
particular ethnic group in order to combat another, to keep it in
a subjugated position, or to keep wages in general low. Thus,
Marxist thinking allows us to speak of a political manipulation
of exploitation and of levels and degrees of exploitation (and
'supra-exploitation').

Perhaps paradoxically, in the area of ethnic tensions (as well
as the study of other forms of social life, such as social structure)
Marxism appears particularly inadequate in offering meaningful
explanations for socialist, regulated societies. One possible
explanation might be that socialist societies are built on principles that supersede Marxist ideas of societal determinism.
As for inter-ethnic conflict, it should be stressed that the
inadequacy stems from the fact that in Yugoslav society, economic relations did not take on an autonomous form, and were
not an independent sub-system regulated by its own logic and
determinism. Yugoslav socialism, possibly more than other forms
of socialism (in Yugoslav parlance 'statist socialism') was
a product of political will, composed of a series of societal
experiments with the force of all-encompassing normative
systems filled with far-fledged utopistic ideas.

FIGURE 4: YUGOSLAVIA

Areas of Yugoslavia inhabited predominantly by ethnic Albanians

KOSOVO - BORDERS

Not only was the sphere of politics dominant, imposing its decision-making power upon other spheres of social life (other societal sub- systems), but other sub-systems were modelled after the political one, and endowed with political and normative institutional criteria. We may speak of the basic 'motive' in the societal system, including its economic sub-system, as the expansion of one's political power. This is the main cause of the inefficiency of capital investment.

Speaking in systems theory language, what happened between the sphere of politics and other spheres of social life (sub-systems) in Yugoslavia was that 'as the political system was not able to master and adequately transform this complexity, it has attempted to compensate this shortcoming by striving to factually de-differentiate the environment [make it less complex]. That means that it endeavours to minimise the number of options at the disposal of the other functional systems.' (Bernik, 1989, p. 37) The relationship between the political and the social system was further burdened by the gigantic and detailed uniform institutional organization of the former, which imposed its models upon the latter. By the last decade, this system had itself become almost unchangeable thanks to its own rules, which created conditions of high integration where dysfunctioning in one part quickly spread to the entire system.

This made the extra-political spheres ever less adaptable and inflexible, bringing them into ever greater contrast with the exigencies of contemporary societal system development. Therefore, we must reject the hypothesis of exploitation – direct or indirect – as the cause of the basic ethnic antagonisms in Yugoslavia. Nevertheless, the idea of exploitation of one ethnic group (or region) by another is something often heard in Yugoslavia in political parlance, in the stance of individual political groups, as such statements have a strong mobilising appeal. Economists like A. Bajt, however, have explicitly spoken against the possibility of economic founding of such an analysis and of the computation of such a 'balance sheet'.

In similar vein, we should note the inapplicability of the theory of culturally split labour markets and middleman positions in explaining the Yugoslav situation. Such approaches offer little by way of explanation, particularly because of the institutionalized policy of ethnic (national) parity and equivalence and equal representation not only in the highest governing bodies, but also at the level of intermediary political management in ethnically mixed areas and at the federal level, which has often worked against professionalism in the functioning of bureaucratic institutions. Therefore, we could speak of institutional barriers to placing members of certain groups in subordinate and unrewarding positions. On the other hand, due to the great inherited cultural differences and inequalities, the distribution of occupations and educational achievement has involved gross disparities.

3. MODERNIZATION AS SOURCE OF ETHNIC TENSION

At first glance – in explaining ethnic conflict in a socialist society like Yugoslavia – the most plausible explanation for what is now happening should be the idea of societal *modernization*, causing a reaction in the form of ethnic resurgence. Firstly, Marxism, which functioned as the official inspiration for Yugoslav socialism, has developed some of the ideas of modernism to the full: that man should be his own master, that he may therefore create a 'transparent' societal organization according to his projects, that no mediation between people in the form of petrified institutions is necessary, that science can be boldly used as an instrument of mastering nature and society by man in this endeavour of his, etc. Nowhere has socialism come close to achieving these final goals as envisioned by Marx. However, in Yugoslavia, attempts have been made to implement some of the most utopist ideas – the system of delegated representation, mastering of the market forces by societal agreements and compacts, and above all self-management as an integral system of governing society and of social relations within society, along with an elaborate institutional scheme covering everything from health to defense – all this accompanied by a system of institutions with a bewildering array of difficult names.

Nevertheless, it would be wrong if we linked modernization in Yugoslavia only to the basic ideological tenets of Yugoslav socialism. Modernization has more to do with empirical social processes, and ethnocentrism could be a reaction to these. Such a reaction arises – according to this line of thought – because of a dislocation of individuals due to mobility, and a lack of security which had earlier (in pre-modern society) been provided by extended family and local groups, religious groups and other forms of primary groups, and which is lacking in modern society.

This emotional lack of security and reliance characteristic of modernity may bring about a resurgence of ethnic identity, inter-ethnic tension; and in cases of economic crisis it may bring about 'scapegoating' in inter-ethnic relations (see the model discussed by Hannan, 1979, and Nielsen, 1980).

Before further analyzing the plausibility of this explanation, we should note that Yugoslavia has in the post-World War II period undergone a series of changes which can be important elements of modernization.

Functional illiteracy has dropped from 30% in 1931 (last preWorld War II census) to 8% in 1981. The share of persons active in agriculture has dropped during the same time-span from 76% to 20% of the economically active population. The participation of the secondary sector in the national income, on the other hand, has risen from 17% to 44% (source: *Statisticki godisnjak Jugoslavije 1918-88*). Though Yugoslavia has undergone significant modernization processes, and it is questionable whether it could have done so at that pace without socialism – contemporary social upheaval and ethnic conflict in Yugoslavia cannot simply be attributed to modernization (in its ideal typical form) and its 'discontents'.

For one thing, modernization in Yugoslavia was not of the type which brought about the 'discontents' which would themselves give rise to ethnic resurgence as a reaction to rationalization, market relations, bureaucratization in the Weberian sense, etc. Yugoslav modernization was in some aspects 'specific', peculiar, unique. Certainly it was a partial, incomplete modernization which lacked those components which give rise to characteristic ethnic reactions – like ethnic gatherings – in order to cope with the situation of a merciless market not recognizing individual ethnicities, a bureaucracy operating solely on the principles of impersonality, prescriptions and orders, professionalism, etc. Yugoslavia's policy of ethnic parity and equivalence made it impossible for universalistic criteria and patterns to achieve greater implementation in cutting across traditional society. Members of different ethnic groups rarely found themselves in a position to compete for the same rewards in a market situation. Nor was there much immigration on economic grounds, except into Slovenia.

It is nevertheless important to examine the problem of modernization in explaining ethnic antagonism in Yugoslavia. What we must primarily address are the impediments to full modernization. If we strip away the institutional and normative masks of the Yugoslav self-management socialist system and look for the true impediments to modernization – after doing away with the basic and other organizations of associated labour, with the system of delegates, social agreements and compacts – we may find the following:

1) There was a lack of bureaucracy in the Weberian sense, as the huge bureaucratic edifice was organised on the principle of more political power to individuals, particularly by manipulating the rule of equal ethnic representation, without producing the greater efficiency in the management of affairs that Weber had stipulated. This edifice was the product of an attempt to bring to life Marx's interpretation of the Paris Commune: it was therefore radically utopistic and at odds with the exigencies of social reality. It served to bring about a two-layered functioning: one at the normatively prescribed level, and another at the means-ends level of 'true' life. Therefore, it was not so much direct favouritism, as general inefficiency due to an irrational organization, that brought about generalized dissatisfaction;

2) The lack of a market was even more pronounced in comparison to bureaucracy. A bureaucracy was present, but it was not of a Weberian nature and therefore did not bring about the processes and reactions otherwise characteristic of it. The market was truly a *faux pas*, a taboo of socialism, including the Yugoslav one, as it was purportedly linked in with the meanest forces of exploitation, oppression and alienation. On the other hand, an independent market of goods, of services and of capital would undermine the rule of the political elite.

Nevertheless, a rudimentary market of commodities did exist. But it was not of dimensions which would bring about the purported discontents of a market economy which leave the individual at the mercy of market forces and sends him running back to his own ethnic group for protection.

3) The basic limits to modernization have been set by the utopistic model of self-management socialism, which not only contains an elaborate system of institutions, but also holds that it is basically unchangeable in the 'mature' 1974 form. The other side of this utopistic institutional arrangement is the political

elite, whose power is legitimated by this institutional arrangement. The system allows as much modernization as can be
absorbed by the normative model and does not seriously question
the legitimacy of the ruling elite. This does open venues for
industrialization, urbanization and the growth of education and
science – but without producing internal movers toward effica-
ciousness. After a certain time, such a model of development
manifests increasingly its internal limitations and weaknesses;
they appear earlier and more acutely in environments with an
industrial and civil tradition. The limits to modernization deepen
along with the routinization of charisma and a certain 'tradition-
alization' of the system, on the one hand, and with changes in
the environment – including multi-national political institutional
arrangements in Europe which Yugoslavia was not able to
accept *in time*. On the other, what was particularly lacking was
space for entrepreneurship, innovation, and the dignity of expert
knowledge and autonomous professionalism. In contrast to the
need for deregulation of society and particularly of the economy,
the Yugoslav system is legally most complex and rigid. Due to
the inflexibility of the institutional system – and the vested
interests of its elite – much time was lost in modernization, both
in the 1970s and in the 1980s.

4.   AUTHORITARIANISM

The 'authoritarian personality' syndrome as formulated by
Adorno and associates (1950) is not really a sociological explanation of inter-ethnic conflict. It is basically the theory of a
personality structure akin to ethnocentrism and via that personality trait akin to inter-ethnic conflictuality. The socio-historical
and cultural situation which Adorno and associates had in mind
was not only that of World War II, but also of the events that
led up to that war in Germany. It should be stressed that a
military defeat, which resulted in a Germany that felt frustrated, complicated by economic transformation (impoverishing
middle strata) and economic crisis, were the social circumstances
that led to German Nazism. And, according to Adorno, this
provides the psychological substance underlying the authoritarian personality.

     In Yugoslavia, authoritarianism has been measured, along
the lines of the Adorno methodology, and found to be high.

Pantic found in Serbia that the aggregate presence of authoritarianism was 4.6 on a scale of 1-7, among adult males in 1974 (Pantic, 1977). Rot and Havelka (1974) found it high among secondary school students. According to recent data (Tos, 1988) among adults in entire Yugoslavia, authoritarianism is high, authoritarian attitudes prevail, without great difference among regions. The lowest region was Slovenia (59%), whereas the highest was Macedonia (67%).

It has often been inferred that authoritarianism had a different meaning in Yugoslavia than the one set out by Adorno et al. It was hypothesized that authoritarianism measured in Yugoslavia should mean traditional patriarchal mentality, respect towards elders, etc. Today, however, there is no reason to believe that authoritarianism has a meaning in Yugoslavia basically different than what it meant to Adorno and associates: we are confronted with an authentic authoritarianism, a socio-psychological regression.

This does not explain the societal sources of ethnocentrism – or ethnocentrically induced conflicts – but an analogy may be drawn with the situation in the German 1930s. Economic troubles during the past decade are similar: the middle strata have been the hardest hit by economic crisis; moreover, three and four digit inflation has its own logic in delegitimizing institutions, bringing about generalized uncertainty and unreliability of behaviour and institutions. Yugoslavia did not lose a war, but ideologically similar phenomena have been at work: 'scapegoating' for the 'unjust' position of one's ethic group, i.e. accusations against other groups (and 'traitors' within one's own) with regard to present political boundaries, historical events and the general unfavourable state of one's ethnic group.

In sum, even authoritarianism cannot provide a general explanation, it may easily be part of one, regarding the psychological content of ethnic resurgence and antagonism.

5. ETHNIC STRATIFICATION

An almost ubiquitous approach in explaining ethnic tension in sociology is the analysis of ethnic stratification (Shibutani & Kwan, 1965). We should note that it has been used in explaining ethnic antagonism mostly in the 'new world', where ethnic tension has little to do with century-long histories of strife.

According to this approach – to put it most simply – ethnic antagonisms and conflicts are the results of the fact that entire ethnic groups occupy systematically different positions on the stratification scale. In itself, this would mean that ethnic conflict boils down to stratificational conflict. But there is more to it: if entire ethnic groups occupy underprivileged positions, in terms of stratification, that would have to be because of structural barriers against achieving equality of opportunity. To put it in more sociological terms, that would mean that a particularistic and not a universalistic mechanism is generating social structure. Furthermore, this would imply a contradiction between how social structure is formed and certain basic tenets of modern democratic society. Ethnic stratification means more than just a stratification conflict, because ethnic groups are collectivities with strong cultural links, enabling a strong mobilization of their members.

In the case of Yugoslavia, social stratification has different dimensions. One could attempt to trace occupational, educational and economic aspects of stratification, but political stratification is clearly the most important, as may be inferred from what has been mentioned earlier. We hasten to point out that the creators of the Yugoslav political system during the 1960s were keenly aware that ethnic conflicts might arise from such a source. They constructed a series of constitutional provisions as to ethnic parity, making equal representation of ethnic groups compulsory at all levels of political life, and even in the distribution of other positions of power. Nevertheless, the matter is of interest. Here we shall draw attention to data on representation of members of the League of Communists – the former ruling political organization – in the different ethnic populations. The justification for taking into account these data is that the League of Communists functioned as a political elite, regardless of the system of self-management. Thus, the membership of all governing bodies was composed almost exclusively of members of the League.

We can note some differences in the volume of League representation among different ethnicities. The incidence of League members was significantly higher among Serbs and Montenegrins, in contrast to the situation among Croatians and Slovenes. According to a survey conducted as recently as 1987 (Tos, 1988, supplement), the membership rate among adults was highest in Montenegro (31%), followed by Serbia proper and by Vojvodina (19% each); the lowest rates were found in Croatia (13%) and Slovenia (9%). Needless to say, none of these regions are ethnically homogenous, but it is clear that in regions where populations of Eastern Orthodox extraction predominate, League membership is more common.

These data, nevertheless, cannot provide an overall explanation of ethnic antagonism in Yugoslavia, though some links appear. We could very loosely speak of ethnic groups where membership is above average as being on one side of the conflict – and those below average as composing the other. But it would be misleading to accept this as an explanation. Firstly, Yugoslav society in the post-War period was basically a segmented society, its institutional component parts were not mutually interlinked, each multiplying the organization of all wider and narrower segments. Secondly, the roots of the ethnic antagonism date much further back than the present period, yet the pattern in which it appears is similar to the previous ones, pointing to deeper roots than contemporary organization. Thirdly, the difference in the rate of membership is related to cultural reasons, with a higher secularization level in Orthodox regions. Fourthly, the degree of dissatisfaction and grievances on the part of the Serbs – concerning internal boundaries and the plight of Serbs in Kosovo – in recent years cannot be regarded as solely of a manipulated nature. The Serbs very much question the allegation that they occupy a favoured position in Yugoslavia. Nevertheless, a small part of the explanation of ethnic conflict may lie in these membership differences, as they are also connected to differences in the ethnic composition of state repressive services.

6. ONE POSSIBLE EXPLANATION

Commenting on the state of contemporary theory and approaches in the study of ethnicity, K. O'Sullivan See and W. J. Wilson point to the 'lack of a single comprehensive framework to integrate these disparate theories and approaches' (1988, p. 238). These authors have mainly in mind the US scene, where synchronic and therefore sociological approaches can do the bulk of explaining. On the Yugoslav scene, the situation is much more complex: the process always has a major diachronic component, a burden of history, challenging the observer with the statement that conflicts are cognitively irreducible, eternal and fateful. We will have to rely on partial explanations and a multi-factor scheme:

6.1. Heterogeneity

Yugoslavia is a very *heterogeneous country* in terms of standard economic, sociological and demographic indicators. We will observe a few:

Let us start by considering the first three columns in Table 1, which contains 'hard' data on modernization. In the first column, we may note the very high birth rate in the Province of Kosovo (predominantly Albanian ethnics) – indicating a population boom – whereas other differentials are not substantial. The per capita income in column two reflects the basic economic disparities in Yugoslavia, where the variability index is high. The ratio between the extremes of Kosovo and Slovenia is 1:8. The illiteracy rate also points to a high differential, with illiteracy almost non-existent in Slovenia, whereas it affects more than one quarter of the population over age 15 in Kosovo. Correlations between these columns are high (r 1/2 .90 = r 1/3 = .72). Later, we seek to explain these disparities in other ways as well.

These demographic and economic disparities appear with respect to modernization in column 1-3. Only a year or so ago, we would have pointed to differences in non-denominationality (non-confessionality) or to the differences in the membership rate in the individual republics and provinces. Both could have been regarded as indicators of modernization: the first indicating a certain emancipation from traditionality, the second representing a 'modernizing elite'. Those disparities were significant, but today their credibility has been superseded by events. On the other hand, one cannot ignore the fundamental fact of the presence of Roman Catholicism, of (Serbian and Macedonian) Orthodoxy, and of Islam on Yugoslav soil as traditional religions, all finding their frontiers in this country/countries, giving the relations between them the very flavour and importance of border-relations, with numerous attempts at forced conversion in the past. The Catholic lands are generally more economically advanced; they have also undergone a protest period which may have left an impact relevant for modernization. Heterogeneity is not by itself necessarily a disintegrative and conflictual factor, though adverse effects seem more probable than favourable ones.

6.2. Recent past

Without entering into an elaborate historical exposition and analysis, a few comments on *the recent past* as to institutional organization should be advanced.

Table 1: *Birthrate per Capita National Income, Illiteracy Rate, and Egaliatrianist Stand, by Republics and Provinces*

	Birthrate	Per Capita National Income	Illiteracy Rate	Egalitarianist Stand
Yugoslavia	15.3	2,101	13.7	36.5
Bosnia & Herzegovina	16.1	1,478	22.2	38.8
Montenegro	16.9	1,495	13.9	45.8
Croatia	12.7	2,702	8.5	32.9
Macedonia	18.7	1,291	14.5	53.1
Slovenia	13.7	4,828	1.4	28.0
Serbia proper	12.6	1,871	15.2	31.1
Kosovo	30.4	601	25.7	60.8
Vojvodina	12.3	2,502	8.4	32.2

Source: *Statisticki godisnjak 1988*. Birthrate represents the number of children born per 1000 inhabitants in 1987. Data for per capita income are computed in Yugoslavian dinars (1987) on the basis of Yugoslav computation of national income (drustveni proizvod).

The Yugoslav system of 'socialist self-management' featured a policy of ethnic and regional parity in political representation, with the cultural advancement of ethnic groups as one of its foremost qualities. This seemed to have functioned well during the period of President Tito's rule.

After his passing away and the unfolding of societal crisis, it became apparent that political and cultural instruments are not sufficient in regulating ethnic relations if they are not part of an overall modernization process – and in Yugoslavia this was limited. Therefore, the lack of overall modernization – in contradistinction to processes in Western Europe – instigated ethnic conflicts through the process of 'scapegoating', i.e. in ideological and ethnocentric explanations of the perceived unsatisfactory position of various ethnic groups.

Disputes arose concerning the ethnic policy during the Tito period, questioning the policy and its instruments. Basic in this framework are the boundaries between the federal units. Boundaries are challenged – between Serbia and Croatia, between Serbia and Bosnia and Herzegovina, between Bosnia and Herzegovina and Croatia. This will become a hazardous dispute not only if Yugoslavia should be dismembered, but also if it should be reorganized in a confederative manner, since entire ethnic groups would then demand to be unified in a single state even though their populations are geographically intermingled. A second major question in this framework concerns the very existence of Macedonia and Montenegro as autonomous legitimate units in Bosnia and Herzegovina, as they are claimed by others.

The sensitive nature of autonomous provinces of Kosovo (Kosova) and Vojvodina which form part of the republic of Serbia, but have direct representation on the federal level of government, is also problematic. Here, Yugoslav federalism has followed the Soviet model with federal units of differing degree (in counterdistinction to other federal systems with only one type of federal unit), where some federal units are both members of another unit and 'members' of the federation. Such a system presupposes an external, extra-constitutional political arrangement for solving political disputes. This used to be found in the principles of 'democratic centralism', but is hardly compatible with the idea of 'civil state' and rule of law.

6.3. Hegemony

A very sensitive matter in ethnic relations in Yugoslavia concerns 'hegemony', i.e. a state of relations contrary to parity and equivalence of ethnic groups and regions. The first Yugoslav state was widely considered to be one of Serbic ethnic hegemony, since it was the Serbs who played the main role in the formation of that state, who gave that state the royal dynasty, whose church was tied to the dynasty. Serbs were also most numerous in the state repressive apparatuses. Accusations of a repetition of such a situation in the second Yugoslav state can also be heard today. We lack analyses of the ethnic composition of various services to justify such statements, but it is a fact that such allegations function in public discussions.

Today, the situation has become even more complex, as reverse accusations as to the subjugation of Serbs may also be heard. The subjugation of Serbs in post-World War II Yugoslavia is purported to have been carried out through the imposition of political boundaries within Yugoslavia in such a manner that Serbs were dispersed in various republics and provinces. Allegations can be heard to the effect that Montenegrins and to a lesser extent Macedonians are not true ethnic groups but artificial ones, 'created' by Communists in order to de-compose the Serbian ethnic unity. Their subjugation is also allegedly shown in their lack of representation at the very top of the Tito era leadership.

It is not possible to give a scholarly assessment of the truthfulness of such accusations concerning the matter of hegemony, but it is certain that such accusations today 'function' ideologically as a factor of inter-ethnic distrust and antagonism.

Instead of general hegemony it may be more correct to speak of the monopolization of certain institutions by certain groups, though we cannot substantiate this statement with precise data. Cases of such a monopolization may instigate, lend credibility to and provoke claims of hegemony. Even more so if the institutions were not Weberian but a 'Balkan type' bureaucracy – with particularism and favouritism instead of universalism, power relationships instead of legalism, and a general lack of professionalism.

6.4. Demographic numbers game

The 'numbers game' of majority and minority enter into these relations not only at the level of Yugoslavia as an entity, but also at the level of the various republics and provinces. To take one example: Serbs are the most numerous ethnic group in Yugoslavia (36% of the entire population, according to the 1981 census), but they are not an absolute majority. They compose an absolute majority within the Republic of Serbia (66%), but not within the Province of Kosovo (only 13% in 1981 and further diminishing).

The 'numbers game' is only part of *demographic problems and processes*. Mass demographic changes have a particular impact. Without going into all the changes which have taken place, we should mention the exoduses of the German and Italian minorities at the end of World War II from different regions in Yugoslavia. These minorities, located mostly in the northern belt of Yugoslavia, were replaced by immigrants mostly from the southern Dynaric mountain areas. A new balance has been more or less reached in those regions.

The chief demographic source of ethnic tension in Yugoslavia is the emigration of Serbs from Kosovo, which is making this area – regarded as the birthplace of Serbian nationhood and statehood – almost empty of Serbs and populated by ethnic Albanians. These demographic changes, which have taken place during the entire post-World War II period, have had political repercussions not only within Kosovo and within Serbia, but have also split the entire Yugoslav polity as to what measures should be undertaken. The consequences have been a shaking up the entire political arrangement, and political reforms drafted by the authorities of Serbia aimed at limiting Kosovo autonomy in favour of jurisdiction by the Republic of Serbia authorities.

Another demographic change of an ethnic nature and with an impact on ethnic structure and political relations is the emigration of Serbs and of Croatians out of Bosnia and Herzegovina, mainly into their ethnic matrices (Serbia, partly Vojvodina, and Croatia).

6.5. Cultural incompatibility
We are on very slippery terrain when we address the question of *social-psychological and cultural homo-heterogeneity and incompatibility* of ethnic groups in Yugoslavia. These matters have not received much attention during the post-World War II period, as the exposition of such differences was not regarded as desirable. On the other hand, lack of scientific data and analyses opens the way for prejudice and stereotypes. Earlier studies (such as Cvijic, 1931, and particularly D. Tomasic, 1950) were also burdened with lack of objectivity and with idealizations as to one's own group. Two main types of differences are evident:

Religious affiliations are much more substantial than the name implies. Although they have to do with differences in doctrine (possibly minimally so), they are also bases of religiously coloured cultures; they relate to some of the basic historical boundaries within Yugoslav lands, and there is a long history of religious warfare and attempts at forced transferrals. Most important – irrespective of intentions – religious boundaries are linked to ethnic constitution, in the case of Serbs, Croats, Muslims (in the ethnic sense), and to a certain degree in the case of Macedonians.

The greater bearing of historical, rather than doctrinal factors in explaining religious differences and relations has come to the fore in relationships between Serbs, Croats and ethnic

Muslims (Bosnjaks) in Bosnia and Herzegovina, where the latter two are closer socially and – it seems – also politically.

There are traditional fundamental differences in culture, understood also as a way of life, between mountain herdsmen and lowland agriculturists. These differences prove to be incompatibilities, particularly when they take on an ethnic colour. The mountain way of thinking include struggle and warfare, a proneness to violence, and power seeking, whereas lowland peasants have traditionally been more peacefully oriented and more industrious, as well as more passive and ready to accept being ruled. This traditional difference has not withered away, but remains relevant.

Not only have differences not disappeared with the modernization process, but according to some opinions, the first psychological-cultural syndrome has formed the basis of the egalitarian syndrome. This has been assessed by J. Zupanov (1977) as one of the conservative factors in modernization in Yugoslavia – a specific cultural factor stemming from traditionality, not imposed by communist ideology, though amalgamating well with it. Egalitarianism implies the idea of a limited pool of goods (without envisaging the possibility of its enlargement) which are to be distributed (and further re-distributed) by a just and authoritarian governor in an even manner. This in turn presupposes the distributive function of the state, which can lead to an obsession about dispossessing private owners, thereby impeding entrepreneurship, professionalism and innovation.

Egalitarianism is not evenly distributed among the regions and ethnic groups in Yugoslavia. In Table I, the last column may be regarded as an independent variable: equalitarianism may function as a restraining factor of modernization in Yugoslavia. We also note that it is unevenly distributed (r with respect to columns 4/3 = -.90, 4/2 = -.78). Both education and authoritarian egalitarianism are complementary factors of a cultural nature that account for disparities in modernization under the circumstances of a 70 year old joint state.

6.6. Diachronic and synchronic levels

Perhaps the most specific type of explanation should be sought in the *relationship between the diachronic and synchronic levels.* In contrast to the US scene, historical grievances and burdens in Yugoslavia are very heavy and make the situation difficult. In further contrast to the USA, ethnic groups in Yugoslavia consider the territory where they live as autochthonously their own, and tend to consider forming their own statehood on that territory. Therein lies a considerable conflict potential, when claims are made for the same territory. We should also note that this trend of forming 'independent' states puts into question the thesis put forward by Rupel (1988), according to which there is a conflict between post-modernist ('defensive') nationalism (held by Slovenians and Croats), modernist ('expansionist') nationalism upheld purportedly by Serbs, and a pre-modernist one ('nation-building') upheld purportedly by ethnic Albanians. We do not deny that different degrees of modernization have been achieved in different regions and within different ethnic groups: but all the ethnic stands fit more into a pre-modern and modern model than a post-modern one, as they all contain ethnocentrism and an inclination to small ethnic statehood. Results of the 1987 study in Yugoslavia as regards e.g. authoritarianism do not confirm his thesis of great differences, nor do the data on ethnocentrism (Tos, 1988, supplement).

At the level of public opinion and its gatekeepers (ideology creators), contemporary events are interpreted through the prisms of history, particularly through the spectacles of historically rooted ethnic grievances and frustrations. The economic crisis – including extended high inflation, a drop of economic activity, high unemployment, a drop in the standard of living, all present for at least a decade (inflation has recently been curtailed) – has given plenty of 'raw material' for the growth of frustrations. These in turn become then transformed into ethnic grievances and interpreted as a repetition of historic injustices towards one's ethnic group. All this gives rise to a structuralist picture of repetition of history without substantial change, where basically identical processes are repeated under different circumstances and by new actors.

7.   CONCLUDING REMARKS

Why did socialism leave such a heritage of ethnic antagonism in Yugoslavia?

One could answer by rephrasing the question and stressing that socialism appeared in Yugoslavia in times of tribulation, because of circumstances which were ethnically and politically (lack of democratic tradition) adverse. Seen that way, it must be considered an accomplishment that socialism was successful in mastering these conflicts for decades. But the possibilities of a politically regulated society decrease together with the exhaustion of legitimacy which in the Yugoslav case rested on a charismatic basis, one becoming later 'routinized' and 'traditionalized'. As for socialism itself as a source of ethnic resurgence, we should note that when an entire polity – if not civilization – disappears in a short time, all values – except for the most firmly rooted ones – become delegitimated. Socialism stressed only political values, and they are totally empty today. It did not attach any relevance to professionalism, to regionalism, to what is called 'civil society'. Not even the once majestic-looking bureaucracy has left a deeper imprint in a cultural sense by leaving a pattern of values which could be upheld by its (former) adherents.

Yugoslav socialism was formally a tightly knit system. But Yugoslav society was not substantially integrated. It retained a basic segmentary quality, lacking the infrastructure of civil society. Normatively uniform but socially separate and culturally different systems co-existed in the republics and provinces. This is reflected in the magnitude of economic disparities that we have indicated, in the persistence of ethnic traditionalism and in the fact that loyalty towards Yugoslavia is disappearing as the legitimacy of the political regime and institutional arrangement is withering away. True enough, there were some attempts to establish a Yugoslav identity as an ethnic identity, but with little success. The only identity which could be found in time of general collapse of institutions and their legitimacy remained religion (partly eradicated) and ethnicity (very much linked to religion, enabling a unique cultural ethno-religious factor to appear in its authoritarian, tradition-invoking form). These have arrived upon a scene full of ethnic conflicts remembered from earlier periods and easily rekindled.

There is much agreement as to solutions to the problem in a sociological perspective: market economy, the civil state, rule of law. On the other hand, there is much disagreement as to solutions to the problem when one observes it *politically*. The basic dispute today is over the form of community (federation or confederation) and furthermore, as to whether any form of union amongst ethnic groups of Yugoslavia is desirable or indeed possible. At this moment, it is difficult to propose a solution in a scholarly manner. We may consider it a success if any lasting solution can be reached without major violence.

NOTES

1. The major ethnic groups in Yugoslavia were the following: Serbs (comprising 36.3% of the population), Croats (19.7%) Muslims (8.9%), Slovenes (7.8%), Albanians (7.7%), Macedonians (5.9%), and Montenegrins (2.6%). According to our findings the denominational composition of Yugoslavia in 1987 involves the following major groups: Roman Catholics 23.8%, Eastern Orthodox 27.8%, Muslims 15.7%, others 1.1%, the rest being without denominational affiliation. Figures from the 1981 census; total population 22,400,000.

REFERENCES

Adorno, Th. et al., 1950. *The Authoritarian Personality*, New York: Harper.

Bernik, A., 1989. 'Socialisticna druzba kot "obmoderna" druzba' (Socialist society as 'marginally modern' society), *Druzboslovne razprave* (Social Science Essays), vol. 7, pp. 31-40.

Cvijic, J., 1931. 'Studies in Yugoslav Psychology', *Slavonic Review*.

Hannan, M.T., 1979. 'The dynamics of ethnic boundaries in modern states', in Meyer J.W. & M.T. Hannan, eds, *National Development and the World System*, Chicago: Chicago University Press.

Jugoslavija 1918-1988. Statisticki godisnjak, Beograd: Savezni zavod za statistiku (Federal Office for Statistics), 1988.

Nielsen, N., 1980. 'The Flemish Movement in Belgium after World War II: A dynamic analysis', *American Sociological Review*, vol.45.

Pantic, D., 1977. 'Vrednosne orijentacije, osobine licnosti i klasna pripadnost' (Value Orientations, Personality Characteristics, and Class Partainance), unpublished Ph.D. thesis, Faculty of Philosophy, University of Belgrade.

Rot, N & N. Havelka, 1974. *Nacionalna vezanost i vrednosti kod srednioskolske omladine* (National Pertainance among Secondary School Youth), Beograd: Institute of Social Sciences.

Rupel, D., 1989. 'Narodno vprasanje v postmodernem casu' (The National Question in Post Modern Times), *Druzboslovne razprave*, 7, pp. 76-83.

O'Sullivan See, K. & W.J. Wilson, 1988. 'Race and ethnicity', in N.J. Smelser, ed., *Handbook of Sociology*, Newbury Park: SAGE Publications.

Statisticki godisnjak 1988 (Statistical Yearbook 1988), 1988. Beograd: Savezni zavod za statistiku (Federal Office for Statistics).

Shibutani, T. & K. Kwan, 1965. *Ethnic Stratification: A Comparative Approach*, New York: Macmillan.

Tomasic, D., 1950. *Personality and Culture in Eastern European Politics*, New York: George W. Stewart.

Tos, N., 1988. 'Klasno bice jugoslovenskog drustva: sumarni prikaz z manjkajocimi vrednostmi' (Class Substanse of Yugoslav Society: Summary Findings with Lacking Values), Ljubljana, Razisklovalni institut Fakultete za sociologijo, politicne vede in novinarstvo.

Zupanov, J., 1977. 'Socijalizam i tradicionalizam' (Socialism and traditionalism), *Politicka misao* (Political Thought), 1, Zagreb: Faculty of Political Sciences.

Index

federal solution 197

federation 1-4, 8, 14-17, 21, 22, 24, 25, 27, 28, 30, 47, 54-56, 58-60, 79, 84, 85, 94, 122, 125, 129, 141, 146, 148, 178, 204, 264, 269

Federation Council 2, 16, 17, 27, 84

Fergana Valley 80, 81, 125, 150, 179, 180

Frunze (Bishkek) 152

Gagauz 5, 12, 28, 50, 68, 72, 73, 75

genocide 117, 120-122, 127-129, 164, 246

Georgia/Georgians 4-8, 11-13, 15, 16, 24, 43, 46, 48, 51, 56, 57, 59, 70-72, 74, 75, 81, 86, 123, 124, 128, 131, 132, 134-137, 149, 180

Germany/Germans 5, 24, 41, 70, 82, 90, 92, 93, 95, 98, 102, 142, 143, 145, 146, 206, 241, 243, 258

Geydar 127

Glasnost 1, 3, 6, 23, 24, 27, 139

Gold 177

Gorbachev, Mikhail 1-3, 6, 7, 9-19, 22-29, 52, 54-56, 84, 120, 122, 127, 147, 180

government 2, 3, 6, 9, 12-19, 23, 26, 27, 49, 54, 68, 78, 81, 82, 85, 86, 87, 91-93, 97, 98, 102, 114, 115, 118, 123, 132, 134, 135, 139, 149, 153, 173, 175-177, 180, 185, 190, 194, 196, 197, 200, 211, 213, 214, 216, 217, 240, 241, 246, 264

group rights 80

guerrilla 13

Gulag 8

Hachkars 116

Han Chinese 187, 189, 191, 192, 195

hegemony 264, 265

history 7, 22, 42, 66, 67, 70, 90, 109, 111, 121, 129, 136, 154, 161, 174, 175, 188, 192, 204, 209, 210, 231, 232, 236, 237, 241-246, 261, 266, 268

human rights 9, 15, 58, 80, 104, 110, 111, 206, 228; violation of 86, 179, 228

ideology 14, 41, 42, 49, 51, 52, 60, 68, 95, 96, 101, 108, 111, 146, 161, 234-238, 241, 244, 249, 267, 268

Immigration 94, 95, 97, 98, 150, 191, 211, 256

India 190

indigenous peoples 60, 109, 151

Ingush 70

intellectuals 8, 42, 43, 46, 48, 60, 61, 69, 70, 139, 162, 169, 201, 205, 241, 242, 244, 248, 249; the role of 50-53

Interfront 9, 15, 97, 110

Intermovement 72, 73

international law 110

Internationalism 21, 48, 109, 139, 212, 240

intervention 10, 22, 26, 30, 251

Iran 7, 8, 117, 124, 194

Islam 6, 7, 10, 142, 146, 147, 151-157, 159, 161, 162, 166-169, 185, 192, 194, 220, 262

Jews 5, 92, 93, 95, 142, 143, 154, 245

Karimov 147, 178

Kazbulatov 85

Kerensky 173

KGB 2, 9, 13, 17, 18, 27, 53, 178

Khiva 144, 172

Kirghizia 4, 5, 7, 9-11, 143-145, 151, 163, 179, 180

274	*Index*

Kishinev 11, 73, 75

Kohtla-Järve 98, 99

Kokand 144, 148, 151, 172, 174,
180

Komsomol 6, 56, 166

Koran 147, 153, 154, 156, 158-160

Koreans 142, 143, 193

Kurds 115, 143

labour 18, 108, 143, 148, 158, 169,
176, 217, 221-226, 252, 254, 257

Landsbergis, Vytautis 10, 57

Language 41, 42, 49, 50, 69-75, 83,
91, 93-95, 98, 100, 101, 104,
108-110, 119, 132, 142, 155, 157,
159, 168, 199-208, 210, 212-216,
218, 234, 235, 247, 254

languages 43, 48, 69, 72, 84, 101,
138, 188, 206, 234

Latvia/Latvians 3-9, 10, 13, 71, 89,
90, 95, 102, 106-112, 207

legislation 9, 60, 140

legitimacy 2, 14, 15, 21, 56, 204,
258, 269

Lenin 27, 46, 48, 52, 79, 80, 114,
121, 152, 160, 171-175

linguistic programme 199-208

Lithuanians 3, 5, 8, 57, 89, 90, 95,
107, 204, 207

Lvov 6

Mafia 48, 113

Market economy 27, 78, 85, 100,
129, 150, 221, 232, 233, 238, 257,
269

Marxism 4, 46, 252, 255

mediation 28, 255

Meskhetian Turks 7, 59, 70, 82,
125, 142, 148, 152, 153, 167, 180

Middle East 194

migration 9, 79, 87, 108, 136, 147,
210-212, 214, 216, 219, 220, 227;
forced 20

minorities 10, 12, 24, 41, 44, 45,
49, 50, 58, 59, 68, 135, 171, 184,
186-193, 195, 196, 206-208,
211-213, 240, 241, 243, 265;
national 24, 79, 80, 89, 91-94,
96-98, 102, 104, 138, 139, 142,
238

minority leaders 193

Minsk 6

modernization 192, 195, 231-235,
249, 255-258, 262, 263, 267, 268

Mohammed 156

Molotov-Ribbentrop Pact 71

Mongolian population 194

Mosques 153, 159-162, 167, 169,
174

Musavat Party 114, 118

MVD (Ministry of the Interior) 53

Nagorno-Karabakh 7, 8, 11, 30,
72, 81, 82, 86, 113, 115, 116, 117,
119, 120, 122, 125, 128, 131,
133-135, 137-140

Nakhichevan ASSR 8, 115, 117,
128, 131, 137

Namangan 151, 152, 154

Narva 98, 99

nation-state 45, 55, 197, 206, 207,
232, 246

national identity 46, 94, 96, 97,
101, 199, 202, 205, 209, 210, 211,
231, 236, 238, 240-243, 246-249

nationalism 6, 10, 12, 21, 41-43,
45-51, 56, 58-61, 110, 113, 115,
116, 171, 189, 194, 197, 204, 232,
235, 242, 268

Nationality distribution 5

natural resources 107, 110, 191

negotiations 27, 54, 179, 212

networks 211

Nomenklatura 3, 17, 18, 206

Novi-Uzen 142

Nuclear testing 7